CW00538153

LONDON RECORD SOCIETY
PUBLICATIONS

VOLUME XX
EXTRA VOLUME FOR THE YEAR 1984

CHAMBER ACCOUNTS OF THE SIXTEENTH CENTURY

EDITED BY
BETTY R. MASTERS

LONDON RECORD SOCIETY
FOR
THE CORPORATION OF LONDON
1984

© *Corporation of London*
SBN 90095220 2

Phototypeset by
Wyvern Typesetting Ltd., Bristol
Printed and bound in Great Britain
at The Pitman Press, Bath

CONTENTS

ABBREVIATIONS

All records cited are in the Corporation of London Records Office unless otherwise stated.

Beaven	A. B. Beaven, *Aldermen of the City of London*, 2 vols., 1908–11.
Birch	*Historical Charters and Constitutional Documents of the City of London*, ed. W. De Gray Birch, 2nd ed., 1887.
BL	British Library.
Cal. Letter Books	*Calendar of the Letter Books of the City of London A–L*, ed. R. R. Sharpe, 11 vols., 1899–1912.
Cal. P & M Rolls	*Calendar of Plea and Memoranda Rolls of the City of London, 1323–1437*, ed. A. H. Thomas, 4 vols., *1437–1482*, ed. P. E. Jones, 2 vols., 1926–61.
Cal. PR	*Calendar of Patent Rolls*.
Cal. SPD	*Calendar of State Papers Domestic.*
Cal. SPF	*Calendar of State Papers Foreign.*
Cal. Wills	*Calendar of Wills proved and enrolled in the Court of Husting, London*, ed. R. R. Sharpe, 2 vols., 1889–90.
CCCLGB, 1	Card calendar to the City Lands Grant Book, no.1, compiled by J. R. Sewell.
CCPR	Card calendar to Property References in the Repertories, Journals and unpublished Letter Books before 1596, compiled by Anne Sutton.
CLRO	Corporation of London Records Office.
DNB	*Dictionary of National Biography*.
Foster	F. F. Foster, *The Politics of Stability: a portrait of the rulers in Elizabethan London*, 1977.
GL	Guildhall Library.
Harben	H. A. Harben, *Dictionary of London*, 1918.
HR	Husting Roll.
Jor.	Journal of the Court of Common Council.
Letter Book	Letter Book of the City of London.
LMAS	London and Middlesex Archaeological Society.
LRS	London Record Society.
Masters	Betty R. Masters, 'The history of the civic plate 1567–1731', *Collectanea Londiniensia: Studies presented to Ralph Merrifield*, LMAS, Special Paper no.2, 1978, 301–14.
PRO	Public Record Office.

Remembrancia	*Analytical Index to the Remembrancia of the City of London 1579–1664*, 1878.
Rep.	Repertory of the Court of Aldermen.
Riley, *Memorials*	H. T. Riley, *Memorials of London and London Life in the XIIIth, XIVth and XVth centuries*, 1868.
Shipley	N. R. Shipley, 'The City Lands Committee 1592–1642', *Guildhall Studies in London History*, ii, no. 4, 1977, 161–78.
Stow	*A Survey of London by John Stow*, ed. C. L. Kingsford, 2 vols., 1908.
Thrupp	Sylvia L. Thrupp, *The Merchant Class of Medieval London*, [1948].
VCH	*Victoria County History*.
Woodfill	W. L. Woodfill, *Musicians in English Society from Elizabeth to Charles I*, 1953.
Wren 1633–42	M. C. Wren, 'The Chamber of the City of London 1633–1642', *Accounting Review*, xxiv, no.2, April 1949, 191–8.
Wren 1633	M. C. Wren, 'The Chamber of London in 1633', *Economic History Review*, 2nd series, i, no. 1, 1948, 46–53.

INTRODUCTION

The City of London's archives are rich in administrative and legal records earlier than the seventeenth century but, with the notable exception of the accounts of the wardens of London Bridge, very few financial records have survived. The main series of city's cash accounts, the annual accounts of the chamberlain which formed the principal record of municipal income and expenditure, begins only with the account for 1632–33. This series is made up of a long succession of engrossed accounts, written on parchment and signed by the auditors. They are bound, usually three accounts at a time, with their accompanying annual rentals. The earlier volumes in this series and other subsidiary financial records were probably lost in the Great Fire of 1666 and in a later fire in 1786.[1] The only earlier chamberlain's accounts to survive are a small number of sixteenth-century paper accounts, most of them drafts and some in fragmentary form, which were drawn as a preliminary to the final engrossed account. These paper accounts are now to be found gathered into two volumes in the Corporation of London Records Office and are hereafter referred to as Chamber Accounts 1 and Chamber Accounts 2.

A calendar of two of these accounts, both nearly complete, for the years Michaelmas 1584–Michaelmas 1585 and Michaelmas 1585–Michaelmas 1586, forms the main part of this present work. These were the third and fourth accounts of Robert Brandon, chamberlain 1583–91, and together with a contemporary but incomplete rental of the city lands they constitute almost the whole of Chamber Accounts 2. The account for 1584–85 is a draft, that for 1585–86 contains particulars of the audit and represents the last stage before the writing of the engrossed account. They serve to show the considerable variations which could occur in certain sections of the account. Extracts from earlier, more fragmentary, accounts of George Heton, chamberlain 1563–77, as well as a subsidiary account kept for the year 1535–36 by Richard Maunsell, clerk to the then chamberlain, George Medley, all of which are now to be found in Chamber Accounts 1, are given as Appendices.

The surviving sixteenth-century accounts are of significance and interest from a number of points of view. First, the form of the account, the headings and sequence of its several sections as we find them in the seventeenth century, is already largely established by the reign of Elizabeth, and, after a brief glance at such slight evidence as remains as to

[1] The principal series of administrative records, the Letter Books, the Journals of the Common Council and the Repertories of the Court of Aldermen, which survived the Great Fire despite being housed at Guildhall, would not have been kept in the chamber, and the bridgewardens' records were always held at the Bridge House in Southwark. The fire of 1786 occurred in the chamber.

the chamberlain's accounts in the medieval period, much of this introduction is devoted to a description of the arrangement of the late sixteenth-century account, which may be of interest also to anyone wishing to use the later material.[2] Secondly, the accounts are a quarry of detailed information on particular topics relating to the years which they cover and in this respect are perhaps even more valuable than their successors since the amount of detail recorded in the chamberlain's account diminishes with time. At a period when city's cash constituted virtually the whole of municipal income and expenditure,[3] the range and diversity of the entries in the accounts is great. It is hoped that the citation in the calendar of originating orders for payment and other references to the repertories of the court of aldermen and journals of the common council may serve to link the accounts with related information to be found elsewhere in the city's archives. Thirdly, it can be discerned that some of the causes of the financial problems which were to beset the city in the seventeenth century were present, in embryo at least, in the preceding century and the introduction includes by way of background an account of the chamber and chamberlains of the sixteenth century.

Medieval Accounts

A little information about the medieval accounts of the period 1321–49 is to be found in the Letter Books which record the audit of almost all the accounts between those dates. The first reference in the city's books to the appointment of auditors of the chamberlain's account seems to be that of 10 December 1298 when the mayor and aldermen nominated two aldermen and six commoners to audit the accounts of William de Bettoyne during the time that he had been chamberlain; on the same day the mayor, aldermen and commonalty ordered that all those who ought to render accounts to the city, including the chamberlains and bridgemasters, should do so in the future twice a year, namely in the first week in Lent and at the beginning of autumn.[4] In September 1300 the mayor and aldermen ordered that the chamberlain should henceforth render an account between Michaelmas and the feast of SS Simon and Jude (28 October).[5] Despite these provisions none of the accounts presented for audit between 1321 and 1349 is an annual account. It is only towards the end of this period that a regular accounting term, in this instance of three years, seems to be emerging.

Andrew Horn was chamberlain 1320–28 and there are entries respecting the audit of three of his accounts, namely for 29 September

[2] Especially that for the period between 1632 and about 1660; there is some re-arrangement later.

[3] In later centuries the city acquired new sources of revenue by the allotment of particular receipts to special purposes, e.g., the allocation by parliament of coal dues towards rebuilding after the Great Fire, and especially by the growth of rates income. In modern times most of the city's expenditure has been rates supported but city's cash remains in being as a separate fund, the principal income of which derives from the city's ancient lands.

[4] *Cal. Letter Book C*, 29–31.

[5] *Ibid.*, 78.

1321–13 October 1323, 13 October 1323–11 November 1324 and 2 February 1326–18 October 1328, this last account for '2 years and 27 weeks less one day' running up to Horn's death and being presented by his executors.[6] Three consecutive accounts of Henry de Seccheford, chamberlain 1328–36, covering 18 October 1328–29 June 1330, 29 June 1330–24 June 1332 ('2 years less 5 days') and 24 June 1332–1 August 1335 ('3 years 5 weeks and 2 days') were presented.[7] No reference has been found to the account covering de Seccheford's last few months in office. He was succeeded by Thomas de Maryns, chamberlain 1336–49, for whom there is a record of the audit of six consecutive accounts.[8] The first three are again quite irregular in term, 29 January 1336–29 May 1337, 29 May 1337–7 September 1339 and 7 September 1339–29 September 1340. The fourth account, however, is for 28 September 1340–28 September 1343 ('to wit, for three whole years'), the fifth for the succeeding three years Michaelmas 1343–Michaelmas 1346 and the sixth account beginning at Michaelmas 1346 was closed within the third year at Easter 1349 by de Maryns' death and was presented by his executors. The practice of annual accounting must have developed within the next quarter of a century. Acquittances to the chamberlain in respect of accounts for one year and the annual appointment of auditors are to be found recorded from 1375 and 1378 respectively[9] and it may be observed that the bridgewardens' accounts which survive from 1381 are annual accounts by that date.

No proper analysis of the accounts between 1321 and 1349 is possible, not only because of the irregular term of the account but also because the amount of information recorded in the Letter Books at the time of audit is so variable, but certain points may be noted. For the first two of Horn's accounts and the last three of Thomas de Maryns we have little more than the total receipts and total expenses with some note of the allowances due to de Maryns upon his fourth and fifth accounts, but in the intervening seven accounts between 1326 and 1340 sub-totals for certain categories of income and expenditure or certain special items are recorded,[10] mention often being made of the roll of particulars or roll of expenses where fuller details were originally entered. On the receipts side, if we set aside such special items as the £77.3s.4d. recorded in the account of 1326–28 as the produce of an aid for making a gift to Edward III's new queen, Philippa of Hainault, and the several sums received for engines of war and other military needs in the account of 1337–39, three regular sources of income are found in every account. Much the most important is the money received in respect of freedom and apprenticeship fees which averaged

[6] Letter Book E, ff.147b, 157, 172b.

[7] Letter Book E, ff.201b–202, 229b–230, 243b–244.

[8] Letter Book F, ff.2b, 9b–10, 40b–41, 73, 128, 166. The initial date is not given for the second and third of these accounts but the sums included for arrears show that there are no gaps between the accounts.

[9] *Cal. Letter Book H*, 14, 83, 105, 169, 250, 284; *ibid.*, 102, 136, 153 and similar entries.

[10] The calendaring of the entries concerning Horn's, de Seccheford's and de Maryns' accounts in *Cal. Letter Books E & F*, which is brief and very selective, does not present all the information. Extracts from the expenses for 1330–32 and 1337–39 are printed in Riley, *Memorials*, 185–6, 206–7.

about £80 a year over this period of fourteen years.[11] By contrast at this date the rental of the chamber lands produced an average of only about £13 p.a.[12] and payments for recognizances of debts, calculated at 2d. per pound of the debt acknowledged, contributed perhaps £4 more. An even smaller sum for the enrolment of documents is found in some but not all of the accounts. Special items also occur among the payments, such as the expenditure upon putting the city in a state of defence which is found in the account of 1337–39 and the presents, whether of money, wine or robes, which figure prominently in some years. Every account, however, contains a separate sub-total for the fees paid to officers and others which averaged about £50 a year and every account contains in one form or another a reference to 'necessary expenses'. In the audit of certain accounts expenditure upon building, reparations or pavements is distinguished either as a sub-total or as particular items.[13]

The variation in financial terms of the total account which could occur at this time is illustrated by contrasting Andrew Horn's second account when both receipts and expenses for a period of some thirteen months were just over £87 with Thomas de Maryns' fifth account for the three years 1343–46 when, swollen by the inclusion of a gift of 1,000 marks and a loan of 2,000 marks raised and paid to the king, receipts were nearly £2,747 and expenditure approximately £2,963.

The Arrangement of the Sixteenth-Century Accounts

The General Account: the Charge

After 1349 no more accounts are entered even in summary form in the city's books although the balance due from an outgoing chamberlain is very occasionally recorded.[14] The surviving accounts for Elizabeth's reign show that by then the arrangement is already established in very much the same form or pattern as is to be found in the engrossed accounts of the 1630s. The nature of the account, however, remained essentially that of a

[11] In the audit of the account covering 24 June 1332–Aug. 1335 four sub-totals for freedom and apprenticeship fees are recorded, one for each complete year from Midsummer to Midsummer and the fourth for the remaining part of a year. The three yearly totals were £86.17s.2d., £85.15s.0d., and £83.17s.10d. Such sums comprised fees paid for admission to the freedom by redemption and apprenticeship (no fees being payable at this date by those admitted by patrimony) and for enrolment of apprentices. For the wide variation in fees paid by redemptioners and for some comparative figures of admissions to the freedom by patrimony, apprenticeship and redemption in 1309–12 and 1551–53, see *Cal. P. & M. Rolls 1364–1381*, xxxii, xxxiv, li–lii; at the former date redemptioners were in a substantial majority, at the later date admission was predominantly by apprenticeship.

[12] A rental of c.1311 (*Cal. Letter Book C*, 237–9) totalled £17.10s.0d. The chamber rental was small compared with that of the Bridge House estates to which in 1358 the properties on the bridge alone contributed £160.4s.0d. (Bridge House Small Register, ff.64v–66v).

[13] See especially the extracts from the accounts of 1330–32 and 1337–39 in Riley, *Memorials*, 185–6, 206–7. Expenditure upon some other building work, including repair of the City wall and the tun and work upon Guildhall chapel, as also the charges of a number of presents to the king and others, was met out of the farm of the profits of murage leased to John Vyncent, clerk, in 1331 and 1332 and did not form part of the chamberlain's account. The entry of the audit of this special account in Letter Book E, f.232b, is partially calendared in Riley, *Memorials*, 186–7.

[14] e.g. Nicholas Mattok (Rep.3, f.220b).

medieval *compotus* designed to show the indebtedness or otherwise of the accountant at the end of the year. First the Charge was totalled, which included all receipts during the year plus the arrears, if any, due from the chamberlain upon the previous year's account, then the Discharge including all the disbursements plus an allowance, if necessary, for any arrears due to the chamberlain from the city upon the last account, and finally, by subtracting one from the other, the amount owed by the chamberlain to the city or by the city to the chamberlain, was established. The city's cash accounts were long to retain this archaic form.[15]

The following description of the arrangement of the account is based upon the accounts of 1584–85 and 1585–86 with some observations as to similarities or variations in the accounts in Chamber Accounts 1, especially those of 1563–67, and in the accounts of the 1630s.[16] The account of 1584–85 begins under the heading of 'The Charge' with four entries for which the totals only of receipts are shown. The first is the sum of the arrears due from the chamberlain upon the foot of the last account (**2**). The second is the proceeds of the rental of the city's general lands and also of the Blanchappleton lands, which had been acquired by the city in 1478,[17] after allowance had been made for unoccupied properties and irrecoverable rents (**3**). The city also held upon charitable trusts certain estates bequeathed by Sir John Philipot, mayor 1378–79, John Carpenter, town clerk 1417–38, and John Reynwell, mayor 1426–27, but receipts and payments in respect of these estates and also of the manor of Finsbury, were still in the sixteenth century being accounted for separately from the general account and are referred to again below. In 1632–33 the total of the general rents is followed immediately as part of the general account by separate totals for the rents of the Philipot, Carpenter and Reynwell estates, of certain other estates acquired in the intervening period, and of Finsbury.

Each of the engrossed accounts of the seventeenth century and later is almost invariably preceded by a detailed rental of city properties, including the estates held by the city upon charitable trusts. A similar rental, compiled for 1584–85 and amended in 1586–87, forms part of Chamber Accounts 2. Although this rental is incomplete, it is evident that the original sequence and the grouping of properties under particular topographical titles or heads were of very much the same pattern as those of the rental of 1632–33 (allowing for the increase in the estate by the later date). Like the accounts the rental must be presumed to have been engrossed on parchment, if not yet annually then every few years.

[15] As new and more modern forms of subsidiary accounts were developed the city's cash account became progressively less detailed but, although increasingly formal in character, the series was not discontinued until 1943. The accounts continue to show a charge, discharge and balance due from or to the chamberlain up to 1858.

[16] The latter were discussed by M. C. Wren (Wren 1633–42; Wren 1633).

[17] Blanchappleton is variously described as a manor, messuage, district, etc. and was situated at the north east end of Mark Lane (Harben, 84). Together with the offices of packer, gauger and garbler it had been acquired in 1478 in satisfaction of debts due by the king (Jor.8, ff.145b, 168b, 169b, 173b, and Birch, 87–9, 90–3). The tenements comprising the Blanchappleton lands formed one section of the chamber rental (e.g. Chamber Accounts 2, ff. 189v–190v; City's Cash 1/1, ff.22r–23r).

The third and fourth totals are the receipts of fees for the enrolment of apprentices and for admission to the freedom respectively (**4, 5**). The former entry refers to the existence of a series of apprenticeship registers, written on paper and distinguished, like so many classes of records in the city archives, by letter references, which by this date had reached the letter P. The latter refers to a series of parchment registers of freemen which had arrived at the letter Q. These registers and many other records were destroyed in a fire in the chamber in 1786. None of the apprenticeship registers before 1786 is known to be extant and only some mutilated portions of a few freedom registers.[18]

By the late sixteenth century the proceeds of the general rental formed a very important element in the city's income which in 1563–67, 1584–85 and the 1630s always exceeded the combined apprenticeship and freedom fees. In 1584–85 the rental yielded £836.18s.8d.[19] as against £211.16s.9d. and £409.13s.1d. from apprenticeship and freedom fees respectively. The first page of the account of 1585–86, which would have contained similar information for that year, is missing but there is no reason to think that the relationship of these three sources of income would have been very different.[20]

The next two sections of the account contain detailed receipts. Of the sixteen items listed under 'Rent Farms' in 1584–85 (**7**), which produced a total of £398.10.1d., fourteen are fixed annual rents payable for leases of the measurage, gauging, packing or sealing of certain commodities and other offices of profit, some of which belonged to the city by virtue of royal grants, and two relate to actual profits received and paid into the chamber. There are corresponding entries in 1563–64 for thirteen of these items, nine of them in rents of the same amount, and eleven of them, seven at the same rent, are to be found in Richard Maunsell's account of 1535–36. 'Casual Receipts Ordinary' (**8**, **154**) contains in the main items which might be expected to recur each year but which would be variable in amount, such as monies received for enrolments of deeds and wills in the husting or for setting over apprentices, but a few fixed sums, such as 6s.8d. received each year under the bequest of Sir Martin Bowes towards repair of the conduits, are also entered here. There appears to be a marked increase in the total of 'Casual Receipts Ordinary' between 1563–64 (£134.19s.8d.) and 1584–85 (£346.13s.0d.) but this is almost wholly accounted for by the inclusion under this head in the latter year of the farm and profits, due to the queen and the city, of the alnagers or searchers of woollen cloth; in the 1560s these are to be found entered

[18] Two mutilated portions of a parchment freedom register (B.L. Egerton Ms.2408 and G. L. Ms.512), probably parts of book N or book O, were edited by C. Welch, *Register of Freemen of the City of London in the reigns of Henry VIII and Edward VI*, LMAS, 1908. Some other mutilated fragments of registers, chiefly of the late 17th century, are in CLRO, the most complete being one for c.1668 which has been repaired and indexed. Bundles of documents, including apprenticeship indentures, which relate to admission to the freedom survive from 1681.

[19] This was still less than the produce of the Bridge House rental which in 1584–85 totalled £1,313.9s.4¼d. (Bridge House A/C 10, f.317v).

[20] The rental yielded £837.0s.8d. in 1586–87 after allowance of £21.0s.8d. for vacations and desperates (Rental, Chamber Accounts 2, f.190v. And see **148–52**).

under 'Receipts Extraordinary', presumably because the city had but lately acquired its interest in the office of alnage (see **8h**).

The next section is headed 'Fines' and once more gives a total only, being the sum of small fines received for market offences, breaches of city ordinances and nuisances (**9**, **155**). The contribution to the city's revenues was small (£36.3s.4d. in 1584–85) but it is the only section in the whole account for which a total alone is recorded where the particular account survives. This is the Book of Fines 1517–1628 in which is recorded annually details of these fines.[21]

'Leases, Incomes, Arrearages of Rents and Venditions' is the somewhat cumbrous title of the next section of the Charge (**10**, **156**). Nearly all the entries relate to admission fines for newly granted leases of city properties and the sums recorded here are either receipts in full or first instalments of such fines received within the year of the account. The total of these non-recurring items was likely to vary considerably from year to year (£53.6s.8d. in 1584–85 and £130.0s.8d. in 1585–86).

Other non-recurring items, sometimes for considerable sums, are recorded in the section which follows, entitled 'Receipts Extraordinary' (**11**, **157**). Here will be found receipt of those fines for refusal to serve the office of sheriff, or occasionally fines for discharge from other civic office, which were imposed within the year of the account and in respect of which monies were received, either in full or by way of a first instalment, before the account was closed. The shrieval fine, which is discussed more fully below, was usually £200. Receipts in respect of any other newly imposed fines or newly created obligations were treated in the same way. In this section also are to be found monies paid into the chamber in consequence of collections by or assessments upon the companies or wards, some of which might be made in respect of expenditure which had occurred some time previously. The expense of rebuilding Ludgate fell within the accounts of 1584–85 and 1585–86 (see below) but the order authorising the levying of two fifteenths for the rebuilding of the gate and the repair of the walls was not made until 6 September 1586 and the proceeds would have been recorded in later accounts no longer extant.[22] In 1584–85 monies were received of the companies for the redeeming of captives in the dominion of Turkey and of foreigners and strangers in the wards for musters of 1578 and 1585. In 1585–86 a ward assessment brought in monies to be used for the purchase of Sir James Croft's interests in the office of garbling. 'Receipts Extraordinary' was also used to record sums, usually small, received towards the 'finding' or maintenance of particular orphans and for a number of miscellaneous items of a non-recurring nature. The total of this section in 1584–85, in which year a number of shrieval fines were paid, was £1,728.3s.5d. but in 1585–86 only £838.13s.11d. By 1632–33 the 'Receipts Extraordinary' is a

[21] R. M. Benbow has pointed out that the fines listed in the book are fewer than the record in the repertory of fines imposed would indicate and suggests that some fines may have been forgiven or returned ('The Court of Aldermen and the Assizes: the policy of price control in Elizabethan London', *Guildhall Studies in London History*, iv, no. 3, Oct. 1980, 110). By 1632–33 the sum received under this head, for which there is no particular account extant, was only £6.13s.4d.

[22] Jor.22, ff.53b, 89b.

very much enlarged section largely due to the inclusion of no less than forty-five entries recording the receipt of interest paid upon loans advanced by the city to merchants and trading companies. Only one such entry is found in 1584–85, in respect of interest on £400 lent to Sir Edward Osborne at five per cent, and the difference vividly illustrates the growth of the chamber of London as a lending institution in the early part of the seventeenth century.

There follows a section headed 'Debts mentioned in the last account and other accounts and since received now being charged' in which are listed any sums received during the year of the account in respect of previously outstanding debts (**12**, **158**). Second or later instalments of shrieval fines, fines for leases or other debts due will be found here as well as outstanding debts being paid off in full. There is no comparable section in the accounts of the 1560s when any such items were entered under 'Receipts Extraordinary',[23] but in 1632–33 this section, which includes receipts for repayment or partial repayment of loans plus accrued interest, is financially by far the most considerable in the whole Charge.

The Charge of the general account is completed by a section headed 'Orphanage', which in 1584–85 and 1585–86 records the totals only of monies deposited in the chamber that year for orphans' portions, £1,743.15s.0d. in the first year and £2,635.8s.4d. in the second (**13**, **159**). Reference is made to two subsidiary accounts where particulars were recorded, the journal and the ledger. The orphans' journals, containing a chronological record of receipts of money for the use of orphans and of payments of orphans' portions and finding money, do not now survive before 1662. The orphans' ledgers, in which such receipts and payments are posted under the name of the deceased father of the orphan or orphans, are extant only from 1627. In the 1560s deposits were still being recorded individually in the chamberlain's account, each entry giving the names of the depositor, the deceased freeman and the orphan or orphans. In 1632–33 the entry for this section is a total only, as in the 1580s, but the sum received has risen to £16,842.6s.6½d.

The Charge upon the general account, excluding the arrears due upon the last account, amounted in 1584–85 to £5,979.6s.8d. and in 1585–86 to £7,182.10s.7½d. It will be observed that for the purposes of the chamberlain's account all the receipts previously described of whatever category, whether monies belonging to the city or orphans' portions held only on deposit, whether a substantial fine payable once only at the commencement of a long lease or an annual rent, were all calculated as current income.

The General Account: the Discharge

As has been seen, the Charge contained some sections for which totals only were recorded, and in other sections the number of individual entries of receipts was not large. By contrast the payments were very much more numerous and diverse and, with the exception of orphanage

[23] In Chamber Accounts 1 only one example of the 'Debts received' section survives and this appears to be for 1576–77.

payments and some weekly payments for wages and minor necessities, are generally recorded in some detail. In consequence the Discharge upon the general account in 1584–85 fills some sixty-seven folios as compared with the mere seven of the Charge.

The Discharge begins with a small and financially unimportant section headed 'Salary of Priests' or 'Salaries of Ministers' (**15**, **161**). Here are entered a small number of regular payments, e.g. to the parson appointed to hold weekday services in Guildhall Chapel, offering money paid to the vicar of St Lawrence Jewry, in the 1580s an annual pension to a former chantry chaplain of Edmonton, and in the 1560s an annual contribution towards the maintenance and exhibition of a student at the university of Cambridge.[24] Single payments, e.g. to individual preachers for preaching before the election of the lord mayor, are usually to be found entered under the 'Foreign Charge'.

The next section, entitled 'Rents and Quitrents' (**16**, **162**), includes such items as the rent paid for the house at St Mary Spital where the lord mayor and other civic dignitaries heard the Spital sermons in the week following Easter and which was held by the city on a 99 year lease, rents for premises leased back from the tenants of Smart's and Somer's quays for the purpose of selling fish, and a variety of quitrents and other annual payments, some of which had been payable by the city since the fourteenth or fifteenth century while others arose from the acquisition in the 1560s of properties needed for the site of the Royal Exchange.[25] This section of the account, amounting to £77.0s.4d. in 1584–85, had increased considerably, both in number of items and in total payments, between the 1560s and the 1580s. In 1632–33 it includes annual payments for the supply of New River water to Guildhall kitchen, the hallkeeper's house and other places.

The next two sections are both concerned in the main with payments to officers. In the first, headed 'Inward Fees' (**17–22**, **163–8**), are entered fees paid annually out of the chamber to the city's own chief officers, namely the recorder, chamberlain, common serjeant, town clerk and comptroller of the chamber, to certain clerks including the clerk of the chamber and the clerk of the works, to the renter-general, and to all the officers of the lord mayor's household. At this date the household comprised the swordbearer, common cryer, common hunt and water bailiff, who were the four esquires, three serjeant carvers, three serjeants of the chamber, two yeomen of the chamber, the serjeant and yeoman of the channel, the under waterbailiff, the four yeomen of the waterside and the several servants or men of the four esquires and the senior serjeant carver.[26] The fees listed here comprise the annual fee or salary out of the chamber,[27] 'rewards at the audit' which were paid to the clerk of the

[24] Chamber Accounts 1, ff.57b, 138, 159, 179b.

[25] For a list of freehold and leasehold interests acquired for the site of the Royal Exchange, with the purchase prices, and of various payments for which the city became due, see Letter Book V, ff.70b–72.

[26] B. R. Masters, 'The Mayor's Household before 1600', *Studies in London History presented to Philip Edmund Jones*, ed. A. J. Hollaender and W. Kellaway, 1969, 95–114.

[27] This was generally only a small part of an officer's remuneration which was derived mainly from a variety of fees and perquisites and payments for particular tasks.

chamber and most of the senior officers of the household, payments in respect of regular responsibilities such as the monies paid to the common hunt for his hounds' meat or to the yeoman of the channel for his duties at Bartholomew Fair, any payments made in lieu of accommodation, and for some officers, principally the serjeants of the household, an additional yearly sum 'in augmentation of their living'.[28] Other payments to these officers which were particular to the year of the account, e.g. monies paid to the recorder for his work in connection with particular law suits or to the serjeants and yeomen for riding to the court or elsewhere on the city's business, will normally be found, grouped with related entries, in the 'Foreign Charge'. The 'Inward Fees' paid in 1563–54 totalled £382.5s.0d. and in 1584–85 £430.5s.0d.

'Outward Fees' are more varied in character but again always comprise regular annual payments (**23–8**, **169–75**). They include the fees paid to the eminent men retained as legal counsel for the city, of whom more is said below, and to the attorneys for the city in the king's courts, and annual fees for the city waits, the chamberlain's clerk, three city artificers, the keeper of Leadenhall, and many minor officials including the keepers of the conduits and a number of rakers and keepers of grates and sluices. Payments are made to twenty-four rakers and keepers of grates in 1584–85 in contrast to nine in 1563–64 and six in 1535–36, an indication of increasing municipal administration. Also included under 'Outward Fees' are pensions granted to retired officers, to the dependants of officers now dead and to others in need, annuities paid to certain officers in respect of special responsibilities and occasionally other annuities.[29] 'Outward Fees', which accounted for expenditure of only £159.9s.0d. in 1563–64 had risen to £355.7s.3d. in 1584–85. Both 'Inward Fees' and 'Outward Fees' in the 1630s follow substantially the same pattern. It should be noted that not all the city officers are listed under 'Inward Fees' and 'Outward Fees'. The pleaders and attorneys of the mayor's court and the undersheriffs, secondaries and clerks of the sheriffs' courts, for example, were not in general in receipt of annual fees payable out of the chamber and will only and rarely be included if they receive an annual fee in respect of additional responsibilities such as the writing up of particular records.

The next section lists week by week throughout the year the total wages paid to the city's labour force of masons, carpenters, bricklayers and other workmen (**29**, **176**). No individuals are named and no information given as to rates of wages or hours worked. The weekly bills themselves have not survived. The heading of the section lists in general terms the works upon which the workmen have been engaged during the year and in 1585–86 such information is also given in more detail for each month in the form of marginal annotations. From the sum total of the weekly wages at the end of the section are deducted any wages for work on properties belonging to the charitable estates or to the manor of

[28] These last had nearly all been granted since 1565. Many of the annual fees are to be found, sometimes in the same amount, in 1535–36 and 1563–64.

[29] 'Pension' and 'annuity' are sometimes used interchangeably in this section although the former is most generally applied to payments with a charitable element.

Finsbury. (These wages are charged to the charitable and Finsbury accounts.) After such deductions the wages in both years totalled a little under £300. The weekly wages are similarly entered by totals only in the accounts of the 1560s and the 1630s.

The section which follows 'Weekly Wages' is the second largest in the whole account. In the Elizabethan accounts the contents range more widely than the title, 'Emptions of reparations stuff and other necessary things bought and provided this year . . .', would suggest. Payments cover workmanship as well as supply of goods and materials, and indeed often combine both, and also extend to major building or other undertakings carried out during the year of the account (**30–62**, **177–202**). In 1584–85 and 1585–86 the gate and gaol of Ludgate were rebuilt by and to the design of William Kerwyn, the city mason, and many of the great conduit pipes were renewed or repaired by John Martyn, the city plumber. No details of the work at Ludgate are given but payments, most of them to Kerwyn, amounted to £321.11s.11d. out of the city's cash in 1584–85 (with a further £100 being contributed this year by the bridgewardens) and to £1,143.6s.8d. in 1585–86 (**38**, **181**, **201**). The difference between these two sums largely accounts for the difference between the sectional totals for the two years, £1,076.18s.3d. in 1584–85 and £2,034.14s.10½d. in 1585–86.

Most of the money paid to Kerwyn consisted of sums due under contract or paid by an order of the court of aldermen specifically quoted as authority in the accounts but in general payments in the 'Emptions' section were made against bills which no longer survive. So far as the artificers were concerned the degree of detail recorded in the accounts seems to have depended on whether the work carried out was of a routine character or particular to the year of the account. Thus there is considerable detail of John Martyn's work in making and laying the great conduit pipes which was included with some other work in his quarterly bills, the information given including weights and prices of lead and sometimes the length of ground dug for the laying of the pipes (**44**, **58**, **191**). Only a total for the year's payments is given for some artificers and suppliers, including the blacksmith, the founder, the ironmonger and the turner, presumably since they provided only routine work and supplies. The paviours received less than a quarter of the sum paid to the blacksmith but the places where paving was done are listed with the total paving executed during the period covered by the bill (**35**, **183**). Similarly the common vaults or vaults belonging to particular properties which were emptied by the nightman are specified, with the amount of soil removed and sometimes the number of nights taken (**46**, **190**). 'Emptions' also covers payments for minor but specific jobs such as painting the pumps, mending the clocks in Guildhall or mending a saddle. Purchases of materials range from quantities of bricks, tiles and timber to a length of crimson velvet for a sword. From the sum total of the section are deducted any payments made in respect of the properties belonging to the charitable estates or the manor of Finsbury, which are to be charged to those accounts.

Those portions of the 'Emptions' which survive for 1563–67 name no major undertakings but the section is otherwise broadly similar to that in the 1580s.[30] By 1632–33, however, this part of the account has undergone one of the few major alterations. The section head, 'Emptions . . .', is still retained for purchases of materials and payments for routine supplies and work by the artificers but is followed by two new sections. The first, and the more important financially, is headed 'Extraordinary Works Buildings and Reparations . . .' and the introduction of this section must indicate a growth in such undertakings by the city. Here in 1632–33 are entered such expenses as repairs to the walks in Moorfields, cleaning and repairing the common sewer, clearing banks of sand and gravel in the Thames and the charges, including casting and laying of pipes, of bringing water from Paddington to the conduit heads near the Banqueting House. The second new section, headed 'Necessary Expenses', is chiefly concerned with expenses in and about Guildhall and repairs and embellishments to the city's plate and insignia, and thus draws together items which in the Elizabethan accounts are to be found variously entered under 'Emptions', 'Foreign Charge' and 'Allowances'.

The 'Foreign Charge' which follows 'Emptions' is the longest section of the whole account (**63–114**, **203–44**). The payments, which are recorded in some detail, are extremely diverse and the 'Foreign Charge' is the residual section for all those items of expenditure which do not fit under the more specific headings of other sections. Here are to be found various expenses in connection with the election, presentation, swearing into office and knighting of the lord mayor as well as his attendance, with other aldermen, at St Paul's and St Mary Spital, payments to the city's four members of parliament, payments under acts of common council to those who accepted the office of sheriff after the refusal of others, and charges for the dinners which were inseparable from so many of the city's activities. Frequent consultations with the court can be discerned in the payments to the bargemen or for boat hire, horse hire, riding and other charges of the aldermen and officers travelling to Westminster or elsewhere and in charges for presents or rewards to great officers of state and lesser officials.

Considerable detail is recorded of arrangements for holding courts of conservancy, and payments are made to the waterbailiff for his searches of the river (**96**, **220**, **221**). The claim of the city to the Thames conservancy, made under its ancient charters and the statute of 17 Richard II c.9, had traditionally extended from Colney Ditch just beyond Staines in the west to Yantlett Creek in the east and to parts of the Medway. The right to the eastern half of this jurisdiction had for some years been successfully challenged by the lord admiral,[31] and in consequence the expenses recorded in the accounts of 1584–85 and 1585–86 relate to searches of the river only west of Blackwall and to the holding of conservancy courts and the summoning of juries for only two of the riparian counties, namely Middlesex and Surrey. This dispute grumbled on for a long time and it was not until 1613 that the city was able to resume its former powers.[32] In the accounts of the 1630s, where the

[30] For the names of artificers and suppliers of goods in Chamber Accounts 1, see **303**.
[31] *Remembrancia*, 500.
[32] Rep.31(1), ff.97, 114b, 125b.

conservancy charges are recorded in even greater detail, the city is once again exercising its full claim and courts are also held for the counties of Essex and Kent.[33]

Charges in many matters of litigation and controversy are to be found entered under the 'Foreign Charge' in these two years. The most important issues appear to have been the case in the exchequer court between the city and Sir James Croft concerning the office of garbling (**79**, **157b**, **174b**, **226**, **251**); the city's defence in the court of king's bench of its claim to the search and survey of hops, butter, oil, vinegar and soap (**76**, **227**); a suit brought against the city in the star chamber for muring up a gate out of the liberty of Christ Church near Aldgate (**83**, **227**); the perennial dispute with the lieutenant of the Tower as to the Tower liberties which reached one of its peaks of acrimony in the years 1579–85 (**82**, **212**);[34] and a suit against the lord mayor and other aldermen by John Mellowes, clothworker (**95**, **228**) which was one of several suits concerning orphanage monies.

The entries in the accounts do not, of course, give the background to these suits and controversies, for which recourse must be had to the repertories and journals and legal sources. Their chief interest lies in the detail they give of the activities of certain of the city's officers and counsel who are seen receiving payments for perusing and drawing up documents, viewing properties, giving advice, conferring in chambers and appearing in the central courts. The recorder, William Fleetwood, was involved in all the important cases, and the number of law suits in which the city was engaged, the responsibility for which fell chiefly on the recorder, was one of the reasons why William Daniel, esquire, of Gray's Inn had been appointed by the court of aldermen on 2 July 1584 to act in Fleetwood's place in the court of aldermen and the court of husting; he was also to take examinations and carry out other duties of the town clerk in the mayor's court in the absence both of the town clerk himself and of William Dalby, the senior attorney.[35] The other reasons for this appointment, to which the recorder and town clerk had consented, were Fleetwood's involvement in the queen's as well as the city's service and his duties as a serjeant at law, all of which made it impossible for him to attend at Guildhall as often as was needful.[36] Daniel's fee of £40 p.a. in respect of these duties, which he continued to exercise until his appointment as one of the undersheriffs or judges of the sheriffs' courts in 1589,[37] is listed under 'Inward Fees' along with the annual fees of the recorder, town clerk and other high officers (**17f**, **163f**) but he is also

[33] The detail is particularly interesting in those years when the holding of the courts was combined with a ceremonial view of the bounds of the jurisdiction as in 1632–33 (City's Cash 1/1, ff.60v–64). The City's Cash accounts appear to provide the only detailed record of such views earlier than the narrative descriptions which survive for the late 18th and 19th centuries.

[34] *Remembrancia*, 426–7.

[35] Rep.21, f.66b.

[36] For some of Fleetwood's activities, see T. Wright, *Queen Elizabeth and her times: a series of original letters*, ii, 1838 (for Fleetwood's letters to Burghley); P. R. Harris, 'William Fleetwood, Recorder of the City, and Catholicism in Elizabethan London', *Recusant History*, vii, 1963–64, 106–22.

[37] Rep.22, ff.95, 101.

among nine men in 1584–85 (eight in 1585–86)[38] who are listed under 'Outward Fees' as receiving annual fees as learned counsel of the city (**23a**, **169a**). In the repertories such men are sometimes described as 'counsel at large'. Of these nine William Daniel was the busiest despite his responsibilities at Guildhall. He became a serjeant at law in 1594 and from 1604 to 1610 was a justice of the common pleas. Thomas Owen, who, after Daniel, was the counsel most actively engaged in the city's legal affairs during these two years, also, like Daniel, held another office under the city. From 1577 to 1589 he was one of the four common pleaders.[39] He became a serjeant at law in 1589 and was also a justice of the common pleas from 1594 to 1598. Three of the city's counsel were called upon in one case only, James Morris in the suit concerning Christ Church Aldgate; Robert Clarke, later Sir Robert, who was to serve as a baron of the exchequer from 1587 to 1607, in the suit over garbling; and Edward Coke, at this time in his early thirties but already with a considerable reputation and destined to be one of the great figures of English law, in the suit brought by John Mellowes against the lord mayor and aldermen. It is clear that the city was adept at engaging rising legal luminaries in its service. The other four counsel who received retainers, Matthew Dale, who was to succeed William Daniel in 1589 as deputy to the recorder,[40] Thomas Bowyer, John Cowper and Richard Shuttleworth, serjeant at law, were not called upon during these two years. In addition to the counsel at large, two other of the common pleaders, James Dalton, who was in office before October 1578 and was to become an undersheriff in 1594,[41] and Nicholas Fuller, who had been admitted as recently as 10 March 1584,[42] were each rewarded for similar activities in three of the city's law suits. Thomas Walmesley, serjeant at law and later a justice of the common pleas, was involved in the matter of the city's title to the search for hops, and Edmund Plowden, the distinguished lawyer and commentator upon the common law, was consulted in the case about garbling.[43]

On 28 October 1581 Robert Smith had been appointed at a fee of 20 marks p.a. to solicit and follow the city's causes at Westminster and

[38] The usual number (Letter Book R, f.310b; Rep.16, f.448).

[39] Rep.19, f.237; Rep.22, f.124.

[40] Rep.22, f.101.

[41] Rep.19, f.385b; Rep.23, f.196b.

[42] Rep.21, f.34b.

[43] In addition to the specific references quoted above, see E. Foss, *Biographia Juridica*, 1870, for Daniel, Owen, Clarke, Coke and Walmesley; *DNB* for Fleetwood, Clarke, Coke and Plowden. The city's success in engaging rising legal talent in its service was not new. Plowden himself had been one of the counsel under retainer in 1563 (**299g**), along with Thomas Carus, later a judge of the queen's bench, Roger Manwood, who was successively a judge of the common pleas and chief baron of the exchequer, Christopher Wray, who was to serve as judge and then chief justice of the queen's bench, Thomas Bromley, who became successively recorder of the city, solicitor general and lord chancellor, and Gilbert Gerrard, already attorney general and later master of the rolls (Foss). Richard Maunsell in 1536 records fees paid to two future judges of the common pleas (**295e**). In July 1554 it was agreed that future recorders, undersheriffs and common serjeants of the city should always be chosen from among the counsel of the city and Fleetwood himself, who became recorder in 1571, had been admitted one of the counsel in 1569 (Letter Book R, f.310b; Rep.16, f.448).

elsewhere, to be attendant upon the learned counsel in all controversies about the liberties of the city, and to engross any collections of documents arising therefrom (**27a**). There are numerous references to Smith receiving reimbursement for his bills of expenses and for the fees which he had paid to the city's attorneys in the central courts as well as payments for making searches and obtaining and copying documents. Before appointment as city solicitor[44] Smith had been one of the under or assistant clerks in the mayor's court; on 29 November 1586 he was given also the office of deputy to the comptroller, William Dummer, and in 1594 he surrendered the post of city solicitor following his appointment as one of the clerks of the mayor's court; from 1597 until his death in 1623 he was also comptroller of the chamber.[45]

Smith also received payments for engrossing various books and documents (**209**, **229**, **214**). The accounts are a useful source of information for the names of writers or binders of particular books or records, most of this information appearing under the heading of the 'Foreign Charge', which also gives, by way of the city printer's bills, the numbers of acts of common council, proclamations, freemen's and constables' oaths and other documents printed (**69**, **229**).

The 'Foreign Charge' also contains payments to the officers of the lord mayor's household for special responsibilities such as procuring venison warrants, delivering the bills of mortality to the court, keeping the door of the council chamber, seeing bills affixed to houses affected with the plague, riding into Kent or Essex to view the stocks of wood or procuring wheat for trial for the assize of bread, while the city's concern for its water supply, already evinced under 'Emptions' in the making of new conduit pipes, is further demonstrated by the many views of the conduits and conduit heads by aldermen, commoners and officers. Routine expenditure about Guildhall is still in the 1580s entered under 'Foreign Charge', as are repairs to the plate and insignia, although, as stated above, by 1632–33 these are recorded in the new section of 'Necessary Expenses'. The 'Foreign Charge' also includes those charitable expenses which took the form of a single payment rather than an annual relief. Thus the pension granted to a former officer of the household while in Bethlem appears under 'Outward Fees' but the 20s. given to his wife for her immediate relief, although granted by the same court order, is entered here.

Many payments in this section are authorised by specific order of the court of aldermen cited in the accounts[46] and a small number by commandment of the lord mayor. Officers of middle and lower rank usually submitted bills in connection with their expenses. It is usual in this section for a number of payments to be grouped together in one entry with a total in the right margin. Such payments are often related, as in an

[44] This was a fairly new office; the first holder was probably Robert Christopher in 1544 (Rep.11, f.152).

[45] Rep.21, f.364; Rep.23, ff.130, 186b. For further references to Smith's career, CLRO, Ms. list of schedules in the mayor's court original bills, introduction by Anne Sutton, pp. xxvii, xxx, xxxii, and for reference to his foundation of Market Harborough School, Ms.53.1.

[46] Often the date of payment is given as well and this is nearly always within a very short time from the passing of the order. In the earlier accounts in Chamber Accounts 1, the authorising order and the date of payment are recorded more rarely.

entry concerning the expenses of a particular law suit or the conservancy charges but a few composite entries are formed of quite unconnected payments (e.g. **85**). The total of this section in 1584–85 was £1,586.16s.1½d. and in 1585–86 £2,119.8s.11d. The average over the ten years 1633–42 was £12,183.[47]

Many folios bearing entries which must be ascribed to the 'Foreign Charge' survive among the draft accounts in Chamber Accounts 1 but almost always in a confused order and in a heavily amended state. Only in 1563–64 does this section appear to be virtually complete (total £737.10s.0½d). Nevertheless it is clear that the 'Foreign Charge' of the 1560s and 1570s was very like that of the 1580s. A small selection of extracts from the 'Foreign Charge' 1563–71 is calendared as Appendix E.

After the 'Foreign Charge' a few sections calling for little explanation conclude the Discharge. 'New Year's Gifts' (**115**, **245**), amounting to less than £100, lists a few payments to high officers of state and £40 p.a. paid to the lord mayor in lieu of wine for his household. 'Liveries' (**116–20**, **246–50**) records both purchases of cloth for making winter and summer liveries and payments to officers who received money in lieu of a livery gown. Deductions are made from the total expenditure upon liveries of those sums which were to be borne upon the charitable or Finsbury accounts. The chamberlain then asks for certain 'Allowances' (**121**, **251**) and, finally, payments made during the year in respect of orphans' portions, £1,411.4s.7d. in 1584–85 and £2,048.4s.7d. in 1585–86 (**122**, **252**) and orphans' finding money, £245.19s.¼d. in 1584–85 and £301.5s.4d. in 1585–86 (**123**, **253**) are given in total only. (As with the receipts of orphanage, these payments were being entered individually in the accounts of the 1560s.)

In the sixteenth century this completes the Discharge upon the general account which amounted in 1584–85 to £6,189.1s.1¼d. and in 1585–86 to £8,273.5s.4d. Again it has to be noted that these figures include all categories of payments made during the year whether in respect of corporate expenses or the payment of principal or interest to orphans. In the accounts of the 1630s, however, a new and financially most important section appears between 'Allowances' and 'Orphanage', which again illustrates the growth of the chamber's banking activities in the seventeenth century. This is headed 'Money at interest lent and paid within the time of this account' and lists monies lent out at interest for six or twelve months.[48] In the 1630s also the orphans' finding money is followed, still as part of the general account, by payments out of the Philipot, Carpenter and Reynwell estates, the more recently acquired Costen estate and the manor of Finsbury, each with its own total, before the total of the whole Discharge is entered.

The totals of the Charge and Discharge now being established, the balance upon the general account due to or from the chamberlain could

[47] Wren, 1633–42, 195.

[48] In 1632–33 there were 36 loans totalling £28,330 but Wren has pointed out this was a very variable section. Some of the loans are marked as repaid and such repayments with accrued interest will be found as indicated under the 'Debts received' section of the Charge; repayments of interest alone are entered under 'Receipts Extraordinary'.

be entered.[49] This balance, since it took account of arrears due from the chamberlain upon the previous year's account, masked the fact that in real terms the payments exceeded the receipts in each of the years 1584–85, 1585–86 and 1632–33.

Accounts for the Philipot, Carpenter, Reynwell and Finsbury Estates

In the 1560s and 1580s the general account is followed by three short accounts relating to the Philipot, Carpenter and Reynwell lands which the city had long held to uses and of which the combined rental amounted to nearly a third of that upon the general and Blanchappleton lands. Each of these three accounts was made up of a charge, which comprised the rental and any other source of income such as admission fines for leases of the property, plus, if appropriate, the arrears due from the chamberlain upon the last account, a discharge containing the disbursements, plus, if appropriate, an allowance for the sum owed by the city to the chamberlain upon the last account, and the balance (**125–33**, **255–63**).

Under the will, with codicils, of John Philipot, mayor 1378–79,[50] proved in the court of husting in 1389, properties which included tenements on the south side of Cheapside, a tenement in Lombard Street near the Stocks, another in Pudding Lane, tenements in and near Lambeth Hill including the premises used in the sixteenth century and later as Blacksmiths' Hall, and tenements on the east side of Queenhithe, came into possession of the city upon the death of Philipot's widow.[51] A number of small payments for obits, which are still to be found in Richard Maunsell's account of 1535–36, were no longer payable by the time of the Elizabethan accounts but the chief charitable bequest of one penny a day to each of thirteen poor people to be chosen after his widow's death by the mayor and recorder remained the principal charge upon the estate. At the opening of the Philipot account for 1563–64 the city was indebted to the chamberlain in the sum of £157.11s.11d.[52] indicating considerable expenditure, perhaps on maintenance of properties, in a previous year or years. Income from the rental, amounting to a little more than £70, exceeded expenditure in the following years and the adverse balance had dropped to £28.13s.4½d. at the close of the account for 1566–67.[53] In both 1584–85 and 1585–86 income from the rental was supplemented by substantial fines for admission to leases while disbursements were less than in the 1560s[54] and the Philipot account was showing a comfortable surplus.

[49] In the draft account of 1584–85 this figure is not entered.

[50] Beaven i, 390; Thrupp 360; *Cal. Wills* ii, 275–7. Margaret Darby, 'John Philipot, a fourteenth century London merchant', unpublished London M.Sc. (Econ) thesis, 1972.

[51] The rental of 1584–85, amended 1586–87, is complete for the Philipot lands although the location of all the tenements is not specified (Chamber Accounts 2, ff.191r–192r). For the rental in the 18th century, see Misc. MSS.354.17.

[52] Chamber Accounts 1, f.108v.

[53] *Ibid.*, f.171.

[54] All four accounts from 1563–64 to 1566–67 show expenditure on building materials and workmen's wages as well as a payment of £6.13s.4d. to the crown, formerly payable under Philipot's will to the convent of St Pancras at Lewes for the maintenance of a chantry. There are no such payments in 1584–85 and 1585–86.

The principal object of the charity of John Carpenter, town clerk 1417–38, was the maintenance and schooling of four boys, originally as choristers in the Guildhall Chapel, and its fame has endured by reason of its absorption into the endowments of the City of London School upon the latter's foundation in 1834. The estate, which was the smallest of the three charitable estates, with a rental in the 1560s of only £26.6s.8d. and in the 1580s of £34, originally comprised three tenements in Thames Street, one in Bridge Street and one in Chancery Lane but the latter was exchanged with Sir Nicholas Bacon, the lord keeper, in 1574 for other premises in Cheapside, Houndsditch and St. Giles in the Fields in a transaction to which reference is made several times in the account of 1584–85.[55] The rental of the Carpenter estate in the second half of the sixteenth century did not exceed the regular outgoings by any considerable amount, and in both 1566–67 and 1584–85 additional expenditure on maintenance of properties resulted in an actual deficit that year although the accounts as presented show only a reduced balance due to the city from the chamberlain.[56]

The most substantial of the three estates was that of John Reynwell, mayor 1426–27,[57] which in the 1560s produced a rental of £123.16s.8d. and in the 1580s of £125.3s.4d. After Reynwell's death in 1445 his property in the parishes of St Botolph Billingsgate, St Mary at Hill, All Hallows the Great and St Andrew Undershaft and elsewhere in the city, and also all his lands and tenements in the town of Calais, had passed upon trusts to the city.[58] In 1447 the property in Calais was granted by the city to William Combes, alderman, for thirty years in recognition of his services in the execution of Reynwell's will.[59] Reynwell's former mansion house in London was held of the city on lease by alderman John Walden and his heirs until 1468. Together with adjoining premises it is to be identified as 'le Styleyerd' or the 'Stilehof' in the parish of All Hallows the Great in the ward of Dowgate, which was described in 1475, when by authority of the king in parliament it was conveyed to the merchants of the Hanse of Almaine in perpetuity for an annual rent of £70.3s.4d., as lately appertaining to John Reynwell and in the occupation of the Hanse merchants.[60] The rental of 1584–85 (amended 1586–87) is complete for the Reynwell lands and shows this rent from the merchants of the Steelyard to be the biggest item in the rental, which also included, among other properties, Somer's Quay leased to Margaret Stockmade for £30 p.a., the Salutation next Billingsgate with an adjoining tenement, and the Blackhoop next St Andrew Undershaft with other premises in St Andrew's parish.[61] The principal uses charged upon the Reynwell estate

[55] The history of the Carpenter estate, including the exchange of lands with Bacon, and of the charity is fully discussed by P. E. Jones, who made use of Chamber Accounts 1 and 2 for his study (*Cal. P & M Rolls, 1458–1482*, xiii–xxi).

[56] Chamber Accounts 1, ff.171v–172; **128–30**.

[57] Beaven ii, 5; Thrupp, 363.

[58] H.R.169(46), Reynwell to feoffees 1441; H.R. 207(31), *Cal. Wills* ii, 576, will of William Stafford, surviving feoffee, 1458 enrolled 1478, reciting the uses of Reynwell's will.

[59] *Cal. Letter Book K*, 322.

[60] *Cal. Letter Book L*, 44, 127; *Cal. PR. 1467–77*, 509; Stow i, 234, ii, 319–21; Harben, 550.

[61] Chamber Accounts 2, ff.193v–195r. No properties in Calais are included in the rental; even before the loss of Calais in 1558 the city was having problems in maintaining its

were payment of the fee farm rent of £10 a year for the borough of Southwark in order to remove the need to collect tolls there, a payment of £8 a year to the sheriffs intended to free Englishmen from paying tolls at London Bridge, and payments which could amount to as much as £65 in relief of the inhabitants of the wards of Billingsgate, Dowgate and Aldgate upon occasions of the levying of a fifteenth. There were also a number of small sums payable to officers and for obits; the latter had disappeared by the 1560s and the former had been modified or regrouped. Any surplus income after payment of the specific trusts could be divided into two and used, one part for the provisioning of the granary in time of need and the other for clearing the Thames of obstructions (e.g. **324 i–m**). The rental of the Reynwell lands was well in excess of expenditure in 1563–64 and the two following years (the account for 1566–67 being incomplete) and again in 1584–85 and 1585–86.

By the 1630s these three accounts were no longer being entered separately. As already indicated, the total of each rental was entered in the general account following the entry for the rents of the general lands and the customary disbursements were recorded elsewhere in the general account, but it would seem that by this date any additional income from admission fines and any expenditure upon materials and wages for the maintenance of properties was no longer distinguished from that in respect of other city lands. The value of each of the three rentals had increased and was to continue to increase whereas most of the charitable trusts remained at a fixed level.[62] The properties comprising each estate continue to be listed separately in the rentals up to 1784; thereafter they are listed with other city lands under the topographical heads of the general rental and their origin is no longer indicated.

A separate account was also kept for the manor of Finsbury which the city held on lease from the prebendary of Finsbury in St Paul's Cathedral. The city had long had interests in Finsbury but the first lease of the prebendal manor was obtained in 1514 and a subsequent lease for ninety years was secured in 1554.[63] Sums to be charged to this account in respect of materials and wages expended upon the properties or for liveries are deducted from the general expenditure under these heads and the balance upon this account is among the list of balances due to or from the chamberlain. The Finsbury account itself, however, was not entered in the chamberlain's account and appears to have been kept as a separate series of subsidiary accounts none of which has survived.[64] In the 1630s

---

interests there although the comptroller of the chamber, accompanied by the clerk of the works, spent three days there in June 1528 viewing the state of the property (Rep.7, ff.262b, 266b–267; Rep.12(2), f.427b; Rep.13, ff.38b, 52b, 54, 60b, 77, 156b).

[62] Save for the cost of educating 'Carpenter's children' which in the early 19th century was considerable (*Cal. P & M Rolls, 1458–82*, xxi).

[63] J. R. Sewell, *The Artillery Ground and Fields in Finsbury*, London Topographical Soc. publication no. 120, 1977, 3. The city continued to hold the manor of Finsbury by lease until 1867.

[64] See **281**. No account for Finsbury is to be found among Chamber Accounts 1 and 2 nor is the rental of the prebendal estate at Finsbury to be found in the city's cash volumes along with the general rental and rentals of the charitable estates before 1649–50.

this account is treated as part of the general account in precisely the same way as the accounts of the charitable estates.

Special Accounts: the Low Countries

In many years that would have concluded the accounts but on occasion a special account would be appended. In 1632–33 there was one for monies received towards the repair of Old St. Paul's. In 1584–85 such a special account related to the transportation of 2,420 men as soldiers to the Low Countries in August and September 1585, the queen having concluded a treaty with Commissioners from the Low Countries in August which bound her to provide an army and the city having already been asked to provide 500 men.[65] The account gives the names of the ships, twelve from London, three from Yarmouth and one each from Blakeney, Colchester and Hull, in which the 2,420 men sailed, the number of men carried in each ship, the name of the captain in charge of each contingent of men (one of whom was John, later Sir John, Norris, commander of the first force to leave for the continent),[66] and usually the name of the ship's master. In addition 400 vagrant and masterless men were taken up and sent as pioneers. Expenditure upon this account totalled £468.13s.4d. and was wholly re-imbursed by the crown (**134–5**). There are further entries in the body of the general account this year concerning the furnishing of 500 men with coats, powder and match, the 50 men who formed the guard of John Norris being given coats of a better quality than the others, and press money paid to the wards (**11q**, **102–4**). In 1585–86 there are two short, special accounts, one for the diet of the masterless men (**264–6**) and the other for the hire of horses provided for the Commissioners from the Low Countries (**267–9**). Upon both these accounts more money was received from the crown than was actually disbursed in this year and the balances of charge over discharge upon these two accounts are listed with the balances upon the general account and the accounts for the charitable estates as part of the final audit of the chamberlain's account for 1585–86 (**270**). The 'Foreign Charge' of 1585–86 also records the payment on 1 December 1585 of £500 in new gold angels to the Earl of Leicester, who had been placed in command of the English army and who was about to leave for the continent, towards his expenses in the Low Countries (**225**).[67]

Debts and Plate

The chamberlain's account is followed each year by two lists of debts, one of sums owed to the city and the other of monies owed by the city. The

[65] Jor.21, ff.454–6.

[66] Norris was appointed 12 Aug. and left England 12 days later (*DNB*). Most of the captains named are included, with others, in a list of 'Names of the [English] Captains in the Low Countries', 31 July 1585 (*Cal. SPF 1584–85*, 635).

[67] With the exception of the monies for horse-hire and of the gift to Leicester, the above receipts and payments are also entered, in a different form and without supporting detail, in the repertory of 30 Nov. 1585 which records an examination to that date of the accounts of the chamberlain relating not only to sending soldiers to the Low Countries but also to musters (Rep.21, ff.242b–243b).

two lists are separated by an inventory of the city's plate, which includes the lord mayor's collar of SS and jewel as well as the bowls, cups, dishes and spoons used for civic entertaining but not the swords or other items of regalia (**143**, **279**). The chamberlain was responsible for the city's plate as he was for the city's cash, and each year the new lord mayor on taking custody of the plate, which remained in his house for the term of his mayoralty, entered into an indenture with the chamberlain for its safe keeping and ultimate return. The few sixteenth-century inventories of plate surviving in Chamber Accounts 1 and 2, of which the earliest is for 1567, provide our earliest knowledge of the size and content of the civic collection although they give no valuation.[68]

Neither list of debts is totalled. The debts owed to the city at the close of the account for 1584–85 (**136–42**) amounted to approximately £6,320, this sum being made up of sixty-two separate items, a marked increase since the close of the account for 1566–67 when only seven items totalling approximately £880 were listed,[69] even though examination suggests that a considerable proportion of the sums outstanding in 1585 were either short-term debts or in a few cases were not yet due for payment. Of the sixty-two, twenty-six may be regarded as 'old' debts originating before 1583 and these totalled approximately £3,362. The first twenty-four are listed in a more or less chronological sequence covering 1558 to 1582 and are followed by two entries concerning a sum of £12.13s.4d. due annually from the merchants of the Steelyard which had been outstanding for thirty-one years and which by now totalled £392.13s.4d. By far the largest of these 'old' debts, which were very varied in character, was £1,463 due from George Heton, the last chamberlain but one, which represented the balance upon his last account for 1576–77,[70] and which was supplemented by two other small debts of £10 and £20 arising from his chamberlainship; the smallest was 30s., the moiety of a freedom fine as yet unpaid. As we have seen, interest at five per cent. was being received on the outstanding loan of £400 to Sir Edward Osborne and three other of the 'old' debts were being paid off in instalments. Two of the debts were in respect of admission fines for leases and of these one was not due until the death of the existing lessee and assurance had been given for payment of the other. Four related to discharge from shrieval or other civic office.

Fines for leases and for discharge from office form the bulk of the thirty-six remaining debts which are here distinguished as 'new' debts since, with the exception of a few of the smaller fines for leases, they had all arisen since 1582. These thirty-six totalled approximately £2,958. The accounts do not record the date and conditions of leases but these can usually be traced through the repertories.[71] Of the seventeen fines for

[68] Masters, 302.

[69] Chamber Accounts 2, ff.196–197. Of this £880, £700 was owed by Sir Thomas Lodge and his sureties. The total did not include the arrears of the annual sum due from the merchants of the Steelyard, referred to below. Two debts listed in 1567 were still oustanding in 1585 (**136a**,**c**).

[70] See p. xxxv.

[71] See CCPR.

leases among the 'new' debts, seven were to be paid off in full during the next year and in four cases the portion of the fine payable at the time of the grant had already been paid and the remainder was not due until a specified date or until the reversion became effective. In conjunction with the evidence of the 'Leases' section of the general account, which records payments in whole or in part of four fines all made within six months of the date of the grant of the lease, and of the 'Debts received' section, which includes several fines in respect of leases none of which had been granted earlier than 1583, it seems clear that debts in this category were not normally long outstanding.

There were twelve fines for refusal to serve as sheriff or for discharge from civic office listed among the 'new' debts in 1585 but this number was probably unusually high. The shrieval fine of £200 was considerably more substantial than the majority of fines for leases but there is evidence that this also was usually paid within a short time. Under the act of common council of 27 May 1585[72] which, among other things, changed the date of the shrieval election from 1 August to 24 June, the lord mayor retained the right, which he exercised from before 1347 until 1694, of choosing one of the two sheriffs, the other being elected by the commonalty, which by now was represented for electoral purposes by the liverymen of the city companies. Between 8 and 24 June 1585, the lord mayor, Sir Thomas Pullison, met with no fewer than ten refusals to serve before his eleventh candidate, Anthony Ratcliffe, accepted office. The first two men elected by the commonalty also refused before the third, Henry Prannell, agreed to serve. A small encouragement to acceptance was given by the payment of £100 under the act of 1585 (£200 under an earlier act of 1 August 1582)[73] to the first person to accept office following a refusal.

Of the ten who rejected nomination by the lord mayor, Richard Hale and Giles Garton paid their fine in full within the account for 1584–85 and so do not appear in the 1585 list of debtors, Thomas Bracy, Richard Gurney and Robert Withens paid half in 1584–85 and half in 1585–86 and had discharged the debt by April 1586, Richard Morris paid one third in 1584–85 and two thirds in 1585–86 and was clear by September 1586, and Edward Elmer paid the whole within the account for 1585–86. John Taylor secured consent to the substitution of a larger fine to discharge him from serving as alderman and mayor as well as sheriff and paid the first of the agreed instalments on 10 November 1585. Apart from the outstanding portion of his debt, this left only William Elkyn and John Ketcher, together with the two men who had refused election by the commonalty, William Gardiner and John Lacy, to be listed among the debtors at the close of the account for 1585–86. The other two debts of this kind listed in 1585 were those of Thomas Gore, who had refused the office of sheriff in August 1584 and who was to pay his fine in full in February 1586, and Richard Barne who, having earlier paid a shrieval fine of £200, secured consent in July 1585 to the payment of a further fine of 200 marks, payable in instalments, to discharge him from shrieval and

[72] Jor.21, ff.437a–438a.
[73] *Ibid.*, ff.226a–227a.

aldermanic office. The customary fine of £200 was payable, it should be said, in respect of a particular election only and did not of itself exempt a man from nomination in future or from a subsequent fine if he again refused to serve. This is well illustrated by the case of the unfortunate Thomas Skinner. He had been chosen by the lord mayor in July 1580 and was not only paying off his fine for refusal in small instalments of £20 a year but was also in debt for a fine for discharge from Newgate where he had been committed for his unwisely expressed exasperation at the lord mayor's nomination on that occasion (**139b**). On 1 August 1584 he was elected by the commonalty, again refused to serve, but this time paid his fine, which is recorded under 'Receipts Extraordinary' in 1584–85, within less than three months. In May 1585 he secured exemption for two years but in June 1587 upon being elected once more by the commonalty he resigned himself to serving.[74]

One of the 'old' debts and fourteen of the 'new' had been paid off before the close of 1585–86 and others had been reduced in amount; five fresh debts had arisen totalling only about £241. The lists of debts owed to the city in 1586 (**272–8**), therefore, was reduced to fifty-two in number and approximately £5,340 in total.

Apart from some monies due to the chamberlain, the list of debts owed by the city at the close of the account for 1584–85 (**144**) contained only four items but in total, at approximately £6,354, these slightly exceeded the sum of the debts due to the city at this date. The largest debt, and the one in which lay the seed of many of the city's financial problems in the next hundred years, was £5,493.17s.10½d. owed to the city orphans.[75] Two debts had originated in the acquisition of property for the site of the Royal Exchange and on both of these outstanding sums interest at five per cent was being paid. The remaining debt was the balance, as yet unspent and remaining in the chamber, of monies raised for the specific purpose of redeeming Christian captives held in infidel hands. All four of these items recur in the list of the city's debts at the close of the next year's account (**280**), the debt to the orphans having risen to £6,092.13s.8½d. and the capitives' money being slightly reduced. Two further debts have been added, each of £100, but both were of a kind likely to be paid off in the next account. The total indebtedness of the city at September 1586 was approximately £7,065.

Reference has been made to the growth of the city's banking activities between the 1580s and the 1630s and this is even more strikingly illustrated in the list of debts due to the city appended to the respective accounts. In 1633 the list includes no fewer than 118 debts, some of them for considerable sums, for money lent by the city at interest, a category of debt which is almost entirely absent in 1585 and 1586. In 1633 there are also twenty-two fines outstanding for refusal to serve as sheriff or discharge from civic office, thirty-one fines for leases and thirty other

[74] Jor.21, f.438 and Jor.22, f.109 for Skinner 1585, 1587. Other references to the journals and repertories relevant to this paragraph are cited at the appropriate points in the text of the calendar.

[75] This debt is given as a total only. In 1567 the debts due to individual orphans are specified but the surviving list may not be complete (Chamber Accounts 2, f.200).

miscellaneous debts. Of the debts owed by the city, the orphans' debt had by 1633 reached the staggering total of £179,300.[76] It is the greater pity that the intervening accounts, which would help to mark the course of these changes, have not survived.

The Chamber in the sixteenth century

The chamberlain was elected or re-elected annually by the commonalty on the day of election of the sheriffs but from 1491 the commonalty's choice was limited to one of two persons nominated by the mayor and aldermen.[77] In the hierarchy of city office he ranked second only to the recorder and of the fourteen chamberlains in office between 1484 and 1603 all but one was a member of one of the twelve great livery companies.[78] His responsibilities were more wide ranging than those of any other officer. As well as his functions concerning the enrolment of apprentices and the admission of freemen and his jurisdiction in respect of apprentices, he was charged by the terms of his recognizance with the oversight of the lands and tenements belonging to the commonalty and responsibility for their maintenance, with the rendering of a true account before the auditors of all the revenues which he received and the payment of all arrears found due upon his account, and with the safe keeping and return of the goods and monies of orphans and others which were entrusted to the city.[79] In consequence of the first of these charges the chamberlain was not only closely concerned with leases and rents[80] but was ultimately accountable for the work of the city artificers and workmen and for the city's store of materials.[81] In the discharge of this latter responsibility he was greatly aided by the comptroller of the chamber[82] who acted in some measure both as a deputy to and a check upon the chamberlain and who was sometimes styled the underchamber-

[76] City's Cash 1/1, f.96; Wren 1633, 52.

[77] Order of common council of 15 April 1491 (Jor.9, f.270b). The date of the annual election was 21 Sept. in the 15th century and up to 1526, 2 Sept. from 1527 to 1537, 1 Aug. from 1538 to 1584 and 24 June from 1585. From 1475 the electoral body was composed of the liverymen (*Cal. Letter Book L*, 132).

[78] Four goldsmiths, three mercers, two merchant taylors and one grocer, fishmonger, haberdasher, vintner and painter.

[79] Recognizances 1490 and 1548 (Jor.9, f.246b and Jor.15, f.383). And see the chamberlain's oath (*Cal. Letter Book D*, 198 and Elizabethan book of oaths, f.6). Before 1462 when the town clerk became keeper of the records, the safe-keeping of the city's muniments had also belonged primarily to the chamberlain (*Cal. Letter Book L*, 17).

[80] For a period prior to 1559 the allocation of leases and setting of rents had devolved upon the chamberlain with the assent of the aldermen, and leases of city property were sealed with the chamberlain's seal. In 1559 the court of aldermen resumed this function and between 1559 and 1592, when the city lands committee was established, control of leases was in the hands of a committee of four to six aldermen together with the chamberlain, which was known as the 'Surveyors of the City's Lands' (Shipley, 161–2; Foster, 21).

[81] Jor.10, ff.203b–207b *passim*.

[82] *Ibid.* And see comptroller's oath (Jor.10, f.200 and Elizabethan book of oaths, f.16). In 1585 'Orders for the city's store and provision in building' specified that the clerk of the works was to certify the labour and wages of the workmen to the comptroller, that any contracts which he negotiated for the purchase of materials had first to be notified to the chamberlain or comptroller, and that no works could be undertaken by the workmen without warrant of the chamberlain (Rep.21, ff.60b–61b).

lain. The breadth of the chamberlain's concerns made him to all intents and purposes the chief executive officer of the city and the repertories of the court of aldermen are studded with executive as well as purely financial orders directed to him.

On 17 March 1490 William Purchas, mercer, who had been chamberlain since 1484, and three fellow mercers as sureties were bound in one recognizance in the very considerable sum of £1,000.[83] In the hundred years which followed, some periodic disquiet about the workings of the chamber is evident, and there are sporadic, if not always specific, hints of irregularities. At the turn of the century, during the chamberlainship of William Milbourne, painter, an investigation into 'Considerations of the decay of the Bridge and Chamber of London and of the yearly profits that of the same should come' resulted in January 1501 in detailed recommendations, the majority of which were intended to remove delay in reparations and to effect more stringent control over artificers, workmen and materials, but which also provided that the mayor and aldermen should assign yearly 'an auditor such as is expert and learned in the feat of audit after the form of the exchequer' to attend upon the elected auditors, that the chamberlain and bridgemasters should present their sureties before the mayor and aldermen within fourteen days of the annual election day, and that each year they should bring their books of account allowed before the auditors and all monies remaining in their hands to the first court of aldermen to be held after Christmas.[84] The appointment during the next two decades of committees to oversee abuses in the office of chamberlain or to see the books of the chamber, and an order for the holding of a weekly meeting of certain aldermen and the town clerk with the chamberlain on matters concerning the chamber, suggest that these recommendations, if implemented, did not succeed in making all well.[85] Complaints were brought against John Barnard, mercer, chamberlain 1517–25,[86] in the course of several disputes concerning money or leases,[87] although the commonalty nevertheless saw fit to elect him as one of the sheriffs in 1525.[88]

Matters seem to have improved for a time thereafter. In 1534 Barnard's successor, John Husee, vintner, chamberlain 1525–32, was

[83] Jor.9, f.246b where the recognizance is set out in full.

[84] Jor.10, ff.203b–207b. No evidence has been traced concerning the implementation of the recommendation concerning an expert auditor at this time. From 1604 to 1750 a 'professional' auditor was appointed annually by the mayor and aldermen to assist the auditors elected in common hall (Misc. MSS.140.10).

[85] Rep.1, f.170; Rep.2, f.163; Rep.3, f.184b.

[86] He was in office for all this period except for a few days in Sept. 1522. Barnard and John Billesden, grocer, were in nomination on 21 Sept., Billesden was elected but successfully pleaded ill health and at a new election on 27 Sept. Barnard was chosen (Jor.12, ff.194b, 203–4).

[87] With Simon Ryce, a former bridgemaster (Rep.4, ff.212b, 214, 214b); with William Dolphin (Rep.5, ff.222b, 225b, 232); and, after going out of office, with John Brown, former alderman (Rep.7, ff.181–250b *passim*). Members of the city companies who were aggrieved with the chamberlain were also ordered on 11 Dec. 1522 to bring their complaints in writing before the lord mayor and aldermen when they would be favourably heard (Rep.6, f.9) but this may have been a matter concerning freedom or apprenticeship.

[88] Rep.7, f.57b.

remitted £50 of the £400 which he owed to the city following the final examination of his accounts.[89] Although the chamberlain's accounts were audited annually, the balance due from or to him was carried forward to his next account, and it was only on going out of office that there was a final reckoning. In 1547 George Medley, mercer, chamberlain 1532–33, 1534–48,[90] was exempted from serving the office of sheriff for seven years in recompense of the exceptional burden of his financial responsibilities during the past few years in connection with the new conduits, the provision of corn for the city, the setting forth of soldiers and other extraordinary business.[91]

When Thomas Hayes, goldsmith, who had been underchamberlain to Medley, was elected to succeed him in 1548[92] he became bound in the sum of £300 and his five sureties, all goldsmiths, in £50 each,[93] a considerably smaller security than had been required in 1491. The financial responsibility of the sureties was a real one. Hayes died in office and a year later, in November 1551, his sureties were given the option of paying £40 each at once or the full sum of their bond by instalments, but it was subsequently agreed that if each contributed £30 immediately towards the payment of the arrears of Hayes' account their recognizances should be discharged.[94] Hayes' successor, John Sturgeon, haberdasher, chamberlain 1550–1563,[95] and his four sureties were bound in similar sums to Hayes and his sureties but it was ordered that future chamberlains should be bound in the sum of £200 and find six sureties to be bound in £100 each.[96]

It was during Sturgeon's tenure of office, on 2 May 1559, that the court of aldermen took back into its own hands the control of the leasing of the city lands which had for a long time been exercised by the chamberlain.[97] Sturgeon resigned in 1563 and in the following year the court of aldermen agreed in view of his long and diligent service to remit the whole of the £291.14s.7d. due upon his last account except for the sum of one hundred marks which was promptly paid.[98] The position was very different when George Heton, merchant taylor, chamberlain 1563–77, went out of office. Heton was first elected on 1 August 1563 and despite the requirement laid down in 1551 order was now given that the chamberlain and his sureties should henceforth be bound in the sum of £1,000,[99] the

89 Letter Book P, f.40b.

90 William Brokett, goldsmith, was in office for the year 1533–34. Medley was in nomination with Brokett at the election in 1533.

91 Rep.11, f.346b; Jor.15, f.325b.

92 Jor.15, f.375. Medley was in nomination with Hayes at this election.

93 Jor.15, f.383 where the recognizance is set out in full. The conditions are the same as in 1491.

94 Rep.12(2), ff.407b, 411, 413.

95 Following Hayes' death the court of aldermen considered nine possible candidates to succeed him, several of whom were put forward by distinguished sponsors, before nominating Sturgeon and Henry Fisher, who had the king's letters in his support, for the commonalty's choice (Letter Book R, f.96b).

96 Rep.12(2), ff.296, 298b; Letter Book R, f.128.

97 See above p. xxxii, note 80.

98 Rep.15, ff.326, 332b, 343.

99 Jor.18, f.137b; Rep.15, f.279.

same sum as in 1491. On 18 January 1565 Heton was required to surrender the office of profit which he enjoyed as one of the alnagers or searchers of woollen cloths but for this reason, and because the chamberlainship was not as profitable as formerly, he was awarded certain fees to his own use.[100] On 13 December 1577 he was dismissed from office by the common council *pro diversis magnis rebus dictam Civitatem et negotia eiusdem tangentibus*.[101] He was heavily in debt to the city and it seems to others also; within a few days of his dismissal he asked that his other creditors might be summoned to the lord mayor's house and persuaded not to press for repayment until he should have settled his account as chamberlain.[102] If they agreed they were destined for a long wait. On 19 October 1580 common council ordered that Heton's sureties should be pressed to pay the £900 for which they were bound and that Heton's own bond should be taken for repayment of the remainder of the debt, 'and he to pay the same as god shall send him able'.[103] It has already been observed that the sum of £1,463 still due from Heton was the largest item in the list of outstanding debts owed to the city in 1585.[104] Committee after committee was appointed to audit Heton's accounts, many of them at his request, but for some unexplained reason no settlement was arrived at and the last reference to the matter is the appointment on 26 April 1598 of yet another committee to examine and close his accounts.[105]

A congregation held on the day of Heton's dismissal, 13 December 1577, elected in his place John Mabbe, goldsmith, who had been an active common councilman since 1573,[106] and in the following July Mabbe delivered ten bonds of himself and his sureties, each in £100, into the custody of the town clerk.[107] He died in office and on 4 June 1583 it was ordered that his account should be audited at a time convenient to his widow and executors.[108]

Robert Brandon, goldsmith, whose two accounts for 1584–85 and 1585–86, are calendared in this volume, was elected in Mabbe's place on 8 January 1583.[109] Brandon became free of the Goldsmiths' Company by redemption on 3 February 1548 and was admitted to the livery on 5 May 1561.[110] From c.1558 to 1580 he was one of the queen's two royal goldsmiths,[111] and in 1582–83 he served as prime warden of his company. The most famous of his many apprentices was Nicholas Hilliard, the

[100] Rep.15, f.413.
[101] Jor.20(2), f.376b. No details of Heton's misdemeanours are specified.
[102] Rep.19, f.275b.
[103] Jor.21, f.76.
[104] See p. xxix.
[105] Rep.24, f.217b.
[106] Jor.20(2), f.376b; Foster, 165.
[107] Rep.19, f.346b.
[108] Rep.20, f.434b.
[109] Jor.21, f.250b; Rep.20, f.387.
[110] Goldsmiths' Company wardens' accounts and court minutes, I, p. 31; K, p. 151.
[111] With Affabel Partridge c.1558–76 and with Hugh Keall 1577–80 (H. D. W. Sitwell, 'The Jewel House and the Royal Goldsmiths', *Archaeological Journal*, cxvii, 1960, 150). At the election for chamberlain following Brandon's death in 1591 Affabel Partridge was the unsuccessful candidate (Letter Book AB, f. 32b).

miniature painter, who married Alice, one of Brandon's daughters by his first marriage, at St. Vedast, Foster Lane, on 15 July 1576.[112]

Concern with the workings of the chamber was particularly evident during Brandon's chamberlainship. In part this related to the administration of the city lands where there was undoubtedly lack of adequate control and supervision and possibly malfeasance. On 29 May 1584 a special court of aldermen was ordered to be held to investigate abuses of the workmen and labourers belonging to the chamber.[113] On 15 January 1589 provision was made that the commoners among the auditors of the chamberlain's account, attended by certain officers including the city carpenter, should meet at least four times a year to view the tenements belonging to the chamber and certify the necessary repairs 'to the end the tenants may be charged for the repairing and amending of the same or other order therein taken', and also to oversee the use of the stores of timber and other materials.[114] On 2 July 1590 the court of aldermen instructed the city's counsel to devise 'some good course' for the leasing of the city's and bridge house lands.[115] This disquiet was undoubtedly a major contributory cause in the establishment of the city lands committee in 1592.[116]

Towards the end of Brandon's chamberlainship there was anxiety about many aspects of the chamberlain's accounts and the city finances. In 1590 an ineffectual attempt was made to advance the date of audit from May or June to two weeks before Christmas.[117] At the audit of the account for 1588–89 held on 3 June 1590 the auditors noted several special matters deserving of consideration.[118] These included a special examination of the allowance of liveries to officers and the increase in fees; the abolition of certain specified payments;[119] a demand that the auditors and two other common councilmen, Thomas Wilford and Humphrey Huntley,[120] should 'look more pertinently' not only at the account for 1588–89 which was under audit but also at both the account for the previous year, 1587–88, which had not yet been signed by the auditors, and Brandon's current account up to the last day of May 1590; and a further demand that the same men should specially consider the

[112] Brandon married Katherine Barber at St Mary Woolnoth in 1548. The younger children of this marriage were baptised at St Vedast, Foster Lane, as also in 1577, Lucy, daughter of his second marriage to Elizabeth Chapman, née Osborne. Both his wives were buried at St Vedast, Katherine in 1574 and Elizabeth in 1588, as was Robert Brandon himself on 8 June 1591 (for Brandon's family, see Mary Edmond, *Hilliard and Oliver: the lives and works of two great miniaturists*, 1983, 34–5, 105–6, 108–9). The Goldsmiths' Company records show him at the sign of the 'Gilt Lion' in Goldsmiths' Row in Cheap where he was living when his will was drawn up. He was survived by a son, Edward, five daughters of his first marriage, including Alice Hilliard, and Lucy (PRO Prob 11/17, ff.339–43. And see below p. xxxvii, note 122).

[113] Rep.21, f.55.

[114] Rep.22, f.18b.

[115] Rep.22, f.186b.

[116] Shipley, 165.

[117] Rep.22, f.175. The audit of the accounts for 1591–2 and 1592–3 continued to take place in May (Rep.23, ff.60b, 214).

[118] Rep.22, f.180.

[119] Including the fee and liveries of John Luck, see **26g**.

[120] Shipley, note 15, for biographical details of Wilford and Huntley.

state of the orphan fund and 'how the chamber might best be brought out of debt'. At the court of aldermen held on 18 June 1590 to which this report of the auditors was submitted, a further provision was made that every Saturday a waste book showing how much orphanage money had been received and paid out should be shown to the lord mayor.[121]

Further than this the city records maintain a discreet silence. No specific charges against Brandon were formulated but rumours must have been widespread. In his will of 8 May 1591, drawn up only three weeks before his death, he protested his rectitude:

> 'I certify and make known to my said executors and overseer, and to all others to whom the same may appertain, and desire them to take knowledge for a certain truth, whatsoever rumours may be blazed abroad to the contrary that touching my state accounts and reckonings appertaining to mine office of chamberlainship of the city of London I stand clear without any just cause of accusation and so I am well assured I shall do unto the end'.

Brandon named two of his Guildhall colleagues in his will. Robert Smith, at this date deputy comptroller and city solicitor, was appointed executor along with Brandon's youngest daughter, Lucy, who was still a minor at the time of her father's death, and John Benson, goldsmith, presumably the same John Benson who is described in the accounts as clerk to the chamberlain and who kept the orphanage accounts, was left a bequest of £10. Among the trusts imposed by his will upon the Goldsmiths' Company was the provision of an annual service at St Vedast, Foster Lane, Brandon's parish church, which was to be attended by the chamberlain and comptroller for the time being who would receive 6s.8d. and 3s.4d. respectively in consideration of their attendance.[122]

Brandon died on 30 May 1591.[123] Despite his assertion of financial probity, the court of aldermen saw fit on 1 June 1591 to order his successor, elected that day, to bring in within fourteen days ten bonds totalling £2,000,[124] double the amount in which Brandon and his sureties had been bound, and on 8 June to order certain aldermen together with Robert Smith to take an inventory of the writings, plate, money and other contents of the chamber at Brandon's death and to deliver them to his successor.[125] The inventory was in the form of a tripartite indenture, one

[121] Rep.22, f.180b.

[122] P.R.O. Prob 11/77, ff.339–43, proved 10 June 1591 and 1 June 1599 after Lucy came of age. Brandon left one half the nett of his personal estate to Lucy, the only one of his children as yet unadvanced, according to the custom of London, and the other half to pay the legacies specified in his will. No personal possessions are mentioned in the will. Monetary legacies were provided for his son, Edward, his five other daughters and his many grandchildren. The Goldsmiths' Company received £20 towards a new gallery intended to be built in the garden of their hall, £6.13s.4d. for distribution among the poor almsmen of the company, and £100 with which to purchase 30 pounds weight of sterling silver to be lent out in parcels of five pounds for terms of three years to poor workmen of the company. Property in the parishes of St Nicholas Acon and St. George Southwark and in Peckham Fields in Camberwell worth £58.16s.8d. p.a. was also left to the Goldsmiths' Company upon trusts which included the payment of £50 p.a. to his son, Edward, to whom he left all his other lands.

[123] Letter Book AB, f.32b.

[124] Rep.22, f.279b.

[125] Rep.22, f.281.

part remaining with the new chamberlain, one with Brandon's executors and the third among the city records. A copy was entered in the repertory.[126] Days were appointed for the audit of Brandon's accounts in September 1591 and again in May 1593.[127]

Brandon's successor was Thomas Wilford, merchant taylor, chamberlain 1591–1603, who seems not to have been the common councilman of the same name mentioned above although both were merchant taylors.[128] Anxiety about finances, particularly the state of the city's debt, was unabated during his tenure of office. In 1595 he was requested to inform the court of aldermen each month in writing of his receipts and payments.[129] A committee was appointed on 13 December 1597 to view the accounts and state of both the chamber and the bridge house.[130] On 29 September 1598 it was ordered that the auditors should close the chamberlain's account for 1596–97, that the chamberlain's clerk should prepare as quickly as possible an abstract of the account for the year just ended for perusal by the auditors, and that any transactions not relating to this last account should be recorded separately 'so as they may be the more easily seen and understood'.[131] The auditors were also instructed to consider how the income of the chamber could be increased and its expenditure diminished but no outcome of their deliberations is recorded. Additional auditors were appointed in October 1598 and in July 1599 Wilford was instructed to find seven new sureties, each to be bound in £100, in place of seven of his existing sureties.[132] On 29 September 1599 auditors were named to examine the accounts and the state of the chamber for 1597–99 and 'to understand what and how much is owing by this city, what in right is due to be paid to the same, what sums remain where and in whose hands the same is'.[133] The financial troubles of the city in the sixteenth century, compounded of inadequate control in the administration of the city lands, accounting procedures which were intended to elicit the personal responsibility of the accountant rather than the true financial state of the corporate body, the failure to distinguish between revenue and capital accounts, the failure to relate costs of maintenance or costs of collecting income to any particular revenue item, dependence upon the unsatisfactory expedient of raising money for extraordinary expenditure for special purposes upon ad hoc assessments upon the livery companies or the wards, and above all the growing debt to the city orphans, all of which can be discerned in the sixteenth-century accounts, laid the foundations of the more serious problems which it was to experience in the seventeenth century.

[126] Rep.22, ff.291b–298.
[127] Rep.22, f.308; Rep.23, f.60b.
[128] Foster, 188.
[129] Rep.23, f.439.
[130] Rep.24, f.170b.
[131] Rep.24, f.286b.
[132] Rep.24, ff.300, 432b.
[133] Rep.24, f.465.

THE MANUSCRIPTS

Dr. Reginald R. Sharpe, the records clerk, concluded his annual report upon the Corporation records for 1889 with the following paragraph:

> 'The attention of your [Library] Committee is drawn to two volumes in the Town Clerk's custody which are of more than ordinary interest, but which in their present state cannot be practically utilised. They contain Accounts of the Chamber of London, temp. Elizabeth, but they have been bound up transversely and used for pasting down a series of Index Slips, of no great value, over the original matter. The Accounts, which, except in a few places, are entirely hidden from view, are probably the earliest Chamber Accounts extant . . . It is for your Committee to consider the advisability of having the Index Slips carefully removed by competent hands and re-laid elsewhere, so that the original matter may be read and utilised and two more volumes added to the City's Archives. It has been ascertained that the whole work of removing and re-laying the slips, cleaning and repairing, where necessary, the pages of the original MSS, and binding them up in their original form, &c, could be done at Her Majesty's Public Record Office, by skilled workmen at a cost not exceeding 50L.'[134]

This programme was approved, and skilfully carried out by craftsmen of the Public Record Office working in a private capacity.[135] The index slips were removed, relaid on cartridge paper, and bound up in two volumes to be identified as two large books with vellum covered boards which are lettered on the covers 'Rough Index to Orphans' and 'Rough Index to the City Records'. Both contain slips giving references to the repertories of the court of aldermen, on orphanage and general matters respectively, between the mayoralties of Sir Martin Bowes 1545–46 and Sir George Bonde 1587–88.

The accounts of the chamber thus revealed to view were guarded and filed and bound up in two other volumes with vellum covered boards which were lettered on the spine 'Chamber Accounts. 16th Century. 1' and 'Chamber Accounts. 16th Century. 2'. All were paper accounts, many of them drafts, drawn as a preliminary to a final engrossed account on parchment such as survives in the main series of city's cash accounts from 1632, and so were able to be discarded once the engrossed account was written up. Only a few lines of text have been wholly lost as a result of the folding of the leaves for the making of the indexes and in both volumes the slips were removed with remarkably little damage to the legibility of the accounts. The edges of many leaves are damaged, particularly in the first volume, where some pages have been trimmed as well as mutilated, but the majority of marginalia were undoubtedly subject headings and in the case of the second volume figures are missing from the right margin in only a small number of instances.

Chamber Accounts 1, foliated 1–240 in pencil at the bottom of the pages,[136] contains leaves from a number of accounts between 1535 and

[134] Report of the Library Committee presented to Common Council 29 May 1890, p. 7.

[135] PRO Office Correspondence (PRO 1/56). I am indebted to Mr. N. Evans of the Public Record Office for this reference.

[136] This numeration runs 1–38, 44, 39–43, 45–240. There is another numeration, also modern, at the top of the page. For much of the book this differs by one from that at the foot.

c. 1578, many of them fragmentary, which are bound up in considerable confusion.[137] The earliest account is for the year Michaelmas 1535–Michaelmas 1536 but this, written on paper of a smaller size than the rest, is not the chamberlain's account but a subsidiary account of certain quarterly receipts and payments kept by the chamberlain's clerk, Richard Maunsell. It is calendared in its reconstituted order as Appendix A where a fuller description is given. Chamber Accounts 1 also contains fragments of two other accounts of the time of George Medley, chamberlain. One, a single leaf, contains a record of sundry payments made in 1538,[138] and the other, comprising two leaves, appears to be part of a weekly record of payments and receipts of small sums.[139]

The greater part of the volume, however, consists of pages from the chamberlain's accounts between 1562 and 1578. These were draft accounts, containing in some sections numerous deletions and amendments, and, as already stated, now bound in considerable confusion. An attempt has been made to reconstruct their order, and a tentative guide to the contents of Chamber Accounts 1 is available in the Corporation of London Records Office. The most nearly complete account is that for 1563–64 where most of the sectional totals survive, but there is no record of the final balances or of the debts due to or by the city at the end of this year and no plate inventory. Considerable sections of the accounts for the three following years also survive, together with more fragmentary portions of some accounts of the later 1560s and the 1570s. Some extracts from the chamberlain's accounts in Chamber Accounts 1 are given as Appendices B–F.

Chamber Accounts 2, as bound in 1890, contained leaves from two chamberlain's accounts, 1584–85 and 1585–86, together with leaves from an incomplete rental of the same date. In addition five leaves from the account of 1566–67, larger in size than the rest, were included at the end of the volume, being guarded and filed by the head and folded. Neither the two accounts nor the rental were bound up strictly in their original order and there was some confusion both within one account and as between the two accounts. Further examination has made it possible to reconstruct the original order with reasonable certainty and to show that the two accounts are very nearly complete,[140] and the leaves of Chamber Accounts 2 have now been re-guarded and filed in their reconstructed order and rebound in the Corporation of London Records Office where tables giving the foliation of 1890 and the new foliation are available.[141]

[137] These accounts were probably already in a disordered and fragmentary state when they were taken as backing for the slips of the indexes.

[138] F.239. Among the payments are plate and money given to the lord chancellor and lord privy seal and their officers as new year's gifts. Three goblets and two salts were sold to provide these gifts.

[139] Ff.28, 29. These pages relate to one week in July and another in September in an unspecified year. Some of the receipts may be fees for enrolments.

[140] The two slip indexes contain no references after 1588 and therefore were probably compiled soon after the paper accounts for 1584–85 and 1585–86 were discarded, hence the comparative completeness of the contents of Chamber Accounts 2.

[141] As well as being rebound in 1982, Chamber Accounts 2 have been further cleaned and repaired, this work including the removal of traces of the backing of the index slips which

The year of the account ran from Michaelmas to Michaelmas but certain payments are dated after the nominal closing date although rarely later than Christmas. Most of these were made to outstanding creditors such as the artificers and others who had yet to submit bills in respect of work done or goods supplied during the last quarter of the year or to the lord mayor who was entitled to an allowance which was paid to him at the end of his term of office. A few such payments, however, were authorised by orders of the court of aldermen passed after 29 September and the reason for their inclusion is not always clear except when they relate specifically to items already in the account (e.g. **201**).

In the second half of the sixteenth century the audit almost always took place in May or June, one or two days being appointed for this purpose, and was followed by the audit dinner.[142] The account was written up in the form to be presented to the auditors during the intervening months, hence the occasional reference to the lord mayor in office during the period of the account as the 'late' lord mayor. References in the account to 'Michaelmas last past' are always to the nominal closing day of the account.

The calendared account for 1584–85 is a draft account. The manuscript is fairly heavily amended but many of the alterations are of a kind inevitable in a draft and of little significance. Several hands seem to have been at work in its compilation and at some stage the folios of this draft were numbered in two sequences, from the beginning of the account to the end of the section entitled 'Emptions' and from the beginning of the 'Foreign Charge' to the end. The draft was perused by an official who has supplied in a small, angular, hand, and usually by means of interlineation, a number of corrections and explanatory additions to the text and the occasional marginal annotation. The same hand has also filled in sums which the original clerk had left blank, including some sums in respect of individual entries and many of the sectional totals. This official also made an occasional re-arrangement of the text, grouping two or three former entries as one paragraph or dividing a long entry into two or three.

There is a strong possibility that the author of this amending hand is John Shaw, draper, who on 14 October 1585, i.e. just after the nominal closing date of the account but long before the audit, which on this occasion took place on 16 May 1586 (**237**), was admitted deputy to Humfrey Wynnington, clerk of the chamber, to carry out all his duties.[143]

---

occasionally adhered to the paper and the removal of tissue used in the repair of 1890 which had badly discoloured with time.

[142] e.g. Rep.16, f.209; Rep.18, f.212; Rep.20, f.191b; Rep. 22, f.173b and many similar entries.

[143] The occasion for this order was Wynnington's 'lewd life and evil behaviour' (Rep.21, f.221). Wynnington, who had been servant to alderman Sir Martin Bowes until the latter's death in 1566, was admitted clerk of the chamber on 6 July 1568 (Rep.16, f.374b). In 1574 an unspecified complaint against him was investigated by certain aldermen and the recorder; in June 1579 he was sequestered from office, retaliated by bringing complaints against the chamberlain and other officers of the chamber, and was restored in Nov. 1579 only upon the suit of the lord chief justice and the attorney general and upon written confession of his offences (Rep.18, f.191; Rep.19, f.462b; Rep.20, ff.14b–15).

In respect of the year 1584–85 the customary fees were split between Wynnington and Shaw, the former receiving the annual fee out of the chamber and the latter the reward at the audit and the fees for drawing and engrossing both the account and the book of fines (**19b**, **74**). The clerk of the chamber was the most important officer in the chamber under the chamberlain, save for the comptroller, and was chiefly concerned with the accounts. The office can be traced back to at least the early fourteenth century. An ordinance of the mayor and aldermen of 23 November 1478 provided that no other clerk in the chamber of the Guildhall should be keeper of the books nor record anything therein nor make the account of the chamberlain except the clerk of the chamber.[144] The number of clerks in the chamber in the late sixteenth century is unknown. The chamberlain himself had a clerk, known as 'Mr Chamberlain's clerk', and by an ordinance of 1492 the clerk of the chamber was allowed a clerk under him[145] but there were almost certainly others.

The account for 1584–85 does not show any final summary of the charges and discharges upon the chamberlain's general account and the other accounts nor the balance due from the chamberlain. It is conceivable that a page is missing but more likely that these totals were not included in the draft.

The draft was re-written, again on paper, preparatory to the audit. The calendared account of 1585–86 represents this stage. It is a tidier manuscript with many fewer revisions although only the folios from the beginning of the account to the end of 'Emptions' are numbered. A few items are annotated, 'stayed by the auditors' or 'disliked by the auditors' and the auditors' names and their findings of the sums due to or from the chamberlain upon the general, charitable, Finsbury and special accounts are all recorded. The engrossed account, now missing, for which John Shaw was paid 53s.4d., would have been copied from this account. Shaw had been admitted clerk in his own right on 20 October 1586 upon Humfrey Wynnington's surrender of office.[146]

Notes on Calendaring

General

In general the calendar has been made by leaving out only those words and phrases of the original which could be omitted without loss of information or intelligibility and, with only exceptions of a minor character, the order of words is that of the original. Since accounts are not a verbose type of record it follows that in certain passages almost the whole of the text is repeated in the calendar. Marginalia have been omitted unless they provide additional information.

[144] *Cal. Letter Book L*, 160. In 1478 the clerk of the chamber, John Hert, also held the office of comptroller, as his predecessor, Robert Langford, had done. The two offices were held by different persons throughout the 16th century. Both the comptroller and the clerk received payments for examining the accounts (**121**, **251**).

[145] *Cal. Letter Book L*, 287.

[146] Rep.21, f.344b.

The layout of the original has not been followed. No brackets linking the lines of an entry are reproduced and the total sum of the entry is given at the end of the text of the entry and not, as in the manuscript, at the right hand of the page. Where the entry comprises a number of receipts or payments this total is preceded by the word 'summa', for the sake of clarity, whether or not this occurs in the original. Occasionally when each item in a succession of payments records only a name and a sum of money these are grouped as a paragraph and not on separate lines (e.g. **117**).

Serial numbers have been allocated to the entries for purposes of reference and indexing and are shown in bold type. Where appropriate one number or a small sequence of numbers has been given to a section of the account with sub-letters for individual entries. In the long sections entitled 'Emptions' and 'Foreign Charge', in which many of the entries are composite ones, each entry has a separate number.

The spelling of place names, which are generally familiar ones, and of common forenames has been modernised but the original spelling of surnames has been retained. Inn or house signs and the names of ships are given as in the original within single apostrophe, thus 'Phenix'. Occasionally the original spelling of a word or place name is shown in roman type within round brackets following the modern form. Editorial annotations are enclosed within square brackets and, to avoid a plethora of footnotes, many brief references, e.g. to an originating order for payment, are shown thus within the body of the text of the calendar.

All figures are given in arabic numerals although the majority in the manuscript are in roman. *Di'* is given as 'half' or '$\frac{1}{2}$' according to context. The standard abbreviations, £.s.d. are used, and also lb. The figures lij^{s} are reproduced as 52s. unless they occur as the final total of an entry; the latter is always given in £.s.d., thus £2.12s.0d. 'C' is retained when this represents a hundredweight. Figures supplied within square brackets which form part or the whole of the sum total of an entry indicate that the right margin of the manuscript is mutilated and no explanatory footnote is appended.

The year has been taken to start on 1 January. Receipts and payments are normally dated in the original only by the day and month and should be assumed to fall within the nominal year of the account, Michaelmas to Michaelmas. The year has been supplied within square brackets only if a payment seems to have been made after the nominal closing date of the account.

The account for 1584–85

In calendaring this draft account many minor corrections in the original have been ignored but those alterations or interlineations which supply additional information or are otherwise significant are included. The great majority are in one hand, which may be that of John Shaw,[147] and in the calendar are enclosed within angle-brackets. Attention is drawn by means of footnotes to the few additions in other hands. Deleted matter, when significant, is given in footnotes.

[147] See above p. xli.

The account for 1585–86

This account contains far fewer amendments than that for 1584–85. The method followed is as above and angle-brackets indicate the same amending hand. Certain sections of this account closely parallel that of the previous year and in such cases a cross reference is given to the comparable entry in 1584–85 with a note, if required, of any variation. Although not calendared, such entries are indexed.

Appendices

Any special features of the calendaring in Appendices A and E are explained there in introductory notes.

CHAMBERLAIN'S ACCOUNT 1584–85

1. [f.1] The third account of Robert Brandon chamberlain of the city of London from Michaelmas 1584 unto Michaelmas last past 1585

The Charge [Receipts]

2. Money due to the city by this accountant as by the foot of his last account appears, ⟨£265.7s.10d. and 8 peppercorns⟩[1]

[1] In this draft account this entry is the fourth item but it and the next three entries are calendared in the usual order of the final account, indicated by letter references A, B, C and D in the margin of the draft. The account for 1583–84 which produced these arrears is not extant.

3. The receipts of the city's general lands and Blanchappleton lands, vacations and desperates allowed, as by the rental[1] appears, ⟨£836.18s.8d. and 4 peppercorns⟩

[1] £3.16s.2d. was allowed for vacations and £9.11s.2d. for desperates (Rental, Chamber Accounts 2, f.190v).

4. The receipts of enrolments of apprentices this year as appears by the paper book signed with the letter P,[1] ⟨£211.16s.9d.⟩

[1] No longer extant, see p. xiv.

5. The receipts of admission of freemen as appears by the parchment book signed with the letter Q,[1] ⟨£409.13s.1d.⟩

[1] No longer extant, see p. xiv.

6. Summa ⟨£1,723.16s.4d. and 12 peppercorns⟩

7. [f.1v] Rent Farms [Receipts][1]

[1] All sums received in this section are in respect of one year unless otherwise stated.

a. The rent farm of Blackwell Hall of the treasurer of St Bartholomew's Hospital in West Smithfield, ⟨£33.6s.8d.⟩[1]

[1] For the history of the complex arrangements concerning the allocation of revenues from Blackwell Hall, the great beam, and other offices of profit to the Royal Hospitals, see *Charity Commissioners' Report*, 32 pt. vi, 1840, 11–12 and *Memoranda relating to the Royal Hospitals of the City of London*, 1836, app. vii and xii. This rent farm was paid by Christ's Hospital to St Bartholomew's which then paid it to the city.

b. The rent farm of measurage of woollen cloths, cotton and friezes of Thomas Port clothworker,[1] ⟨£10.0s.0d.⟩

[1] See **8h** note.

c. The rent farm of custom of rushes at Broken Wharf gathered by Anthony Percye for ⟨three quarters and a half [*of a quarter of a year*] ended at Michaelmas 1585 after £14 per annum⟩, ⟨£12.5s.0d.⟩[1]

[1] In 1562 a space at Broken Wharf was allotted for the sale of green rushes, which had formerly been sold at Queenhithe and for a short time at Bridewell, and the farm thereof set at £20 p.a. (Rep.15, f.110). In 1582 the farm was set at £16 p.a. and in 1584 at £14 p.a. (Rep.20, f.322b; Rep.21, f.108). There were recurring problems with arrears of this rent farm (cf. **137e** note, **137f**, **153c**, **278g**).

d. For the sealing of tanned leather at Leadenhall by the hands of Thomas Wheeler currier,[1] ⟨£10.0s.0d.⟩

[1] Elected sealer of tanned leather, 30 June 1573 (Rep.18, f.34).

e. Of Thomas Wattes carpenter for rent reserved for passing of barges to and from Gravesend, ⟨£30.0s.0d.⟩[1]

[1] There had been a ferry between Billingsgate and Gravesend since at least the late 13th century (J. G. Broodbank, *History of the Port of London*, i, 1921, 372–3). It was owned and let to farm by the city and watermen were forbidden to solicit fares for this journey until such time as the barges belonging to the farmer of the ferry had departed (Rep.29, ff.183–4). On 15 May 1578 Thomas Wattes was granted a lease in reversion of the 'Meyremayde' near Billingsgate, where passengers embarked, for 21 years from the expiration of a lease to his brother Roger, deceased (Rep.19, f.330). Roger was paying the same farm in 1563–64 (Chamber Accounts 1, f.113v). Jacob Watts, and then his widow, held the farm early in the 17th century (CCLGB 1, Kent: Gravesend, 1603, 1609. And cf. **288**, **291**, **294**).

f. Of ⟨George Ferrand haberdasher⟩[1] for the wharfage of strangers at Billingsgate and for Romeland[2] which Elizabeth Haywarde ⟨late held⟩ by a lease for 21 years or life ⟨and which Ferrand holds for 21 years beginning immediately after her decease⟩, ⟨£20.0s.0d.⟩

[1] Written above 'Elizabeth Haywarde widow ⟨deceased⟩'. For Elizabeth's lease to continue as farmer for life and the grant of the reversion to Ferrand (Farrand), 16 Jan. 1584, see CCPR, Billingsgate, 1583.
[2] The open space at the head of Billingsgate dock used for discharge and sale of cargoes. The name was also given to a similar space at Queenhithe.

g. [f.2] Of the treasurer of St Bartholomew's Hospital for the farm of the great beam, ⟨£50.0s.0d.⟩[1]

[1] The profits of the king's or great beam, used for the weighing of heavy merchandise, which had long belonged to the city, were among revenues allocated to the hospitals, see **7a** note.

h. Of Richard Young grocer for the farm of the office of package of woollen cloths and other merchandise, ⟨£66.13s.4d.⟩[1]

[1] Young was admitted as packer on 2 June 1580 (Rep.20, ff.78b–79).

i. Of James Harman yeoman of the chamber for sealing of weights and measures ⟨£3.2s.6d.⟩,[1] and for wine pots weighing ⟨31½⟩lb seized and brought in by the wardens of the Vintners for that they were not sealed at ⟨4d.⟩ the lb⟨10s.6d.⟩; summa⟨£3.13s.0d.⟩

[1] James Harman was admitted one of the 2 yeomen of the chamber with the keepership of Guildhall and the sealing of weights and measures on 7 June 1576 (Rep.19, f.86b). These duties became traditionally combined(CLRO list of keepers of Guildhall; *Second Report of the Municipal Commissioners*, 1837, 100, 118).

j. Of George Heton merchant taylor for gauging of wine and oils, ⟨£40.0s.0d.⟩[1]

[1] Heton was admitted gauger of wine, oil, honey and all things gaugeable for 30 years or life on 24 Jan.1569 (Rep.16, f.437).

k. Of Edmund Johnson for gauging of small barrels for oil, honey and train under the quantity of 38 gallons which he holds by lease for 31 years from Michaelmas 1572, ⟨6s.8d.⟩[1]

[1] Edmund Johnson, joiner, was granted the office of petty gauger of 'honey and such other petty things' for 30 years [*sic*] or life on 8 Oct.1573 (Rep.18, f.80b).

l. Of Richard Wystowe for standing of wool and lead at Leadenhall[1] as by his account appears, ⟨£21.12s.1d.⟩

[1] Richard Wystowe, barber surgeon, was admitted keeper of Leadenhall, 14 May 1562 (Rep.15, f.72).

m. [f.2v] Of George Southwyk[1] garbler for the office of garbling, ⟨£20.0s.0d.⟩

[1] Written over 'Thomas Saunders' deleted. Saunders' widow and executrix, Mary, was ordered on 2 Oct. 1584 to set over his term of years in the garbler's office to George Sowthacke, grocer (Rep.21, f.102). For other particulars as to Southacke, see *Remembrancia*, 273–4.

n. Of Thomas Eveley haberdasher, measurer of linen cloth, for the farm of his office, ⟨£50.0s.0d.⟩[1]

[1] Eveley (Iveley) was granted a lease of this office on 19 Feb. 1583 (Rep.20, f.401). This rent farm was paid over to the lord mayor, see **106**, **243**.

o. Of John Clarck and William Clarck for gauging of fish, ⟨£4.0s.0d.⟩[1]

[1] William Clerke, fishmonger, was admitted gauger of fish on 31 March 1584 (Rep.21, f.43b).

p. Of John Cockes farmer of the profits of meal and other things put to sale at Queenhithe, housing of wheat and other grain in the new storehouse there, and wharfage of oysters at Queenhithe, ⟨£26.13s.4d.⟩[1]

[1] Cockes (Cox) had paid this rent as tenant at will of the market houses at Queenhithe since 1578 and was to be given an allowance for 2 lofts which the companies of Grocers and Salters had for their corn (cf.**68**, **231**; CCPR, Queenhithe, 1578). He had been overseer of the market since 1566 (Rep.16, f.134b).

q. Summa ⟨£398.10s.1d.⟩

8. [f.3] Casual Receipts Ordinary

a. The fines of beerbrewers, innholders and tipplers for breaking their assize in victuals and gathered by the 3 serjeants of the chamber, ⟨£10.16s.8d.⟩

b. For the court of pie powder at Bartholomew (Bartilmewe) Fair, ⟨nil⟩

c. ⟨Of the Merchant Taylors for suffering the botchers strangers, 13s.4d.⟩[1]

[1] Inserted entry. A fuller version, 'Of the Wardens of the Merchant Taylors for suffering of strangers botchers to occupy their art within the city of London, 13s.4d.', entered as the last item of this section, having presumably been omitted in error from its customary place, has been deleted. Botchers were tailors who undertook repairs but were not permitted to make new clothes. Their numbers were limited and they paid fines on admission, see Rep.3, f.198b and the Book of Fines.

d. Of the city of Canterbury for one annuity to be paid by composition at the feast of St Luke the Evangelist [18 Oct.] and first charged in the account of George Medley late chamberlain ended in 30 Henry VIII [1538],⟨4s.0d.⟩[1]

[1] An agreement of 2 July 1536 exempted freemen of Canterbury from taxes, tallages and customs upon goods carried to or from Billingsgate or other wharves in the city of London in return for this payment of 4s.0d. a year (Deed 17.13).

e. For standing of butchers at Leadenhall as by the particulars appears,⟨£85.11s.0d.⟩

f. For commissions of ⟨61⟩ apprentices before enrolled and after set over, viz. for every commission 2s., ⟨£6.2s.0d.⟩

g. [f.3v] Of oystermen at Billingsgate and Queenhithe by the hands of Henry Woodwall[1] for their signs, ⟨8s.0d.⟩

[1] A yeoman of the chamber, see **20b**.

h. Of Peter Worlich, John Leake, John Nicolles and William Packington, searchers of woollen cloth, for the profits of the office due to the queen as by ⟨13 bills⟩ appears ⟨£20.13s.4d.⟩, and for the profits due to the chamber of London as by the said bills appears ⟨£114.7s.6½d.⟩, and of the said alnagers for the farm of the office due to the queen ⟨£60⟩; summa ⟨£195.0s.10½d.⟩[1] [cf.**113**]

[1] In 1560 the city had bought out the interests of the then alnagers, who held office under a grant from the crown, and itself appointed the searchers and sealers of woollen cloth (Rep.14, ff.199b, 293b, 335, 341, 364b, 386b, 396b–7, 399). Thomas Port's interests in the office of measurage of cottons (cf. **7b**) were preserved (Rep.14, f.429). In 1564 the terms of the grant of alnage to the city were revised and the rent farm due to the crown increased from £50 to £60 (Rep.15, ff.338b, 359b; Chamber Accounts 1, f.55v).

i. Of ⟨Thomas Wylbram deputy to⟩ John Fludd ⟨2nd⟩ clerk of the lord mayor's court for enrolments of deeds and testaments,[1] ⟨£1.3s.4d.⟩

[1] Enrolments of deeds and testaments in the husting were traditionally the responsibility of the second most senior of the 4 clerks of the mayor's court (Rep.9, f.251b).

j. For the pickage in Smithfield at Bartholomew (Bartilmewe) Fair, ⟨£22.19s.11½d.⟩

k. [f.4] Of Adam Copcote, keeper of the bayhall market for strangers,[1] for the city's part at ½d. the bay, being the fourth part of the profits of the market, ⟨£17.0s.6d.⟩

[1] Adam Copcote, merchant taylor, was admitted keeper on 7 June 1576 (Rep.19, f.86b).

l. Of William Norton stationer and treasurer of Christ's Hospital towards the repairing of the conduits and conduit pipes by the bequest of Sir Martin Bowes knight late alderman deceased, ⟨£6.13s.4d.⟩[1]

[1] Bowes died in 1566, having executed in the previous year two deeds conveying properties of the annual value of £24 to the hospital upon certain charitable trusts, which included this payment (*Charity Commissioners' Report*, 32 pt vi, 1840, 92–3).
A deleted entry, see **8c**, note, follows.

m. Summa ⟨£346.13s.0d.⟩

9. [f.4v] Fines [Receipts]

Received for the city's part of persons breaking and disobeying customs, ordinances and laudable acts ordained for the commonwealth of the city, and for fines taken of persons committing offences within the market of the city by way of forestalling and regrating, and for wares hawked in the streets, and for wares and merchandises foreign bought and sold within the liberties of the city, 'mispitching' of cloths in inns out of the common markets, breaking of ordinances in fellowships, making of unlawful wares, breaking of the assize of bread, annoyances done in the river of Thames with filth and ordure, for burying of jakes (jaques) within the liberties of the city, and for the admission of persons to occupy the feat of cobbling and botchers within the city and liberties, as more particularly appears by the book of fines called the journal,[1] of all which fines the presenters have the moiety and the city the other part, whereof the city's part amounts to ⟨£36.3s.4d.⟩

[1] The Book of Fines 1517–1628, ff.200r–202r.

10. [f.5] Leases, Incomes, Arrearages of Rents and Venditions [Receipts]

a. 28 Jan. of William Lucas mercer for a fine for the lease of a garden without Aldgate late in the tenure of John Christian joiner, deceased, £5.0s.0d.[1]

[1] Grant of lease approved 10 Sept.1584 (CCPR, Aldgate, 1584).

b. 4 March. Of William Offeley merchant taylor, Richard Wyseman goldsmith, William Quarles mercer, Nicholas Berry and Edward Lawson fishmongers, and Richard Venables merchant taylor, parishioners of St Lawrence Pountney, for a fine for a lease of two houses within the same parish, £13.6s.8d.[1]

[1] Grant of lease approved 8 Oct.1584 (CCPR, Lawrence Pountney, 1584).

c. 19 March. Of William Hichecock fishmonger in part of £100 for a fine for a lease of his house wherein he dwells at Billingsgate, £30.0s.0d.[1]
Margin ⟨Rest £70⟩

[1] Grant of lease approved 10 Sept.1584 (CCPR, Billingsgate, 1584).

d. 22 March. Of William Tybald dyer for a fine for the lease of a cellar within Leadenhall now in his tenure, £5.0s.0d.[1]

[1] Grant of lease approved 8 Oct. 1584 (CCPR, Leadenhall, 1584).

e. Summa ⟨£53.6s.8d.⟩

11. [f.5v] Receipts Extraordinary

a. 3 and 17 Oct. Of Mr Thomas Skynner clothworker for a fine for that he refused to be sheriff* of London ⟨and Middlesex⟩ being thereunto lawfully elected,*[1] £200.0s.0d. [1 Aug. 1584, Jor.21, f.371b]

[1] The words between the asterisks are omitted from the calendar of later entries of a like character. For the shrieval fine, see p. xxx.

b. 3 Dec. Of William Rowse of Leicester vintner for a butt of muscadel ⟨by him forfeited as foreign bought and sold⟩ and coloured by Stephen Hosyer cooper ⟨and assessed by a jury and to him sold by this accountant⟩, £13.0s.0d. [cf. **71**]

c. 24 Dec. Of Edward Palmer haberdasher for the finding of the orphans of Henry Austen baker for half a year ended at Christmas 1584 £5; 3 Feb. Of Stephen Somes girdler for the same £5; 26 June. Of Edward and Stephen for the half year ended at Michaelmas 1585 £10; summa £20.0s.0d.

d. 28 Jan. Of Thomas Lutwich joiner, keeper of the gaol of Ludgate, in part of £100 due by Robert Thrower waxchandler, late keeper, ⟨appointed to be paid by order of court 6 [*recte* 26] Jan. last [Rep.21, f.132b] and the rest payable at 2 payments, viz. in 2 years after⟩, £33.6s.8d.

Margin ⟨Rest 100 marks⟩

e. [f.6] 29 Jan. Of Lawrence Mellowe clothworker for the finding of the orphans of George Saunders merchant taylor for one year ended at Christmas 1584, £10.0s.0d.

f. 27 March. Of Alexander Lockwood merchant taylor for the finding of the orphans of William More merchant taylor for ⟨half a year⟩ ended at the Annunciation 1585 22s.6d.; 5 Oct. Of him for ⟨half a year⟩ ended at Michaelmas 1585 22s.6d.; summa £2.5s.0d.

g. 10 April. Of Richard Hilles merchant taylor for the finding of Luce the daughter and orphan of Lambert Thomas scrivener for 10 months ended the 7 April 1585, £2.16s.8d.

h. 28 April. Of William Felles, one of the yeomen of the waterside, towards £6 which the city pays yearly for a warehouse at Smart's Key called the 'Beres Fote' ⟨occupied by the yeomen of the waterside⟩, £2.10s.8d. [cf. **16b**]

i. [f.6v] 8 May. Of John Gybson barber surgeon for his part towards the cleansing of a vault belonging to his house and to the house of Henry Mathewe grocer in the parish of St Michael le Querne, £1.8s.3d. [cf. **46**]

j. 11 May. Of George Pullyard, executor of Elizabeth Somer widow, deceased, towards £20 which the city pays to Nicholas Wyllye gentleman due for half a year ended at the Annunciation 1585, £5.0s.0d. [cf.**81**]

k. 27 May. Of the companies of Drapers, Mercers and Grocers collected on Good Friday towards the redeeming of captives in the dominion of Turkey £15.0s.11¼d., of the Fishmongers, Goldsmiths and Haberdashers collected on Monday in Easter week £20.12s.3d., of the [f.7] Skinners, Salters and Merchant Taylors collected on Tuesday in Easter week £23.14s.6½d., of the Ironmongers, Vintners and Clothworkers collected on Wednesday in Easter week £16.14s.5¼d., and of the Mercers, Fishmongers, Goldsmiths, Skinners and Merchant Taylors collected on Low Sunday £24.6s.7½d.; summa £100.8s.9½d.[1]

[1] A committee appointed to devise means of redeeming captives held in infidel hands reported to the court of aldermen on 12 Nov. 1585 on monies remaining in the chamber for this purpose. This particular sum is stated to have been collected at the earnest suit of the poor wives of the captives (Rep.21, ff.168b, 219, 237, 237b).

l. 28 May and 16 August. For collections in the several wards received and assessed (sessed) upon foreigners and strangers inhabiting the said wards towards the charge of mustering and training up of 4,000 men with gun shot and pikes which made show before the queen at Greenwich, viz. of Aldersgate £9.14s., Aldgate £11.6s.4d., Bassishaw 23s.4d., Billingsgate £23.6s.8d., Bishopsgate [f.7v] £16.3s.6d., Bread Street 34s., Bridge Within £10.4s., Broad Street £8.19s., Candlewick Street £17.10s., Castle Baynard £12.0s.2d., Cheap 50s., Coleman Street £12.6s.4d., Cordwainer Street £3.15s., Cornhill £3.16s.8d., Cripplegate £17.18s.2d., Dowgate £12.11s.10d., Farringdon Within £10, Farringdon Without £20, Langbourn £40, Lime Street £3.8s., Portsoken £5.0s.2d., Queenhithe £5.2s.10d., Tower £34.6s.8d., Walbrook £3.13s., and Vintry £3.14s.2d.; summa £290.3s.10d.[1]

[1] In view of the increasing likelihood of involvement in the struggle of the Low Countries against Spain, orders were addressed to the city in April 1585 for raising 4,000 men, who were later to muster before the queen at Greenwich. Mayoral precepts were directed to the city companies specifying the number of men each should raise and to the aldermen of the wards to raise contributions from strangers born and Englishmen not being freemen (foreigners). The chamberlain was later ordered to pay these contributions to the companies in proportion to the number of men each raised but this is not reflected in these present accounts (Jor.21, ff.421b, 426–7, 454b).

m. 28 May and 2 July. Of Richard Cotton leatherseller for a collection of foreigners and strangers by him made in certain parishes in the ward of Cripplegate Within towards the training up of 2,000 men in gun shot in 1578,[1] £4.2s.0d.

[1] For the raising of men for the queen's service in 1578, see Jor.20(2), ff.388b–389, 394–6, 404–12 *passim*. Those born in the Low Countries were exempted from the assessment upon foreigners and strangers.

n. 16 Aug. Of Mr John Hyllard, deputy of the precinct [f.8] without Cripplegate in the ward of Cripplegate, towards the charge of training up the said 2,000 men in 1578 being collected of foreigners and strangers inhabiting the same ward, £4.6s.6d.

o. 7 Oct. [1585]. Of Thomas Pullison knight, lord mayor, being collected of foreigners and strangers inhabiting the wards hereafter mentioned towards the charges of training up 2,000 men in gun shot in 1578, viz. of Aldgate £4.2s.2d., Bridge Within £3.9s.2d., Candlewick Street £3.10s., Coleman Street 56s.6d., Cordwainer Street 44s., Farringdon Without £3.2s.6d., Lime Street 16s.2d., and Walbrook £4.2s.6d.; summa £24.3s.0d.

p. 22 July. Of the rulers of waterbearers for the city's moiety of £5.17s.5d. for the admission of freemen to be of their fraternity and for fines by them levied upon offenders in their fraternity for one year ended 22 July 1585, £2.18s.8½d.

q. [f.8v] 14 Aug. Of Richard Huddulstone, treasurer of the queen's wars in the Low Countries of Flanders, towards the furnishing of 500 coats for soldiers sent into the Low Countries for her majesty's service at 4s. the coat £100, and of several companies of this city towards the same at 5s. the coat £125; summa £225.0s.0d.[1]

[1] See p. xxviii.

r. 27 Aug. Of Mr Richard Hale grocer for a fine for that he refused to be sheriff, £200.0s.0d. [23 June 1585, Rep.21, f.183][1]

[1] In this and similar references cited below, the date and first folio reference relate to the refusal to serve; a second folio reference, if any, relates to an arrangement arrived at for paying the fine, e.g. by instalments.

s. 3 Sept. Of Mr Richard Gurney haberdasher in part of £200 for a fine for that he refused to be sheriff, £100.0s.0d. [19 June 1585, Rep.21, ff.181, 204b]

t. 23 Sept. Of Mr Thomas Bracye haberdasher in part of £200 for a fine for that he refused to be sheriff, £100.0s.0d. [17 June 1585, Rep.21, ff.178b, 210b]

u. [f.9][1] [Of Richard Morrys ironmonger in part of £200 for a fine for that he refused to be sheriff, £66.13s.4d.] [22 June 1585, Rep.21, ff.181b, 206]

[1] The upper part of this folio is missing. Entries **u** and **v** have been deduced from the list of debts owed to the city at the end of the year, see **141e**, **f**.

v. [Of Robert Withens vintner in part of £200 for a fine for that he refused to be sheriff, £100.0s.0d.] [21 June 1585, Rep.21, ff.181, 206]

w. [Of Giles Garton][1] ironmonger for a fine for that he refused to be sheriff, £200.0s.0d. [24 June 1585, ff.183b–184]

[1] The only ironmonger other than Morrys to be chosen sheriff in June 1585.

x. 5 Oct.[1585] Of Sir Edward Osborne knight in consideration of £400 to him delivered out of the chamber due for one year ended at Michaelmas 1585, £20.0s.0d.

y. Summa ⟨£1,728.3s.5d.⟩

12. [f.9v][1] [Debts mentioned in the last account and other accounts and since received now being charged]

[1] The upper part of this folio is missing. Heading supplied from the account for 1585–86.

a. [Items missing from the beginning of this section total £18.13s.4d., a sum which should include £6.13s.4d. paid by Thomas Wrighte, see **136e** note.]
b. 6 Feb. Of Sir Edward Osborne knight and alderman for a fine for a lease of his garden without Aldgate late in the tenure of Richard Markam, £10.0s.0d.[1]

[1] Grant of lease approved 26 Feb.1583(CCPR, Minories, 1582).

c. 8 Feb. Of Thomas Westmerlond cordwainer in part of a fine for a lease of his house in the Old Bailey, £4.0s.0d.[1]

[1] Grant of lease approved 16 Jan. 1584 (CCPR, Old Bailey, 1584).

d. 2 April. Of Elizabeth Can widow in part of £57 due to this city as by one obligation appears, £6.13s.4d.
Margin ⟨[Rest] £43.13s.4d.⟩[1]

[1] This is the second instalment of the debt to be received.

e. [f.10] 30 April. Of Francis Brampton and John Warter merchant taylors for one obligation due to be paid on 30 April 1585, being the 9th payment of £1,000 to be paid by £100 yearly, £100.0s.0d.[1]
Margin ⟨[Rest] £100⟩

[1] Brampton and Warter were the principal sureties under several obligations for the repayment of £1,000, which was lent out of the orphans' monies in the chamber by order of court of 10 April 1576 to the then chamberlain, George Heton, and which was to be repaid by £100 a year upon the last day of April from 1577 to 1586 (Rep.19, ff.67b–68b).

f. 30 July. Of Mr Thomas Skynner clothworker in part of £160 being the rest of £200 due for that he refused to be sheriff, £20.0s.0d.[1]

[1] Skynner refused to serve on 21 July 1580 (Rep.20, f.95b). His fine of £200 was still outstanding on 26 April 1582 when the court of aldermen agreed that it should be paid at £20 p.a. (Rep.20, f.318).

g. 25 Sept. Of Mr Thomas Bayard clothworker in part of ⟨£80 parcel of £100⟩ due for a fine for that he refused to be sheriff, £20.0s.0d.[1]
Margin ⟨Rest £60⟩

[1] Bayard refused to serve on 24 July 1581 (Rep.20, f.222). The original fine of £200 was reduced to £100, to be paid at £20 yearly, on the ground of poverty on 15 Feb. 1582 (Rep.20, f.292b). For a suit against him for recovery of a debt of £20, see **92**.

h. ⟨Of Katherine Crowther widow of William Crowther clothworker in part of £40 being the rest of £50 lent to William and due at Michaelmas last as appears as well by act of court as by one obligation wherein William with his two sureties stands bound, £35.0s.0d.⟩
Margin ⟨[Res]t £5⟩
i. Summa ⟨£214.6s.8d.⟩

13. [f.10v] Orphanage [Receipts]
Money received from Michaelmas 1584 unto Michaelmas 1585 to the use

of divers orphans, as particularly appears by an account thereof kept by ⟨John Benson⟩[1] in two books called the journal and the ledger,[2] £1,743.15s.0d.

[1] Written over 'James Peele' deleted. See **27d**.
[2] No longer extant, see p. xvi.

14. Summa totalis declaro is ⟨£6,244.14s.6d. and 12 peppercorns⟩

[f.11] The Discharge [Payments]
15. *Margin.* Salary of Priests [Payments]
a. To John Peereson clerk, late one of the chantry priests in the parish church of Edmonton (Edelmeton), Middlesex, for one yearly pension granted for life by act of court, £6.0s.0d.[1]

[1] An endowment of £13.6s.8d. p.a. towards the maintenance of 2 chantry chaplains, established in 1417 by John Church, grocer, out of property in London, was being paid out of the city chamber before the Suppression (*VCH Middlesex*, v, 182; *London and Middlesex Chantry Certificate*, ed. C. J. Kitching, LRS, xvi, 1980, no. 173). On 14 Nov. 1570 the chamberlain was instructed to take the best order he could with the auditors and the queen's officers for answering John Pierson, late chantry priest at Edmonton (Rep.17, f.73b).

b. To Roger Greene, parson of the parish church of St Michael Bassishaw, appointed by order of court [28 Aug. 1576, Rep.19, f.110] to say service in the Guildhall chapel on the [ferial days and to attend upon the lord mayor and aldermen at other solemn feasts],[1] £5.0s.0d.

[1] Ms defective; words supplied from the account for 1585–86. Probably the only other item missing is the total of entries **15a** and **b** supplied in **c** below.

c. [Summa £11.0s.0d.]

16. [f.11v] Rents and Quitrents [Payments][1]

[1] Unless stated otherwise these were paid in respect of the year ending Michaelmas 1585. References to the existence of acquittances, usually quarterly, have been omitted unless a rent gatherer or other collector is named.

a. 26 Oct. To Mr John Harte alderman for quitrent out of tenements in the parish of St Swithin sometime paid to the Earl of Oxford[1] and due for 2 years ended at Michaelmas 1585, £4.0s.0d.

[1] And before the Dissolution to the prior of Tortington in Sussex, see **295d**. By his will enrolled in the husting in 1286 Sir Robert Aguylun bequeathed to the prior of Tortington his mansion house in the parish of St Swithin, probably the house near London Stone lived in by Henry Fitz Ailwin, first mayor of London. In 1539 the premises were granted by the crown to the earls of Oxford and in 1641 were acquired by the Salters' Company as their hall (*Cal. Wills*, i, 75; Stow, i, 224, ii, 315–16).

b. To Richard Thomkyns cordwainer for rent of a warehouse at Smart's Key called the 'Beares Fote' occupied by the yeomen of the waterside for the bestowing [of salt fish by them put there to sale],[1] £6.0s.0d.

[1] See **15b** note.

c. [To William Garforth, collector of the dean and chapter of St Paul's, for quitrent out of two tenements in St Lawrence Pountney, 3s.0d.][1]

[1] See **15b** note.

d. [f.12] To William Ashebold parson of St Peter's in Cornhill for offering money due out of Leadenhall, £4.0s.0d.[1]

[1] Property was acquired by the city from St Peter Cornhill for part of the site of the new granary at Leadenhall erected c.1445 (A. H. Thomas, 'Notes on the history of the Leadenhall 1195–1488', *London Topographical Record*, xiii, 15–19) but the sum agreed in 1456 to be paid annually was £5 (Jor.6, f.88b).

e. To Master Henry Mackwilliams bailie of St James, due to the queen for the Conduit Meads which the city holds by a lease made to Sir John Browne knight and other aldermen and commoners for 180 years beginning at Michaelmas 1491, £4.0s.0d.[1]

[1] In 1491 the Conduit Meads were leased by Sir John Fortescue to the city for 180 years (*Cal.Letter Book L*, 283–4). They were among lands conveyed by him to Lady Joan Bradbury and by her to the Mercers' Company (information from Miss Anne Sutton, Archivist to the Mercers' Company) and in the account of the chamberlain's clerk for 1535–36 the first three quarterly payments of the rent are made by the city direct to the Mercers (**286c**, **289c**, **292c**). By a deed enrolled 3 June 1536, made under statute 28 Hen.VIII, c. xlii, the Mercers conveyed the lands to the crown and with other lands they became known collectively as the bailiwick of St. James. And see C. L. Kingsford, *The early history of Piccadilly, Leicester Square and Soho*, 1925, 1–2, 7–12, 15.

f. To this accountant by the bequest of the Lady Wiche,[1] 10s.0d.

[1] Alice Wyche, third wife and widow of Sir Hugh Wyche, lord mayor 1461–62. Her will, proved 1476, *Cal. P & M Rolls, 1458–82*, 101–4.

g. To the parson and churchwardens of St Dunstan in the East for a quit rent for a parcel of ground late called Horse Alley and now part of Leadenhall as by four acquittances made by Thomas Gyles the rent gatherer appears, £4.0s.0d.[1]

[1] A tenement called 'le Horsmylle' in Gracechurch Street, the site of which was needed for the new granary at Leadenhall, was granted to the city by the rector and churchwardens of St Dunstan in the East in 1444 for an annual payment of £4 (*Cal. Letter Book K*, 313; Stow, i, 153. And see A. H. Thomas, 'Notes on the history of the Leadenhall 1195–1488', *London Topographical Record*, xiii, 16–19).

h. [f.12v] 8 Oct. To William Norton stationer, receiver of the church of Canterbury, for a quitrent out of tenements in the parish of St Leonard Eastcheap, 10s.0d.[1]

[1] On 21 March 1565 the court of aldermen ordered examination to be made of the title of the dean and chapter of Canterbury to 10s. a year which they claimed 'out of a parcel of the city lands' and, if found correct, the rent was to be paid with reasonable arrears (Rep.15, f.431. And cf. **295d**).

i. To Stephen Vawghan gentleman for one year and a half ended at Michaelmas last for the house and ground adjoining in St Mary Spital and used chiefly for the ease and sitting of the lord mayor, aldermen and others repairing thither in Easter week to hear the sermons and by him demised to the city for [99][1] years beginning at [Michaelmas 1568],[1] £3.15s.0d.

[1] Blank in the Ms; particulars supplied from Rep.16, f.400b, 18 Sept.1568. George Heton, the chamberlain, was given use of the house for term of his office upon condition of making it available to the lord mayor to hear the sermons.

j. [f.13] To Walter Agard haberdasher, for the use of the queen, for a rent charge out of tenements in Cornhill, now parcel of the soil of the Royal Exchange, £2.6s.8d.

k. To Bartholomew (Barthilmewe) Smithe gentleman, the queen's receiver, for a quitrent out of tenements in Cornhill sometime Mr Pawn's, now parcel of the soil of the Royal Exchange [13s.4d.], and more to him for his acquittance 4d., 13s.8d.[1]

[1] The rents in the last two entries probably represent the £3 p.a. payable to the queen for 'obit money' out of the lands late Mr. Pawn's which were acquired for the site of the Royal Exchange (Letter Book V, f.71b).

l. To the dean and chapter of Canterbury for one annuity to continue until they be paid of £600 as appears by a pair of indentures made between the mayor, commonalty and citizens of London and the dean and chapter in consideration of lands, tenements and rents now parcel of the soil of the Royal Exchange,[1] as appears by 2 acquittances made by William Norton their receiver, £30.0s.0d.

[1] After considerable negotiation the agreement between the city and the dean and chapter was embodied in 3 documents, which are mentioned but not recited in the repertories: a deed of covenant dated 4 April 1566, a deed of feoffment to the city of messuages in the parishes of St Bartholomew the Less and St Michael Cornhill dated 5 April, and a grant by indenture of the same date of an annuity of £30 to be paid by the city until such time as the sum of £600 be paid (Rep.15, ff.422, 431, 433b; Rep.16, ff.38b–39, 59b–60. And see **144b**). The property comprised 13 tenements, one storehouse, one garden and a voidway leading to a well (Letter Book V, f.70b).

m. [f.13v] To Helen Romforde wife of Stephen Romforde goldsmith, and late the wife of Ralph (Raffe) Burton deceased, by order of court [28 Jan. 1580, Rep.20, f.34] in recompense of her title and dower to and in messuages and tenements late situated where the Royal Exchange is now built which sometime were Burton's, £3.6s.8d.

n. To John Powell of the borough of Southwark brewer, to the use of Thomas Denbighe and Katherine his wife, executrix of Elizabeth Hilles widow deceased, in full payment of one annuity granted in respect of her interest of years in a tenement taken into the Royal Exchange [26 July 1566, Rep.16, f.89b] and is due for one year ended at the Annunciation 1585 ⟨at which time her interest was determined and so the further payment ceases⟩, £1.11s.0d.

o. [f.14] To Francis Cromewell esquire for the third part of tenements in Aldermanbury late in the tenure of Henry Wrest carpenter and now of Robert Maskall carpenter, £3.6s.[8d.][1]

[1] Negotiations with Cromewell for the purchase of his part of these premises, described as on the backside of Guildhall, were initiated on 15 Nov. 1576 (CCPR, Guildhall, 1576). For other references to this and other shares in the premises, see CCPR,

Aldermanbury, 1578–91. Cromewell is often named as Francis Williams alias Cromewell (Crumwell).

p. To Margaret Stockemead widow, the city's tenant at Somer's Key,[1] according to an act of court 8 June 23 Elizabeth [1581] [Rep.20, f.204b] in discharge of the yeomen of the waterside which they heretofore paid her for a room (rome) that they occupy for the bestowing of fish,[2] £1.0s.0d.

[1] By a lease for 31 years from 1576 (CCPR, Somar's Key, 1576).

[2] According to the order of court the room at Somer's Key, which lay to the west of Billingsgate, was used by the yeomen for the stowage of baskets and fresh fish. There was a warehouse for salt fish at Smart's Key to the east of Billingsgate, see **16b**.

q. To the master and governors of St Bartholomew's Hospital for a benevolence given to the use of the poor there by order of court 7 Oct. 4 Edward VI [1550] [Rep.12(2), f.270b], as by the acquittance of John Hyll[1] skinner one of the governors appears, £5.0s.0d.[2]

[1] 'Hilles' in 1585–6.

[2] According to the order of 1550 the £5 to be handed over to the hospital was rent received of Sir John Aylyf (d.1556) for the library of Guildhall chapel. It was subsequently received of Blackwell Hall (Rep. 13(2), f.572).

r. [f.14v] To the bridgemasters for quitrent out of tenements sometime the 'Horsehead' in the parish of St Dunstan in the East 4s.8d., and out of tenements in Short Lane by St Lawrence Pountney in the parish of All Hallows the Less 10s., and out of a tenement in the same parish sometime of Roger Depeham 19s.8d., as by the acquittance of William Dalbye the rent gatherer appears, £1.14s.4d.[1]

[1] The rent of 4s.8d. was payable out of a house bequeathed to the city by Henry Wymond (Wymund) by will enrolled in the husting in May 1349 (*Cal. Wills* i, 577; rental of bridge house properties 1358 in Bridge House Small Register, f.73d). The rent of 10s. was payable out of property belonging in 1358 to William de Leyre, subsequently to Adam Faunceys (d.1375) and before 1404 to the city (Rentals of bridge house properties 1358, f.77d; 1404, f.11v). The rent of 19s.8d. was due out of a tenement belonging in 1358 to Roger de Depham, who by his will enrolled in the husting in Feb. 1359 left all his lands and tenements in the city to the mayor, aldermen and commonalty (*ibid.*, 1358, f.78; 1404, f.11v; *Cal. Wills* ii, 7).

s. To Thomas Pursell of Clements Inn gentleman to the use of Richard Browne gentleman for a quitrent of the ground where the conduit heads at Paddington stand in the name of 2 pounds of pepper at 3s.4d. the year[1] and due for 7 years ended at Michaelmas 1585, £1.3s.4d.

[1] In 1440 the abbey of Westminster had granted the city licence to erect conduit heads in a close within the manor of Paddington and to conduct water from thence to the city for an annual payment of 2 lb of pepper (*Cal. Letter Book K*, 233).

t. Summa ⟨£77.0s.4d.⟩

[f.15] Inward Fees from Michaelmas 1584 unto Michaelmas 1585 [Payments]*

*Many of these fees were traditional sums. Where originating orders for particular payments are cited it should be noted that in some cases they may have been first made in respect of a predecessor of the office holder named in this account.

17.a. To Mr William Fletewood esquire serjeant at law and recorder of London for his year's fee, £80.0s.0d.
b. To this accountant for his year's fee, £23.6s.8d.
c. To Mr Thomas Kyrton common serjeant for his year's fee, £20.0s.0d.
d. To Mr William Sebright common clerk for his year's fee, £20.0s.0d.
e. To Mr William Dummer comptroller of the chamber for his year's fee, £30.0s.0d.[1]

[1] Dummer became comptroller in 1544. In 1563 he was granted £10 above the customary fee in respect of his long service (Rep.15, f.278b).

f. To Mr William Danyell by order of court 2 July 1584 [Rep.21, f.66b] for giving his attendance and supplying the room of Mr Recorder and Mr Town Clerk in the inner chamber, the husting and the lord mayor's court as judge there for his year's fee, £40.0s.0d.[1]

[1] See p. xxi.

g. To James Smithe now the third clerk of the lord mayor's court for his year's fee, £1.0s.0d.
h. To him for keeping the journal in parchment[1] and to engross therein as well all acts of common council as also recognizances for orphanage and other orders and decrees mentioned in the repertory concerning the causes and matters of the city, due for one year, £10.0s.0d.

[1] i.e. the Letter Book. And see **163h**.

18.a. [f.15v] To Mathew Sturdevant swordbearer for his year's fee £20, and for like time for the tenement over Aldersgate now in the tenure of the late wife of John Daye £3,[1] and for his reward at the audit £3.6s.8d.; summa £26.6s.8d.

[1] Sturdevant received this sum in lieu of accommodation (Rep.17, ff.124, 131, March–April 1571). John Daye, stationer, was granted a lease in reversion of Aldersgate on 3 Aug. 1571 (Rep.17, f.201b).

b. To John Deywell common hunt for his fee £10, for hounds' meat 53s.4d. [4 Oct. 1552, Rep.12(2); f.531] and for fuel for the hounds' meat 26s.8d. [30 May 1500, Rep.1, f.70], and in consideration for his house for his better relief £5[1] and for the keeping of a long winged hawk or a goshawk or a tercel (tassell) of a goshawk and a kennel of good spaniels £3.6s.8d. [30 April 1584, Rep.21, f.49], and for his reward at the audit £3.6s.8d.; summa £25.13s.4d.

[1] Deywell was to receive this sum until provided with a house (Rep.21, f.49).

c. To John Northage common cryer for his year's fee £3, and for his reward at the audit £3.6s.8d.; summa £6.6s.8d.
d. To Robert Skarborrowghe waterbailie for his year's fee £10, and for his reward at the audit £3.6s.8d.; summa £13.6s.8d.
e. [f.16] To Edward Ap John, Robert Hyde and John Vyncent serjeant carvers, to every of them £5 for his year's fee £15, and 33s.4d. in

augmentation of their living £5 by order of court *tempore* Richard Champion knight mayor [15 Nov. 1565, Rep.15, f.495], and 40s. for their reward at the audit £6 [31 May 1580, Rep.20, f.76b], and to Edward Ap John for weighing bread for one year 26s.8d.; summa £27.6s.8d.
f. To Richard Foster, Edward Lyle and James Lorde serjeants of the chamber, to every of them £3 for his year's fee £9, and 33s.4d. in augmentation of his living £5 [15 Nov.1565, Rep.15, f.495], and 13s.4d. for gathering the ale silver 40s., and 6s.8d. for his reward at the audit 20s.; summa £17.0s.0d.

19.a [f.16v] To the renter general for his year's fee £10, and for potation money 53s.4d., and for the receipts of Blanchappleton lands 30s.; summa £14.3s.4d.
b. To Humfrey Wynnyngton ⟨late⟩ clerk of the chamber for his year's fee £10.6s.8d., and ⟨to John Shaw now clerk of the chamber⟩[1] for his reward at the audit 40s.; summa £12.6s.8d.[2]

[1] See pp. xli–xlii.
[2] A deleted entry follows: 'To [*blank*] keeper of the reparation stuff and clerk of the works for his fee £10'.

20.a. To James Harma[n yeoma]n of the chamber[1] for his year's fee 26s.8d., and for attending upon the lord mayor and aldermen at St Paul's and the Spital and keeping clean the place and setting up and laying down of cushions there 10s., and for keeping the clock in the Guildhall 26s.8d., and for trying of weights and measures 20s., and for keeping the Guildhall clean 13s.4d., and for his reward at the audit 6s.8d.; summa £5.3s.4d.

[1] See **7i** note.

b. [f.17] To Henry Woodwall yeoman of the chamber for his year's fee 26s.8d., and for his reward at the audit 20s., summa £2.6s.8d.
c. To Leonard Lorgyn serjeant of the channel for his year's fee 40s., and by act of court 14 June 1565 [*recte* 17 July 1565, Rep.15, f.454] over and besides his charges weekly sustained in carrying certificates[1] to the court 33s.4d., and by order of court 25 Oct. 1580 [Rep.20, f.130b] in augmentation of his living 20s.; summa £4.13s.4d.

[1] The bills of mortality. Lorgyn (Largen) was a yeoman of the market, for which yeoman of the channel was an alternative title, when he first received this payment in 1565.

d. To William Lathes ⟨under waterbailie⟩ for his year's fee, £2.13s.4d.
e. To Henry Byrun yeoman of the channel for his fee ⟨33s.4d.⟩, and for service done at the wrestling and shooting at Bartholomew (Bartilmewe) Fair and towards his apparel, horse, minstrel and other charges by order of court 22 March 1577 [*recte* 1569, Rep.16, f.457b] 50s., and more by act of court 14 June 1580 [*recte* 25 Oct. 1580, Rep.20, f.130b] 20s. during the pleasure of the court; summa £5.3s.4d.
f. [17v] To William Felles, John Smythe, Henry Ravenscroft and Ralph

(Raphe) Shepparde yeomen of the waterside, to every of them 26s.8d. for his year's fee £5.6s.8d., and 26s.8d. for a yearly augmentation by act of court [4 June 1557, Rep.15, f.79b] £5.6s.8d., and 26s.8d. by act of court of Michaelmas 1571 [Rep.17, f.205b] £5.6s.8d. ⟨to have continuance while the intercourse was stayed⟩ and by order of court of 21 June in the mayoralty of Sir Nicholas Woodrouf knight [1580, Rep.20, f.86] to continue during pleasure of the court,[1] and to William Felles and Henry Ravenscroft to either of them 53s.4d. for considerations moving the court £5.6s.8d.; summa £21.6s.8d.

[1] The extra allowance granted in 1571 was made in recognition of loss of profits occasioned by interruption of the Flanders trade. In 1580 the allowance was continued because of the decline in the quantity of fish brought by strangers.

g. To John Savage the swordbearer's man for his year's fee 40s., and to Thomas Sympson the common cryer's man for his year's fee 40s.; summa £4.0s.0d.
h. [f.18] To William Ravenscrofte the common hunt's man for his year's fee 40s., and to Richard Grewe the common hunt's second man for his year's fee 40s.; summa £4.0s.0d.
i. To Robert Lyddys and Richard Dod, to either of them being the waterbailiff's men for his year's fee 40s.; summa £4.0s.0d.
j. To Philip Treherne the carver's man for his year's fee 40s., £2.0s.0d.

21. To John Smithe the elder, appointed to call upon such as ought to cleanse the lanes and streets in the city to do their duties and to kill dogs going at large unled, to him given by act of court 1 Aug. 1563 [Rep.15, f.279] for his year's fee £6, and in reward for carrying away the dead dogs and cats and other carrion laid in the streets and burying the same 20s., and by order of court 24 March 22 Elizabeth [1580, Rep.20, f.57b] for a further augmentation of 5d. [f.18v] the week and due for 52 weeks 21s.8d.; summa £8.1s.8d.[1]

[1] *The Diary of Henry Machyn, citizen of London, 1550–1563*, ed. J. G. Nichols, Camden Soc., 1847, under 4 Aug. 1563, reports a mayoral proclamation that 'there is one man hired to kill dogs as many as he can find in the streets'. John Smith, who in 1563 was servant to the common hunt, was instructed to bury the dogs near the windmills without Cripplegate. In the order of 1580 Smith is described as late servant to the common hunt. For the numbers of dogs killed in 1584–85 and 1585–86, see **107**, **238**.

22. Summa ⟨£430.5s.0d.⟩

Outward Fees [Payments]

23.a. [1]To Henry Beauemont,[2] late deceased, for his year's fee due at Michaelmas 1584 40s., to Mr Thomas Owen, Mr William Danyell, Mr Thomas Bowyer and Mr Matthew Dale to every of them 40s. for his year's fee due at Michaelmas 1585 £8, to Mr Richard Shuttleworthe serjeant at law, Mr Robert Clark, Mr James Morrys, Mr Edward Cooke and Mr John Cowper to every of them £4 for his 2 years' fee due at Michaelmas 1585 £20, being all of the learned counsel of the city,[3] and to Mr John Kytchin ancient pleader[4] for his year's fee due at Michaelmas 1585 20s.; summa ⟨£31.0s.0d.⟩

[1] This entry, preceded by an instruction ⟨Follow as in the journal for these counsellors' fees underwritten⟩, is written in the margin in a different hand in substitution of the original entry, already containing some amendments, in the text. The original entry contained the same names and fees in a different order but did not refer to Beauemont's death.
[2] 'the younger' in the original entry.
[3] For biographical references to these men and for the city's counsel in general, see pp. xxi-xxii.
[4] The most senior of the four common pleaders.

b. To Mr William Butler attorney in the exchequer and to Mr George Kempe attorney in the king's bench, to either of them 20s. for his year's fee 40s., and to Anthony Clypsham under exchequer[1] for his year's fee 40s., and to the keeper of the star chamber for his year's fee 6s.8d.; summa £4.6s.8d.

[1] *Sic.* Under escheator?

c. [f.19] To Mr William Sebrighte common clerk and clerk of the peace of this city and to Henry Clarke clerk of the peace of the county of Middlesex and to William Dyoys keeper of the gaol of Newgate, to every of them £3.6s.8d. for a yearly reward granted by act of court [27 June 1581, Rep.20, f.214 confirming 16 March 1557, Rep.13, f.487b][1] in recompense of such fees as to them belong by reason of their offices by the poor prisoners of Newgate at the time of their deliveries for that such as are not able to pay their fees shall not remain prisoners for the same; summa £10.0s.0d.

[1] These orders specify only the payments to the common clerk and to the clerk of the peace of Middlesex.

d. To the 6 waits, to every of them £11.13s.4d. for his year's fee £70, and to Anthony Tyndall one of the waits by order of court 29 Aug.1583 [Rep.20, f.453] to be paid during the apprenticehood of Robert Baker his apprentice £5[1] and due for one year; summa £75.0s.0d.

[1] For his charges in instructing Baker in the skill and knowledge of music for the service of the city. For the London waits see Woodfill, 33–53.

e. To John Benson this accountant's clerk for his year's fee, £3.6s.8d.
f. [f.19v] To William Kerwyn master mason for his year's fee, £1.0s.0d.
g. To Robert Mascall master carpenter for his year's fee, £1.6s.8d.
h. To John Martyn master plumber for his year's fee, £2.0s.0d.
i. To Richard Wistowe keeper of Leadenhall for his year's fee, £5.0s.0d.

24.a. *Margin* ⟨Follow the journal⟩
To the raker of Coleman Street ward for his year's fee 6s.8d., to the keeper of the grate at Lothbury 6s.8d., to the raker of Broad Street ward 6s.8d., to the keeper of the sluice at Moor Lane and the postern called Moorgate 13s.4d., to John Kinge for keeping clean the ditches there 13s.4d., to the keeper of the grate at Aldgate and the late Crossed Friars 6s.8d., to the keeper of the new grate at Bishopsgate 5s., to the keeper of the sluice at Holborn Bridge 6s.8d., to ⟨Dobson⟩ for keeping clean the channel between Bishopsgate and St Mary Axe 13s.4d., to the scavenger

of Tower ward ⟨for keeping clean the grate at Petty Wales⟩ 20s., to the keeper of the grate at Fleet Lane 10s.,[1] to the raker at Dowgate for carrying the soil away gathered at the new grate in Walbrook 20s., to William [f.20] Johnson for keeping clean the same grate for 3 quarters [of a year] 15s. and to Daniel Wauden for one quarter 5s., to Elizabeth Ball widow for keeping clean the grate near St Bartholomew's 3s.4d., to the keeper of the grate at Queenhithe 26s.8d., to John Chamber for keeping clean the doors and stairs at the new brick wall against Bridewell 6s.8d., to Francis Bates for keeping clean the kennel within and without Aldgate 6s.8d., to Martin Howe girdler for keeping clean the grate near St Mary Spital 6s.8d., to the keeper for keeping clean the grate into Water Lane in Thames Street and over against St Dunstan's Church in the East 6s.8d., to William Johnson for keeping clean the watergate at Dowgate and for carrying away the soil gathered there for 3 quarters £3 and to Daniel Wauden for one quarter 10s.,[2] to Lawrence Ponder for keeping clean the ditch between Aldgate and [f.20v] the postern 20s., to keeping clean the house of the common privies within Leadenhall 10s., to keeping clean the grate ⟨near⟩[3] Broken Wharf 13s.4d., to the scavenger of Lime Street ward and Leadenhall ⟨for carrying away the soil there made⟩ 20s., to the ringer of the market bell at the standard in Cheap 6s.8d.; summa £17.5s.0d.

[1] 'to the keeper of the sluice at Fleet Bridge', deleted.
[2] Annual fee reduced from £4 to £2 (Rep.21, f.59).
[3] Written over 'at', deleted.

b. To the keepers of the conduit of Gracechurch, the conduit at Cornhill, the great conduit at Cheap, the standard in Cheap, the little conduit in Cheap, the conduit in Aldermanbury, the conduit in Holborn, the conduit in Lothbury, the conduit at Bishopsgate, the conduit without Cripplegate, the conduit in Fleet Street and the conduit at Aldgate, to every of them 6s.8d. for one year £4, and to William Palmer founder for overseeing the said conduits for one year 26s.8d.; summa £5.6s.8d.

25.a. To William Browne foreign taker for his year's fee, £2.0s.0d.
b. [f.21] To John Evans and Stephen Cowlye mealweighers for the markets at Leadenhall and within Newgate, to either of them £5.4s. for his year's fee, summa £10.8s.0d.
c. To the widow Farrer for her yearly annuity, 13s.4d.[1]

[1] The order initiating this payment has not been traced but it was already being paid in 1563 (**301h**). A Thomas Ferrer, under porter of the lord mayor's house, was granted 26s.8d. p.a. for life in 1551(Rep.12(2), f.402).

d. To Lawrence Nashe farmer of Finsbury[1] for his pains to see that the fields be not annoyed by the rakers and others resorting thither, 13s.4d.

[1] The lessee of the manor of Finsbury. Nashe was granted a new lease in 1588 upon surrender of an earlier lease (CCPR, Finsbury Manor, 1588. And see **301k**).

e. To James Mase beadle of the beggars in full recompense of all such charges as he shall sustain about the punishment of vagabonds and idle persons, £1.0s.0d.

f. To David Manninge and Thomas Redknighte, searchers at the waterside of the ordering of billets, faggots and tall wood and other fuel brought by water to the city, to either of them £4 for his year's fee, summa £8.0s.0d.
g. To Peter Meadcalf clocksmith for tending the clocks in the Guildhall and orphans' court, 6s.8d.
h. [f.21v] To Anne Colsylle widow for a yearly relief, £1.0s.0d.
i. To Anthony Castell drum player and Richard Oker fife player, to either of them 20s. for his year's fee, £2.0s.0d.
j. To Clement Forman and Michael Wrighte bellmen of the city, to either of them for his year's fee £4 for watching and sounding of a bell and for uttering certain speeches nightly,[1] summa £8.0s.0d.

[1] 'Remember the Clockes/Loke well to your Lockes fyre and your light and god geve you good night/for nowe the bell ringeth', to be pronounced in a loud voice in every street and lane in which the bellmen watched (Rep.16, f.439, 17 Jan. 1569). They were to watch, one in the east part of the city and one in the west, from 11 p.m. to 4 a.m. in winter and 11 p.m. to 3 a.m. in summer (Rep.16, f.422b, 7 Dec. 1568). By order of 12 Dec. 1570 each received an additional 13s.4d. bringing his annual fee to £4 (Rep.17, f.84b).

26.a. To Phyllis Hawes widow[1] for her year's pension by order of court 15 March 1569 [Rep.16, f.455b], £1.0s.0d.

[1] Of one of the sheriffs' serjeants.

b. To Richard Darrell in respect of his poverty for one year's pension by order of court 28 Oct. 1573 [Rep.18, f.96b], £2.13s.4d.
c. To David Hewes woolman for his year's pension by order of court 8 June 1574 [Rep.18, f.219], to continue until a carroom to him granted falls void, £1.6s.8d.
d. To Elizabeth Hillary widow[1] for a weekly pension of 20d. granted 10 Feb. 18 [*recte* 17] Elizabeth [1575] [Rep.18, f.345] towards the relief of her and her poor children and due for 52 weeks, £4.6s.8d.

[1] Of Andrew Hillary, serjeant of the chamber.

e. [f.22] To Alice Straunge widow of Doctor Straunge in consideration of her poverty and great charge of children by order of court 16 Aug. 1577 [Rep.19, f.231b] for one year's pension, £4.0s.0d.
f. To John Marten late a yeoman of the waterside for one daily pension of 4d. granted by order of court 7 March 1577 [Rep.19, f.179b] and due for 52 weeks, £6.1s.8d.
g. To John Luck[1] by order of court 7 March 1577 [Rep.19, f.179] and is due for one year, £2.0s.0d.

[1] Described in the repertory as 'servant' to William Fletewood, the recorder. By the same order he was granted a livery gown. For his summer and winter liveries, see **89**, **116c**, **118b**, **231**, **246b**, **248b**.

h. To William Edwyn barge master for a yearly pension granted by decree of court [28 June 1582, Rep.20, f.338], £1.6s.8d.
i. To Annes Cottrell widow of Thomas Cotterell late one of the bailiffs of Southwark for a weekly pension of 8d. granted by order of court 21 July

1579 [*recte* 1580] *tempore* Nicholas Woodrooff knight mayor [Rep.20, f.95b] and due for 52 weeks, £1.14s.8d.
j. [f.22v] To the late wife of John Asplyn, late a yeoman of the waterside deceased, for one annuity to her granted by order of court the day of Simon and Jude [28 Oct.] 1577 [Rep.19, f.254b], £4.0s.0d.
k. To Simon Cordell late one of the yeomen of Mr Sheriff by order of court 13 July 1581 [Rep.20, f.219] in respect of his poverty and for one annuity to him granted quarterly, £2.0s.0d.
l. To the late wife of Peter Browne deceased for one annuity of 20s. granted by act of court 1581 [19 Oct., Rep.20, f.242b] for keeping the Sessions house and charge of fires, candles and drink at the time of the sessions there, £1.0s.0d.[1]

[1] The grant of 1581 was made to Peter Browne and Elizabeth his wife. By order of 24 Feb. 1584 she was allowed to keep custody of the Sessions house while she remained a widow (Rep.21, f.33).

m. To William Crowther clothworker, late keeper of the gaol of Newgate, for one annuity of £40 granted by order of court 26 April 1582 [Rep.20, f.317] for his life, £40.0s.0d.[1]

[1] Crowther had been dismissed from misdemeanours on 31 Aug. 1580 (Rep.20, f.103). He petitioned the queen against his removal and an inquiry into the cause between him and his successor as keeper, William Dayos, was conducted by Sir Thomas Bromley, the lord chancellor. It was finally agreed that he should have a pension of £40 p.a. (*Remembrancia*, 369–71; Rep.20, ff.104b, 138, 154–5, 227, 230, 243b, 299, 317).

27.a. [f.23] To Robert Smithe, late one of the under clerks of the outer court of the lord mayor and aldermen, for one annuity of 20 marks granted by act of court 28 Oct.1581 [Rep.20, f.245b] in consideration that he shall solicit and follow the city's causes in law at Westminster and elsewhere and shall be attendant upon the learned counsel of the city at such times as any controversy shall arise about the liberties of the city, and shall engross all such collections as shall be made for and about the same, £13.6s.8d.[1]

[1] See p. xxii.

b. To Mr Julius Cesar doctor of the civil law for one annuity of 40 marks granted by order of court 11 June 1583 [Rep.20, f.436b] in gratification of the queen's letters and others written in commendation to the lord mayor and alderman for his apt and worthy service for the city,[1] £26.13s.4d.

[1] He was retained as counsel for the city. The annuity was granted 'only in respect of the queen's satisfaction' and was not to be a precedent. It was far higher than the usual fee paid to the city's counsel, cf.**23a**.

c. [f.23v] To Christopher Fowlkes late common cryer in consideration of one yearly pension of £8 granted by order of court 23 July 1583 [Rep.20, f.446b], and by order of court 20 Oct.1584 [Rep.21, f.98] £6, and by order of court 29 Sept.1585 [Rep.21, f.211b] £6 and due for one quarter ended at Michaelmas 1585 30s.; summa ⟨£15.10s.0d.⟩
d. To James Peele now clerk of Christ's hospital for one annuity of 20s.

granted for that he shall perfect and make up the books of accounts of orphans' portions wherewith the chamberlain is charged, £1.0s.0d. [cf.**13**]
e. To Matthew Sturdyvante swordbearer for one daily pension of 4d. granted by order of court 10 Sept. 1583 [Rep.20, f.455b] for divers considerations in the same expressed, and partly that he shall not henceforth make any further suit to the court for himself, and due for one year, £6.1s.8d.
f. [f.24] To Joan Lune, widow of John Lune late common hunt, for one yearly pension of 40s. granted by act of court 24 Sept. 1584 [Rep.21, f.88], £2.0s.0d.
g. To William Seger horner for one annuity of £4 granted by order of court 28 Oct. 1584 [Rep.21, f.105] to continue until he shall be otherwise advanced by this city or Christ's Hospital, provided that he be always attendant upon the court days and to engross all letters which shall be sent from this court or lord mayor, ⟨due for 3 quarters at Midsummer last⟩, ⟨£3.0s.0d.⟩
h. To Andrew Sare salter[1] for one annuity granted by order of court 19 Nov. 1584 [Rep.21, f.112b] for his life, £20.0s.0d.

[1] 'Haberdasher' in the order of court.

i. [f.24v] To Vincent (Vycent) Hill late one of the officers of the sheriffs, who is very aged, blind and impotent, for one annuity of 4 marks granted by order of court 2 Sept. 1585 [Rep.21, f.204b] for his life, and due for one quarter ended at Michaelmas 1585, 13s.4d.
j. 10 March. To George Nicholles tailor in right of Alice his wife, daughter of Robert Fisher haberdasher deceased, by order of court [9 March 1585, Rep.21, f.148b], to them due by the bequest of Alice Smarte widow deceased for her interest in tenements and gardens in Chancery Lane which she held of the city by lease to her and to Robert Smarte her husband and since by them surrendered, which lands were or are exchanged with Sir Nicholas Bacon knight lord keeper of the great seal of England, and to them payable during the lease to Robert Smarte and his wife which ended at Michaelmas 1579 ⟨£11.19s.2d. whereof £5.19s.7d. borne by this account and the rest in the account of Mr Carpenter⟩, £5.19s.7d.[1]

[1] And see **129i**. The lands in Chancery Lane were part of the Carpenter estate, see p. xxvi.

28. Summa ⟨£355.7s.3d.⟩

29. [f.25][1] Paid weekly for the wages of masons, carpenters, sawyers, bricklayers (bricklers), plumbers and labourers working on the new gate,[2] at Bishopsgate, making ladders, mending the gin, repairing the Guildhall, mending of decayed places and conduit pipes, masons working at the Guildhall, for drawing of water at Dowgate, at the tenement near Leadenhall making penthouses there and at Mr Haughton's,[3] mending of necessaries at Newgate, setting up of three posts at Ludgate, Aldersgate and Cripplegate, at the pond in Smithfield, mending the tenement at

Finsbury and the docket for prisoners, at the house at Billingsgate, at the cage at Cripplegate, St Lawrence Pountney, at Fleet Bridge and at other sundry places belonging to the city as by the week[ly] bills hereafter appears.

[1] The following passage is unpunctuated in the Ms.
[2] Ludgate, then being rebuilt.
[3] Near Pye Corner without Newgate? The pages of the contemporary rental for this area are missing but Mrs Haughton held a tenement here in 1608 (CCCLGB, 1, Pye Corner 1608).

a. 3 Oct. £4.18s.2½d., 10 Oct. £5.0s.8d., 17 Oct. £4.6s.4d., 24 Oct. £4.6s.4d., 31 Oct. £4.2s.7½d. Summa £22.14s.2d.
b. 7 Nov. £5.2s.0d., 14 Nov. £5.13s.6d., 21 Nov. £6.4s.8d., 28 Nov. £5.15s.3d. Summa £22.15s.5d.
c. 5 Dec. £4.1s.1d., 12 Dec. £8.4s.11d., 19 Dec. £6.14s.6d., 24 Dec. 58s.2d. Summa £21.18s.8d.
d. [f.25v] 2 Jan. 56s.5d., 9 Jan. £4.9s.3d., 16 Jan. £4.13s.6d., 23 Jan. £5.19s.1d., 30 Jan. £5.5s.1d. Summa £23.3s.3d.
e. 6 Feb. £4.1s.4d., 13 Feb. £6.18s.11d., 20 Feb. £6.18s.11d., 27 Feb. £7.8s.4d. Summa £25.7s.6d.
f. 6 March £13.3s.8d., 13 March £14.15s.2½d., 20 March £8.16s.1d., 27 March £9.10s.1d. Summa £46.5s.0½d.
g. 3 April £9.14s.8d., 10 April £7.5s.1d., 17 April £5.8s.2d., 24 April £7.3s.6d., 30 April £5.14s.7d. Summa £35.6s.0d.
h. 8 May £5.5s.9d., 15 May £7.11s.11½d., 22 May £7.0s.5d., 29 May £8.2s.10d. Summa £28.0s.11½d.
i. [f.26] 5 June £4.3s.9d., 12 June £6.2s.1d., 19 June £6.0s.0d., 26 June £4.6s.10d. Summa £20.12s.8d.
j. 3 July £3.8s.4d., 10 July £4.9s.7d., 17 July £4.17s.10½d., 24 July £4.9s.5½d., 31 July £4.13s.10d. Summa £21.19s.1d.
k. 7 Aug. £5.1s.7d., 14 Aug. £6.2s.9d., 21 Aug. £4.8s.11½d., 28 Aug. £5.18s.11d. Summa £21.12s.2½d.
l. 4 Sept. £4.8s.8½d., 11 Sept. £4.12s.8d., 18 Sept. £3.13s.2d., 25 Sept. £3.17s.0d. Summa £16.11s.6½d.
m. Summa totalis £306.6s.7d.
⟨whereof to Mr Carpenter £5.17s.11d. and for Finsbury £3.15s.6d., Summa £9.13s.5d.⟩
⟨Summa [. . .][1] declaro £296.13s.2d.⟩ [f.26v blank]

[1] Illegible word.

[f.27] Emptions of reparations stuff and other necessary things bought and provided this year for the service of the city whereof part is spent about the building and necessary reparations before mentioned in the weeks' bills and the rest remaining in store.*

*Most of the payments in this section were made against bills submitted by the artificers or suppliers of materials. The frequently recurring phrase 'as by a bill appears' has not been included in the calendar. In many paragraphs each subdivision by date or subtotal represents one bill, e.g. the total of entry **34** is the payment of 3 bills. The bills are not extant.

30. 15 Oct. to Stephen Cowley one of the meal weighers for 6 half C weight of iron to weigh meal within Newgate market at 6s.4d. the C weight, 19s.0d.

31. 11 Nov. to Richard Isackson painter stainer for stuff and workmanship bestowed in painting and beautifying the conduit near Dowgate by order of court [8 Oct. 1584, Rep.21, f.92][1] £3.6s.8d.; ⟨to the same for painting the pump at Milk Street 20s., and to Robert Maskall carpenter for mending the pumps at Dowgate, Leadenhall and Newgate market, the pump in Fleet Street and pumps at St Antholin and at Dowgate 20s.⟩;[2] summa ⟨£5.6s.8d.⟩

[1] The order authorises expenditure for this purpose but does not name Isackson. The conduit was before the house of the lord mayor elect, Thomas Pullyson.
[2] This insertion is a condensed version of a deleted entry on f.32.

32. 21 Nov. to my lord mayor in consideration of one dozen buckets to him due and being thereof provided beforehand 26s.8d.; 23 Aug. to Robert Aplebye saddler for four dozen leather buckets at 26s.8d. the dozen £5.6s.8d.; summa £6.13s.4d.

33. [f.27v] 28 Nov. to Michael Mellyn stranger for one new lock and three keys for the bookhouse door near the treasury, 7s.0d.

34. The same day to Randolph Bull goldsmith for stuff and workmanship bestowed upon the clock in the council chamber 6s.; 14 Dec. to Peter Medcalff clocksmith for stuff and workmanship bestowed on the clocks in the Guildhall 4s.6d.;[1] 5 June to Randolph Bull for stuff and workmanship in mending the clock in the council chamber 7s.4d.; summa 17s.10d.

[1] Peter Metcalfe, blacksmith, was paid £5 for a clock for the council chamber in 1566–67 (Chamber Accounts 1, f.215v).

35. 11 Dec. to Edward Nashe paviour for work at the suspiral (sesperall) at St Martin in the Field, at the suspiral at St Dunstan in the West, at the suspiral in the Old Bailey, at the common stairs in Trigg Lane, at, on and about Broken Wharf the dock and rush rooms (romes) there, at Mr. Edmoundes' in Thames Street,[1] the waterhouse at Dowgate, the suspiral in Walbrook, the cage at Blanchappleton and the [f.28] pump at Aldgate, containing in all 143½ 'tesse' at 8d. the 'tesse' £4.15s.8d., and for a labourer's wages for 36 days at 9d. the day accounting four 'tesse' for every day 27s., and for gravel and sand and carriage of rubbish and stones to and from the said works 50s.4d., summa £8.13s.0d.; 10 April to John Ramsbury for paving work at the conduit in Fleet Street, Ivy Bridge and the Old Bailey containing 134 yards at 1½d. the yard 16s.9d., and for gravel and sand 17s., summa 33s.9d.; [f.28v] 22 July to Nashe for paving work at Dunghill Lane near Broken Wharf, at Billingsgate, the 'Green Dragon' on Fish Street Hill,[2] Ivy Bridge,[3] over against the lord treasurer's,[4] the suspiral at St Dunstan's, the Old Bailey, Newgate without, the meal market within Newgate, the little conduit in Cheap, the cross there, the standard there, the great conduit there, the pissing conduit near the

Stocks, the conduit in Cornhill, the conduit at Gracechurch, Queenhithe, Smithfield pens, Ludgate, Aldgate and Bishopsgate, containing in all 87½ [*sic*][5] 'tesse' at 8d. the 'tesse' £3.5s., and for a labourer's wages after the rate of 9d. for every 4 'tesse' 18s., and for 25 loads of gravel and sand 25s., and for carriage of 28 loads of stones to the same works 10s., and for the carriage of 38 loads of rubbish to and from the works 12s.8d., and for carriage of 10 loads of stones to Fleet Bridge where the new pipes were laid 3s.4d., summa £6.14s.0d.; [f.29] 16 Oct. [1585] to Edward Nashe for paving 140 yards against Mr Isam's[6] house near St Mary Spital at Easter 1584 at 2½d. the yard 29s.2d., and for 33 loads of gravel to the same work 33s., summa ⟨£3.2s.2d.⟩ over and above 45s. for 18 loads of stones occupied at the work. Summa totalis £20.2s.11d. ⟨whereof owing [by] Mr. Isham[6] £5.7s.2d. for the which remains a tablet of gold with Mr Chamberlain in store⟩.[7]

[1] 'The Pecocke', belonging to the Carpenter estate, held by John Edmondes (Rental, Chamber Accounts 2, f.192v).
[2] Part of the Carpenter estate (*ibid.*).
[3] A footbridge at the northern (Strand) end of Ivy Lane. The name was later accorded to the landing place at the southern end of the lane (*Notes & Queries*, 10th series, v, 81, 136).
[4] Burleigh House, on the north side of the Strand, opposite the Savoy.
[5] *Recte* 97½?
[6] Henry Isham, mercer and common councilman? (Foster, 166).
[7] Cf. **142e**.

36. 12 Dec. to William Edwyn bargeman for 6 new bails for the great barge at 2s.6d. the piece and for 6 new bails for the little barge at 2s. the piece, for 4 oars for the great barge at 3s.4d. the piece and for 2 oars for the little barge at like price, summa £2.7s.0d.

37. 19 Dec. to Davy Parr joiner for a table with a crest for orders for fishwives 2s.6d.; 23 Jan. for a mould for the casting of signs appointed to be worn of all such as are allowed to sell fish, oranges and such like victuals in and about the city[1] 2s.6d. ⟨as by the journal appears⟩; 10 April to him for work done at St Mary Spital 11s.10d.; ⟨and more to him for 3 frames for 3 windows at the conduit heads 8s.⟩;[2] ⟨summa £1.4s.10d.⟩

[1] Metal badges hung round the neck (Jor.21, f.418).
[2] This insertion is a condensed version of a separate, deleted, entry on f.33v in which the frames are said 'to serve 3 windows under the Banqueting House at the conduit heads'. For the Banqueting House, see P. E. Jones, 'The Estates of the Corporation of London: property records as a source for historical, topographical and economic research', *Guildhall Miscellany*, i, no.7, Aug. 1956, 10–14.

38. [f.29v] 21 Dec. to William Kerwyn mason for 141 foot of arch stone delivered towards the new building of Ludgate at 2s.6d. the foot as by a bill appears, £17.12s.6d.; 29 March to the merchants of the Steelyard (Stilliarde) for 2,294 foot of ashlar stone, 86 foot of jamb (iame) stone and arch stone, 269 foot of table and 'skewe' stone, 89 foot of vent and crest stone, 2 door rooms 28 foot and one window 11 foot, for the use aforesaid £103.19s.5d.; and more to William Kerwyn in part of a sum for the new building of the jail of Ludgate according to an act of common council and a pair of indentures made between the mayor, commonalty and citizens of the one part and William Kerwyn of the other part £200; summa £321.11s.11d.[1]

[1] The rebuilding of Ludgate was under discussion from March 1584. On 13 March 1585 the common council approved a 'plot or module' made by William Kerwyn (Jor.21, f.420). The indentures between him and the city (no details given) were sealed on 26 Aug. 1585 (Rep.21, f.202b). In addition to this £321.11s.11d., £100 was paid towards the work out of the Bridge House estates (**181**). The greater part of the expenditure fell in 1585–86 (**181**, **201**).

39. 19 June to William Kerwyn for 77 foot of purbeck (purpickt) paving stone at 4½d. the foot 28s.10½d. and for 22 foot of hollow channel [f.30] stone at 6d. the foot occupied at Newgate 11s., summa £1.19s.10½d.

40. To George Michell limeman for 82½ C of lime at 6s. the C due for one year ended at Michaelmas 1585, £24.17s.0d.

41. To ⟨Richard⟩[1] Awsten of Hoxton (Hogsdon) for 34,250 bricks delivered at 10s. the thousand to the Guildhall, to the city's storehouse at Leadenhall, to the tenement 'Peacock' in Thames Street and to the conduit heads, for one year ended at Michaelmas last, £17.2s.6d.

[1] Written over 'Robert' deleted. The whole entry is written following and in substitution for a deleted and incomplete entry respecting delivery of a smaller quantity of bricks, probably Awsten's bill for one quarter only.

42. [f.30v] 3 Feb. to Thomas Ruddick carpenter for 13 loads and 17 foot of oaken timber at 14s. the load £9.6s.11d., and for the carriage and cranage of the same from the '3 Craines'[1] to Leadenhall at 20d. the load 22s., £10.8s.11d.; 29 May to Lewis Gardner for 9 loads of elm timber lacking (lack) 5 foot delivered into the Greenyard[2] at 13s.4d. the load £5.18s.9d.; 7 Aug. to Thomas Rudduck for 26 loads and 26 foot of oaken timber and 13 loads 19 foot of elm timber delivered into the Greenyard at 16s.7d. the load £33.1s.8d.; summa £49.9s.4d.

[1] Three Cranes Wharf in Vintry Ward.
[2] The Greenyard at Leadenhall was the city's principal store for materials.

43. [f.31] 13 Feb. to Mote bellfounder for a new bell to be used by Clement Forman [cf.**25j**] nightly over and above the old bell being mended ⟨delivered in exchange⟩, 2s.6d.

44. 3 and 9 Feb. to Christopher Webb salter for 10 fother (fodder)[1] ¼C 25 lb of lead at £8.18s. the fother and for other charges £89.8s.8d.; to John Martyn plumber for 84 great conduit pipes in lead weighing 25 fother 12½C 9 lb at £9 the fother £230.13s.3d., and for casting and burning the pipes at £7 the fother £179.8s., and for 23¾C of solder for the same pipes, accounting 112 lb to the C, at 56s. the C, viz. 6d. the lb (le pounde), £66.10s., and for wood and digging 520 yards of ground for laying of the pipes at 12d. the yard £26, [f.31v] summa £502.11s.3d., whereof received of John Martyn for 22 fother 13¼C 15 lb of lead to him delivered at £9 the fother £204.0s.6d., so rest due to John Martyn £298.10s.9d.; to John

Martyn for 16C 9 lb of new lead, accounting 112 lb to the C, at 9s. the C £7.4s.10d., and for casting the same at 2s. the C 32s.2d., and for 4C 20 lb of lead to him due upon his account ended at Michaelmas 1584 at 9s. the C 37s.10d., and for 3½C 12 lb of old lead by him delivered to the mason for the yoking of stones at like rate 32s.9d., and for 1¼C 14 lb of solder by him delivered as aforesaid at 6d. the lb £3.17s. [f.32] due for a half year ended at the Annunciation 1585, summa £16.4s.7d. Summa totalis £404.2s.11d.[2]

[1] The fother is here equivalent to 20 cwt.
[2] An instruction in the right margin ⟨Follow as in fol.34 plumber⟩ indicates that in the final account entry **58** on f.34 was to be entered at this point. There follows a deleted entry, see **31** note 2.

45. 2 April to John Cox for 2 ropes for the crane at Queenhithe weighing 80 lb at 4d. the (le) lb 26s.8d.; to Richard Hewghson skinner for a white rope weighing 104 lb at 2½d. [f.32v] the lb to serve the gin at Ludgate 24s.2d.; summa £2.10s.10d.

46. 10 April to Edward Downes nightman for cleansing the common vault at Leadenhall containing 17 tuns (tonnes) at 22d. the (le) tun 31s.2d., and for cleansing a vault belonging to the tenement of William Anthony at St Lawrence Pountney[1] containing 4 tuns at like rate 7s.4d., and to a labourer seeing the same tuns filled 18d., and for 4 lb of candles 12d., summa £2.1s.0d.; 8 May to him for cleansing a vault belonging to the tenements of John Gibson and Henry Mathew in the parish of St Michael le Querne[2] containing 30 tuns at 22d. the tun 55s., and to a labourer for watching 3 nights seeing the same tuns filled 18d., summa £2.16s.6d.; 29 May to him [f.33] for cleansing the common vault within Blanchappleton containing 148 tuns at 22d. the tun £13.11s.4d., and to a labourer for watching 12 nights seeing the same tuns filled 6s., ⟨summa £13.17s.4d.⟩. Summa totalis £18.14s.10d.[3]

[1] A tenant of the city (Rental, Chamber Accounts 2, f.180).
[2] Gibson and Mathew were both tenants of the city (*ibid.*, f.187). Mathew dwelt at the sign of the 'Talbott' (CCPR, St. Michael Le Querne, 1587). For Gibson's contribution to this sum, see **11i**.
[3] From time to time the court of aldermen regulated the hours during which the night carts removing ordure from the city could operate, e.g. in 1600 between 10 p.m. and 4 a.m. (Rep.25, f.83b).

47. 4 Oct. for mending one of the city's saddles against Bartholomewtide (Bartholmewtide) to be used by Henry Byram ⟨yeoman of the channel⟩, 4s.6d.

48. 24 April to Robert Northe of Shootup Hill (Shoote Uphill) in the parish of Hampstead, Middlesex, yeoman in part of £10 for 20,000 tiles to be delivered between this and St James day next [25 July], £5.0s.0d.

49. 10 May to Mr John Lacy clothworker for one yard and 1½ nails[1] of crimson velvet for the covering of the sword carried before the lord mayor at 26s. the yard, £1.8s.6d.

[1] Nail: 2¼ inches.

50. [f.33v] 5 June to Thomas Bennet ironmonger for locks, staples, hooks, spikings and nails of sundry sorts with other iron work occupied and bestowed about the necessary business of the city for one year ended at Michaelmas 1585, £17.5s.5½d.[1]

[1] There follows a deleted entry, see **37** note 2.

51. 18 June to Richard Pike of Rudgwick (Ridgwick), Sussex, yeoman for 3,425 foot of plank (planche) and quarter board at 4s. the (le) C £6.17s., and for wharfage and carriage thereof from Paul's Wharf to the Guildhall at 6d. the load 5s.6d.; summa £7.2s.6d.

52. [f.34] 7 Aug. to John Porter for 21 fir poles at divers prices, 13s.3d.

53. 10 Aug. to Richard Payne joiner for stuff and workmanship in repairing the city's wagons, 8s.10d.

54. 28 Aug. to William Shawe armourer for oiling and trimming 86 calivers, harquebuses (hargabusshes) and half ⟨pikes⟩[1] and 146 morions (murryons), for 16 days' work at 14d. the day 18s.8d., and for one gallon of oil occupied about the same 3s.4d., summa [£1.2s.0d.]

[1] Written over 'axes' struck through.

55. 2 Oct. [1585] to Richard Sampson blacksmith for hasps, hinges, staples, spikings, bars, bolts, locks, cramps and dogs of iron and other stuff and workmanship, due for one year ended at Michaelmas 1585, £84.16s.5d.

56. [f.34v] 29 Nov. [1585] to John Frenche girdler for 77 foot of great wire by him set up at the conduit and conduit heads since Midsummer last at 8d. the foot 51s.8d., and for 2 days' work 2s.4d., and for wire 6d., summa £2.14s.6d.

57. To John Edredge of Croydon collier for 8 loads of great coals at 30s. the load, £12.0s.0d.[1]

[1] The first version of this amended entry read, '13 Dec. to James Harman for 8 loads of great coals by him bought of John Eldridge of Croydon collier. . . .'

58. 14 Dec. [1585] to John Martyn plumber for 16¼C 8 lb of sheet lead, accounting 112 lb to the C, and for casting the same at 11s. the C £8.19s.6d.; to him for 2½C 9 lb of solder, accounting 112 lb to the C, viz. 6d. the lb £7.4s.6d., and for 5¾C 6 lb of burnt pipes at 16s. the C £4.12s.10d.; [f.35] to him for 4¼C 14½ lb of leaden weights for the meal markets at 14s. the C £3.14s.10d. due for half a year ended at Michaelmas 1585; summa £24.1s.8d.

59. 14 Dec. [1585] to William Palmer founder for a new washer for the conduit heads, mending, tinning and setting in cocks, wastes, washers and stoppers at sundry conduits, and for mending and scouring the city's latten squirts, due for one year ended at Michaelmas 1585, £4.1s.10d.

60. To Barnaby Bestowe turner for shovels, tampions, scoops, stoppers, staves, lime sieves (lymesyves), racks and pump boxes for one year ended at Michaelmas 1585, £4.6s.10d.

61. To John Smithe glazier for glass stuff and workmanship bestowed about the house at St Mary Spital, the Sessions house, the Guildhall and other places, due for one year ended at Michaelmas 1585, £1.7s.7d.

62. [Estimated total of 'Emptions' *c.* £1,083, less deductions amounts to £1,076.18s.3d.][1]

[1] The total of the 'Emptions' is missing but as so far calendared is £1,045.4s.2d. Ff.35v–37v contain entries, deleted and not calendared here, relating to canvas, tallow, cords, candles, meat and drink for workmen, and other minor necessities and works which are grouped by one paragraph per month with weekly sub-totals. No suppliers are named. The bottom portion of f.36 is missing and in consequence the paragraph for Dec. is incomplete and those for Jan. and Feb. are missing. The surviving entries total £31.12s.3½d. and the missing items probably accounted for approximately £6. All these monthly entries have been deleted, possibly with the intention of substituting therefor a short composite entry for the whole year such as occurs in the account for 1585–86 (and which totals £35.10s.5d.), see **199**. On the above calculations the total would be *c.* £1,083 (i.e. £1,045.4s.2d. + £31.12s.3½d. + *c.* £6) but certain deductions would be made in respect of the special accounts. There were no deductions this year for the Philipot and Reynwell accounts (see notes to **126c** and **132h**) but £5 was charged to the Carpenter account (see **129h**) and perhaps something for Finsbury. The total required for the 'Emptions' on the general account after deductions in order to make the total of the Discharge correct is £1,076.18s.3d.

[f.38] The Foreign Charge [Payments]*

63. To Mr Browghton[1] for preaching in the Guildhall chapel on Michaelmas day 1584 before the election of Sir Thomas Pullyson knight late lord mayor[2] 10s.; to Leonard Largyn serjeant of the channel (cannell) riding to the court to deliver the weekly certificates made to the queen and the lord mayor of all such persons as are weekly born and buried within the liberties of the city and other out parishes near the city as due at the said feast of St Michael ⟨£9⟩; to the vergers of St Paul's for opening and shutting the door of St Dunstan's chapel in St Paul's[3] at the repairing of the lord mayor and aldermen thither on Sundays and other days ⟨there⟩ tarrying till the sermon time 20d.; to the yeoman of the waterside for keeping clean the said chapel 6s.8d.; to a poor man for keeping clean the circuit of the place where my lord mayor's officers and others sit and stand at the sermon time[4] 8s.; summa ⟨£10.6s.4d.⟩

[1] Possibly Hugh Broughton, puritan preacher and Hebrew scholar, who had recently come to London from Cambridge (*DNB*).
[2] Knighted during his mayoralty on 14 Feb. 1585 (cf.**86**).
[3] On the south side of the Lady chapel (William Benham, *Old St Paul's Cathedral*, 1902, plan, illus. 10).
[4] In St Paul's churchyard (see **304** where comparable payments in 1563–64 to those listed in the above entry are recorded).

*Many of the payments recorded were paid against bills of charges, particularly in the case of junior officers. The frequently recurring phrase 'as by a bill appears' has generally been omitted from the calendar. References to payment by court order, commandment of the lord mayor or in accordance with the journal are always noted.

64. [f.38v] ⟨5 Oct. for going with the lord mayor elect to the lord chancellor after his election 9s.8d. and given in reward there 2s.6d.⟩;[1] 23 Oct. to William Edwyn bargeman for serving my lord mayor and my lord mayor elect to the lord chancellor's 13s.6d.; 22 March to him for serving my lord mayor and certain aldermen to and from the lord chancellor's 9s.2d.; 16 April to him for serving certain aldermen to and from the court 13s.10d.; 15 May to him for serving divers aldermen to and from the court twice 16s.8d.; 15 July to him for serving my lord mayor, divers aldermen and Mr Recorder to and from Woolwich (Wollwich) 19s.8d.; 7 Aug. to him by commandment of my lord mayor for making ready and giving attendance with a barge for the Estates of the Low Countries 5s.;[2] summa ⟨£4.10s.0d.⟩

[1] Inserted entry. According to a fuller version originally entered on f.44v and deleted, 9s.8d. was paid, by a bill, to William Edwyn, bargeman, and 2s.6d. was given to the lord chancellor's porter at the watergate.
[2] See p. xxviii.

65. [f.39] 23 Oct. to William Edwyn for stuff and workmanship bestowed in dressing the city's great barge 33s.5d.; 6 Feb. to him for dressing the city's 2 barges 35s.2.; 20 April to him for dressing the 2 barges 34s.10d.; 5 July to him for dressing the 2 barges 35s.1d.; summa £6.18s.6d.

66. For the boat hire of divers aldermen and their servants as also for sundry officers of the city travelling about the city's affairs within the time of this account as by the journal appears £10.6s.7d.; [f.39v] 19 Oct. by order of court to William Ravenscroft the common hunt's man and Robert Lyddyas the waterbailie's man, to either of them 20s. for seeing the bills be fixed and continued 28 days on such houses as are and have been infected with the plague 40s.; 27 Feb. for 100 proclamations to be proclaimed against eating of flesh in Lent 8s.; for 100 exhortations ⟨against conspirators⟩[1] to repent 8s.; summa £13.2s.7d.[2]

[1] Written over 'for traitors' struck through.
[2] Following this entry in the right margin, '⟨Pag'1 £34.17s.5d.⟩' which sum is the total of the preceding four paragraphs. Throughout the Foreign Charge similar annotations from Pag'1 to Pag'17, with totals as appropriate, are to be found. They presumably indicate a sequence of leaves, for a rewriting of the account, perhaps the engrossed account on parchment.

67. 25 Jan. to William Prestwood leatherseller[1] for one roll of parchment, 2 paper books for my lord mayor, 6 quires of parchment for the account, 6 quires of parchment for the journal of letter Z, 6 quires of parchment for freemen,[2] 2 quires of paper royal, 6 quires of parchment for common council[3] and for a second book of parchment covered with leather to serve the lord mayor's court for entering [f.40] of reprieves (repryes) of prisoners to actions commenced in the said court, £6.10s.10d.; 17 March to Hugh Singleton stationer for stuff and workmanship bestowed in binding of the book of Z serving the lord mayor's court[4] 29s.2d.; 17 July to William Prestwood for one roll of parchment, 5 quires of royal paper, 8 quires of parchment for common council, one skin of vellum and one forel (forrell) of vellum, 4 quires of parchment for the journal of the repertory[5] and 6 quires of parchment for freemen £4.2s.4d.; summa £12.2s.4d.

[1] *Margin* stationer (cf. **229**).
[2] The register of freemen, see **5.**
[3] Presumably for the book of acts of common council referred to in **209** and **229**.
[4] Presumably Letter Book Z, which covers the 5 mayoralties Nov. 1579–Oct. 1584.
[5] Presumably for the new Letter Book, the repertory itself being always of paper.

68. [f.40v] 8 Jan. allowed to John Coxe merchant taylor, farmer of the customs and profits at Queenhithe, as well for the garners (garnerdes) there as other profits, in consideration of the lack of one of the lofts of the garner which the company of Grocers withhold to lay their corn in without anything allowing therefor, for one year ended at Michaelmas last past 40s.;[1] to sundry persons for 14 otter heads at 3s.4d. the head as by the journal appears 46s.8d.;[2] and for 3 cormorants' heads as by the journal appears 12d.;[3] summa £4.7s.8d.

[1] See **7p**, note.
[2] Payments at the same rate were made for 23 otters' heads in 1563–64, 48 in 1565–66 and 32 in 1568–69 (Chamber Accounts 1, ff.122, 193v, 11v). And see **216**.
[3] This last item added in a different hand. Payments at the same rate were made for 36 cormorants' heads in 1563–64, 42 in 1565–66 and 31 in 1568–69 (*ibid.*) And see **216**.

69. 24 March to Hugh Singleton stationer[1] for printing 450 acts of common council for the queen's great beam [7 Oct. 1583, Jor.21, ff.322b–324 amended 6 Aug. 1584, f.370b], 500 rates for weighing at the same beam, 350 proclamations against casting abroad of libels [13 Feb. 1585, Jor. 21, f.407b], 1,000 freemen's oaths, and 300 proclamations for fishwives [4 March 1585, Jor.21, f.418], summa £3.18s.5d.

[1] *Margin* printer. Hugh Singleton had been appointed printer to the city on 4 Aug. 1584 (Rep.21, f.78).

70. [f.41] 23 Oct. for a dinner for divers commoners appointed by my lord mayor for the search of naughty and corrupt hops 15s.2d., and for further charges in law for condemning the same being found out by the searchers 17s.4d., and for carriage and burning of the same 6s.10d.; 29 Oct. to Sir Edward Osborne's man for the carriage of certain seditious books to the court 6d.;[1] 20 Nov. by order of court [19 Nov. 1584, Rep.21, f.112b] to Andrew Saires salter for divers considerations moving the court £8.6s.2d.;[2] summa £10.6s.6d.

[1] Edward Osborne was lord mayor 1583–84. A royal proclamation concerning seditious books was dated 12 Oct. 1584 (Jor.21, ff.387–8; Hughes and Larkin, *Tudor Proclamations*, ii, no. 672).
[2] This sum was orphans' finding money outstanding. See **27h** for an annuity granted to him by the same order.

71. [f.41v] 4 Dec. to 14 persons ⟨being sworn on a quest of office⟩[1] to enquire and present a butt of muscadel seized and found by them to be foreign bought and sold ⟨at 8d. apiece and coloured by Stephen Hosyer cooper⟩ 9s.4d., to Mr Kitchen for his pains and counsel therein 10s.[2] and to William Dalby for further charges in the law 18s., to James Harman for carriage and other charges for the same 2s., by order of my lord mayor to Thomas Redknight and Charles Lockey for their part of £13 received for the same muscadel £4, and [f.42] by order of court to Stephen Hosier for so much to him allowed towards the loss he sustained for that he coloured the butt of muscadel contrary to his oath and the laws and customs of this city £4, summa £9.19s.4d.[3]

[1] Written over 'of a jury being sworn', struck through.
[2] This clause, giving in addition the date of payment as 4 Dec., was originally the first entry on this page, but was deleted.
[3] See **11b** for receipt of £13 for this butt of muscadel and Rep.21, f.123b for the distribution to Hosier, the informers and others.

72. ⟨For 25 reams of paper bought of sundry persons at divers payments as by the journal appears⟩[1] ⟨£5.18s.6d.⟩[2]

[1] This entry is written in substitution of a deleted paragraph listing 10 items of paper totalling 25 reams. The names of the suppliers are not given in the deleted passage.
[2] In the right margin '⟨pag'2 £46.12s.9d.⟩' which sum is the total of **67–72.** See **66**, note 2.

73. [f.42v] 16 March to Mr Alderman Martyn ⟨by order of court⟩ for 2 pieces of gold of 30s. the piece by him given in reward to 2 clerks of the council and for the charges of himself and Mr Alderman Barnes with their servants at the court the same time £3.8s.4d.; 3 April by 2 orders of court to Mr Town Clerk by him to be delivered to Mr Wilkes clerk to the council 40s.[1] and to the keeper of the council chamber 40s. [16 March 1585, Rep.21, f.150b]; 22 March to Mr Town Clerk for so much by him given to the lord chancellor's [f.43] secretary and porters 13s.; 14 June by order of court [27 May 1585, Rep.21, f.173] to Mr Alderman Bond by him to be delivered for the city's service to a person whose name the court will not for divers considerations have known £50; 30 Jan. by like order [4 Feb. 1585, Rep.21, f.134b] to Mr Town Clerk by him to be bestowed upon a person whose name the court will not have known £10; 30 Dec. by order of court [15 Dec. 1584, Rep.21, f.122b] to Mr John Eve deputy in the crown office as of the free gift of the city £3.6s.8d.; summa £71.8s.0d.

[1] Thomas Wilkes (*Acts of the Privy Council, 1586–87*, 239, 395). Order for payment not traced.

74. 21 Nov. to Henry Bryam for his charges riding into Surrey to Mr Lyfeilde and Mr Vincente justices of peace there for the certifying of my lord mayor what store of wood there is there 11s.4d.; 13 Oct. to Edward Wallys carpenter which he ⟨before⟩ paid ⟨in the name of a fine⟩ by order of my lord mayor for breaking the price of faggots set down by the [f.43v] court ⟨and by order of court [8 Oct. 1584, Rep.21, f.92] to him restored⟩ 40s.; 25 Nov. by like order [19 Nov. 1584, Rep.21, f.113] to David Manninge and Thomas Redknight the 2 yeomen of the woodwharf for the moiety of such fines as were levied ⟨and charged as well in the last as in this account⟩ upon divers woodmongers for breaking the price of billets and faggots set down by the court £14; to Humfry Wynnington late clerk of the chamber[1] for writing one pair of indentures between this accountant and my lord mayor for the city's plate delivered to the lord mayor 2s.6d., and for the carriage of the plate from the old lord mayor's to the new 12d; to Wynnington for writing such presentments of wardmote of inquests as are to be reformed by Mr Chamberlain 30s.; to John Shawe [f.44] now clerk of the chamber[1] for drawing of this account 13s.4d. and for engrossing the same 53s.4d.,[2] and for drawing the book of fines and engrossing the same 3s.4d.; summa £21.14s.10d.

[1] Description inserted above the line.
[2] In the 1560s, the fees for drawing and engrossing the account were 6s.8d. and 26s.8d. respectively and that for writing the plate indenture was 12d. (Chamber Accounts 1, ff.110v, 194, 214).

75. In reward to the poor at Westminster when my lord mayor went to take his oath there 50s.6d., to the keepers of the chapel door[1] 2s., to the queen's bedemen 2s., to the vergers 3s.4d., to the sexton 2s., to the keeper of the exchequer 2s., to the marshal's men 5s., to the keeper of Baynard's Castle 10s., and for the boat hire of this accountant's clerk from Westminster 4d.; to William Edwyn bargeman for serving my lord mayor, aldermen and others in the city's 2 barges and 2 other barges at the same time £6.2s.6d., and in reward to the said bargemen 2s.; summa £10.1s.8d.[2]

[1] 'old palace there' struck through.
[2] In the right margin '⟨pag'3 £103.4s.6d.⟩' which sum is the total of **73–5**. See **66** note 2. There follows [f.44v] a deleted entry, see **64** note.

76. 25 Nov. to Robert Smithe for money by him laid out in the suit of quo warranto brought against the city for the search of hops, butter, oil, vinegar and soap 33s.8d.;[1] 4 Dec. to Mr Eve of the crown office for charges in the suit 7s.8d.; to Mr Serjeant Wamsley[2] [f.45] for his pains in the matter 30s.; 16 Jan. to Mr Recorder, Mr Daniell and Mr Owen to every of them 20s. for his pains in the suit £3; 4 Feb. to Mr Recorder, Mr Daniell and Mr Owen to every of them 20s. for perusing the books of answer to the quo warranto ⟨as by the journal appears £3⟩; to Robert [Smithe for his further][3] charges in the suit £3.18s.8d.; 5 June to Robert Smithe for money by him laid out and for writing 2 copies of the quo warranto 27s.4d.; 5 July to him which he paid to Mr Kempe and Mr Reve[4] the city's attorneys in the crown office for their fees for the matter in Trinity term 13s.4d.; summa £15.10s.8d. [cf.**227**]

[1] The search was a matter of dispute between the city, which had long exercised the right of appointing searchers, and the company of tallow chandlers, which obtained a grant by letters patent in 1577. The controversy continued for many years (R. Monier-Williams, *The Tallow Chandlers of London*, iv, 1977, 142–67).
[2] Thomas Walmesley, serjeant at law and later justice of the common pleas.
[3] Ms mutilated.
[4] *Sic. Recte* Eve?

77. [f.45v] 21 Oct. to Mr Henry Billingsly haberdasher and one of the sheriffs for so much to him due by act of common council [1 Aug. 1582, Jor.21, ff.226a–227a] for that he took upon him the office of shrievalty [10 Aug. 1584, Jor.21, f.371] in place of Mr Thomas Skynner clothworker who lately refused the same £200; 22 Oct. by act of court [20 Oct. 1584,

Rep.21, f.99b] to Edward Maryner and Arthur Warde officers to Mr Sheriff Billingsly for their charges and hindrances in the time of their imprisonment in the Marshalsea (Mershalsey) £4, and by commandment of my lord mayor for the charges of Edward Bassaney, Arthur Bassany and Jeronomy Bassaney, 3 of the queen's musicians, in the compter (counter) being committed thither by my lord mayor ⟨for their misdemeanour used against the lord mayor and others at Christ Church 12s.⟩;[1] summa £204.12s.0d.

[1] The occasion of the musicians' imprisonment was their violence and insolence towards John Spencer, the sheriff (1583–84), and the recorder, and their obstruction of the officers muring up a way and gate at Christ Church, Aldgate (see **83**; *Cal. SPD, 1581–90*, 202, 204). For the Bassano family of court musicians, see *New Grove Dictionary of Music and Musicians*, ii, 1980, 253.

78. [f.46] 30 Sept. to Robert Hide for his charges riding to the court with letters 6s.2d.; to Henry Ravenscroft for his charges riding to the court with letters 6s.8d.; to Robert Smithe for the charges of himself and of Leonard Largen riding to the court 7s.2d.; to him for his charges and the charges of the servants of Mr Dixey, Mr Bond and Mr [. . .][1] 13s.11d.; to him for money by him laid out in riding to the court with Mr Bond, Mr Martyn, Mr Allett and Mr Spencer aldermen and others 25s., and for the charges of Mr Allott and Mr Rowe, aldermen, Mr Town Clerk with divers officers and servants to ⟨Hampton⟩ Court 21s.6d.; to James Harman for horse hire for ⟨Mr Bukle, Mr Humfrey Smyth, Mr Secondary and other officers⟩[2] to and from the court ⟨at Hampton⟩ for the inviting of the lords of her majesty's council to my lord mayor's feast £3.4s.6d.; [f.46v] to Leonard Largyn for his charges riding to the court at Theobalds (Tibballes) to the lord of Leicester touching Mr Ketcher late elect sheriff 5s.; to James Harman for horse hire for one of my lord mayor's officers being sent to Mr Brasey late elect sheriff 2s.3d.; to Henry Raynescroft for his horse hire and other charges to and from the court 3s.6d.; to Leonard Largen for his horse hire to and from the court at [. . . 5s.6d.];[3] to Mr Waterbailiff for horse hire and other charges for himself and Henry Ravenscroft to and from the court 10s.2d.; to Henry Ravenscroft for his horse and other charges to and from the court 4s.; summa £8.17s.4d.[4]

[1] Ms. mutilated; one line missing.
[2] Written over 'divers officers'. Below is written 'Mr Bukle', struck through, 'alderman, Mr Humphrey Smyth Mr Secondary Fytton'.
[3] Ms. mutilated; one line missing.
[4] In the right margin '⟨[pag']4 £229.0s.0d.⟩' which sum is the total of **76–78**. See **66** note 2.

79. [f.47] 12 Oct. to Mr Plowden, Mr Daniell and Mr Owen to every of them 20s. for his pains taken at Mr Plowden's chamber in conferring together touching the quo warranto by Sir James Acroft brought against the city for the office of garbling[1] ⟨as by the journal appears⟩ £3; 13 Oct. to Mr Recorder for perusing the books penned by Mr Plowden, Mr Daniell and Mr Owen 20s.; 29 Oct. to Mr Clerk for his counsel 20s.; 5 Nov. to Mr Owen for moving the court of exchequer for a longer day for the answering of the quo warranto 10s., and to Mr Plowden, Mr Clark, Mr Daniell and Mr Owen to every of them 20s. for his pains taken at Mr Plowden's chamber touching the quo warranto £4; to Sir James Acrofte [f.47v] by order of the court ⟨of exchequer⟩ by reason of putting in a new answer to the quo warranto £3.6s.8d.; 25 Nov. to Mr Plowden for his pains taken in the city's answer upon a demur for the same office 10s.; 16 Dec. to Robert Smithe for his pains and for money by him laid out in the matter £4.12s.10d.; 24 Dec. to Mr Recorder, Mr Daniell and Mr Owen to every of them 40s. for his pains £6; 26 Jan. to Mr Clark for perusing the books of the answer 20s.; 30 Jan. to Mr Recorder for his pains taken at the exchequer bar 30s., and to Mr ⟨Danyell, Mr Owen and Mr Clarke to every of them 20s. for their pains then and there £3; 1 Feb. to Mr Recorder for his pains at the exchequer bar 30s., and to Mr⟩ Clark for his great pains then pleading there 40s., [f.48] and to Mr Daniell and Mr Owen for their pains then and there 40s.; 9 Feb. to Mr Recorder, Mr Daniell, Mr Owen and Mr Clark to every of them 20s. for their pains taken at the exchequer bar £4; 23 Feb. to Robert Smithe for writing of divers copies and for money by him laid out in the suit £3.3s.6d.; 4 May to Mr Recorder for his pains taken at the exchequer bar 20s., and to Mr Daniell for his great pains in drawing and penning a book for answering the writ of quo warranto and for pleading then and there to the same £3, and to Mr Clark then and there 10s., and to Mr Daniell's man for engrossing the book of answer 10s.; [f.48v] 10 May to Mr Recorder for his pains taken at the exchequer bars pleading and answering the writ of quo warranto £3, and in reward to the ushers there 2s.; 1 June to Robert Smithe for money by him laid out and for writing divers copies 43s.3d.; 5 July to Robert Smithe which he paid to Mr Solloway and Mr Godfry Fanshaw the city's attorneys for their fees in Trinity term touching the matter 16s.8d.; summa £53.5s.0d.[2]

[1] Sir James Croft, comptroller of the queen's household, had acquired the interest in a grant made under letters patent of 17 June 1567 to Anthony White of the office of garbling throughout the realm, whereas the city under letters patent of 20 June 1478 had long held the right to the office within London. The matter was to be resolved in 1586 by the city purchasing Croft's interests for 1,000 marks, the money being raised by an assessment upon the wards, and taking over Croft's obligations for the payment of an annuity to Joan, widow of Anthony White (cf. **157b**, **174b**, **226**, **251**; Jor.22, ff.9b, 10; Rep.21, ff.268–9).

[2] In the right margin '⟨5 £53.5s.0d.⟩'. See **66** note 2.

80. 7 Nov. for a dinner at St Giles in the Fields for Mr Chamberlain, Mr Dommer and other officers to view the conduit heads 11s.7d.; 27 March for 2 dinners at the conduit heads the 8 and 9 March for Mr Chamberlain, Mr Domer and the [f.49] city's workmen in surveying the conduit heads 26s.9d.; 21 Jan. for a dinner for this accountant, and theodory,[1] the surveyor of Middlesex and others at the viewing and measuring out a plot of ground near Tyburn for the burying of prisoners which shall be executed there ⟨as by the journal appears⟩ 10s.; 14 Aug. for a dinner at the conduit heads for Sir Rowland Hayward, Mr Woodcock, Mr Roe and Mr Buckle aldermen, Mr Chamberlain, Mr Dommer and other commoners appointed by order of court [1 Aug. 1585, Rep.21, f.202] to survey the small conduit pipes being greatly decayed 37s.6½d.; 19 June for a dinner at James Harman's house for the auditors of the second account of this accountant[2] 30s.2d.; 11 Dec. for a dinner at the 'Flying Horse' in Maiden (Meaden) Lane for Mr Chamberlain, Mr Dommer and others at the cutting out of winter liveries 22s.2d., summa £6.18s.2½d.

[1] *Sic.* For feodary?
[2] The account of the previous year, 1583–84.

81. [f.49v] 9 Dec. to Nicholas Willy gentleman in consideration that he did resign the office of waterbailiff unto Thomas Sommer deceased, due ⟨for one year ended at Michaelmas last £20⟩,[1] 26 Nov. by order of court [24 Nov. 1584, Rep.21, f.114] to John Younge of Newport, Salop, gentleman towards his relief 20s.; 28 Nov. by like order [24 Nov. 1584, Rep.21, f.114] to Margaret Plane widow towards her relief 20s.; 21 [f.50] July by order of court [20 July 1585, Rep.21, f.192] to William Ryder draper in respect of his hurt and hindrance which he sustained by a foreign tapster whom he sued (shewed) in Mr Chamberlain's name as of the free gift of the court 20s.; to Robert Smithe for the fee of Mr Kemp attorney in the king's bench in the suit against Ralph (Raffe) Sheppard for seizing of eggs 3s.4d.; 18 Dec. [1585] by order of court to William Ravenscroft the common hunt's man for keeping the door leading out of the council (counsell) chamber into the outer court for one year ended at Michaelmas last 40s.;[2] summa £25.3s.4d.

[1] Written in substitution of entries for four quarterly payments, deleted. In consideration of Willy's surrender, Sommer (Somers) had undertaken to pay him £20 p.a. for life (Rep.19, f.498b, 6 Oct. 1579). After Sommer's death, the contribution from his estate was reduced by half (Rep.20, f.183b (cf.**11j**)).
[2] An order of 17 December 1583 provided that one of the officers of the lord mayor's house, nominated by the lord mayor, should always carry out this duty and be paid 40s. a year (Rep.21, f.15).

82. [f.50v] 20 Oct. to Mr Recorder for his pains taken in the matter of controversy between this city and the lieutenant of the Tower[1] 20s., and to Mr Daniell and to Mr Owen to either of them 10s. for his pains therein 20s.; to Mr Recorder, Mr Daniell and Mr Owen to every of them 20s. for his pains taken at Serjeants' Inn before the 2 lords chief justices and the master of the rolls in the matter £3, and to the porter there in reward 12d., and for the dinners of certain officers attending and warning divers aldermen and counsellors there 2s.10d.; 31 Oct. to Mr Town Clerk for his charges to and at the court touching the matter 13s.1d.; 12 Nov. to Christopher Carlton, Richard Hollon, Jonas Keffer, William Norton, Robert Payne, Widow Fisher, Thomas Norton and Thomas Mason inhabitants [f.51] of the ward of Portsoken towards their pains taken 3 several times attending at Serjeants' Inn to give evidence 6s.8d.; 16 Dec. to Robert Smithe for his pains and for money by him laid out in the matter £8.12s.2d.; 29 Dec. to Robert Payne carpenter for his charges in the Tower of London being committed thither by the lieutenant for that he wrought in one of the city's gardens on Tower Hill ⟨as by the journal appears⟩ 7s.8d.; to Mr Daniell and Mr Owen to either of them 20s. for their pains taken at Sir Francis Walsingham's house 40s., and to the keeper of his chamber door 2s.6d., and to his porter 12d.; 23 Feb. to Robert Smithe [f.51v] for his pains and charges in the said suit 13s.2d.; to Mr Daniell and Mr Owen to either of them 10s. for penning an order to be set down by the lords of the council betwixt this city and the lieutenant of the Tower 20s.; summa £19.0s.1d.[2] [cf.**212**]

[1] For the perennial dispute over the Tower liberties, see *Remembrancia* 426–7.
[2] In the right margin '⟨6 pag' £51.1s.7½d.⟩' which sum is the total of **80–82**. See **66** note 2.

83. 29 Oct. to Mr Heckes and Mr Milles attorneys in the star chamber, to either of them 10s. being retained for the city for a suit commenced against my lord mayor, aldermen and divers others for muring up a gate made out of the liberty of Christ Church near Aldgate[1] 20s., to Mr Morrys for his counsel therein 20s., and to Mr Daniell and Mr Fuller to either of them 10s. for his counsel therein 20s.; 5 Nov. to Mr Daniell and Mr Fuller to either of them 10s. for perusing and penning the books of answer 20s.; [f.52] 17 Nov. to Mr Morrys, Mr Daniell and Mr Fuller to every of them 20s. for their pains £3; to Mr Recorder for perusing the said answer 20s.; to Robert Smithe for money by him laid out and for divers copies by him written touching the matter £5.16s.4d.; to Mr Lynton examiner in the star chamber for examining of Sir Edward Osborne, Mr Chamberlain, Mr Town Clerk and 5 others at 4s.4d. the piece touching the said suit 34s.8d.; to Mr Morrys for his advice in penning a rejoinder to the replication 10s., and to Mr Lynton for the copies of the said articles and examinations 40s., and to his clerk for writing the same 3s.; [f.52v] 23 Feb. to Robert Smithe for his pains and charges 40s.2d.; to Mr Daniell and Mr Fuller to every of them 10s. for their pains 20s.; to Robert Smithe for money by him laid out and for writing divers copies £3.1s.8d.; to Robert Smithe for his boat hire and for money by him paid to Mr Heckes and Mr Milles for their fees in Trinity term for the said suit 15s.4d.; summa £25.1s.2d. [cf.**227**]

[1] On 28 Oct. 1584 the Recorder, Daniel, Owen and Nicholas Fuller were ordered to draw an answer to the bill exhibited in the star chamber by the Lord Thomas Howard against the lord mayor, sheriffs and other officers (Rep.21, f.104b). Howard was in possession of the whole site of the dissolved monastery of Holy Trinity, Aldgate (Christ Church) which he sold to the city in 1592 (Harben, 592; CCPR, Aldgate within, 1586, 1592).

84. 5 April to Robert Smithe for the fee of Mr Salowaye attorney in the exchequer in the suit brought against the city's tenants of the Conduit Meads (Conductes Meades) 3s.4d.; to him for drawing and engrossing a conveyance from this accountant unto divers aldermen and commoners of the lease of the Conduit Meads 6s.8d.; summa 10s.0d.[1]

[1] The term of the lease of the Conduit Meads demised by Sir John Fortescue in 1491 to certain aldermen and commoners was still running, see **16e**. In the court of aldermen on 26 April 1586 it was said that it was difficult after so long to know in whom the interest rested, the original lessees having made no 'meane' conveyances to the city's use, and that a suit in the exchequer was likely to call the title in question (Rep.21, f.289. And see **227**).

85. [f.53] 11 Dec. to ⟨Humfrey Murson servant to Mr Payne serjeant of the king for his master's fee for entering the city's warrant⟩[1] 3s.4d.; to Hugh Shingleton stationer for 13 gallons of ink delivered this year at

3s.4d. the gallon (gallande) 56s.4d.; to Thomas Childe servant to Mr Town Clerk for writing into Mr Chamberlain's book to remain with him such orders of court and decrees out of the repertory as concern this accountant, due for one year ended at Michaelmas last past 20s.; 23 Dec. and 29 May for 12 badges for the six waits as by the journal appears 24s.; summa £5.3s.8d.[2]

[1] Written in a space left blank for the name of the recipient and over 'for the warrant of attorney in the king's bench by the hands of Mr Dommer', struck through.
[2] In the right margin '⟨pag 7. £30.14s.10d.⟩' which sum is the total of **83–5**. See **66** note 2.

86. [f.53v] 14 Feb. paid at the court at Somerset House at which time my lord mayor was knighted, viz. to the heralds 20s., the gentleman ushers of her majesty's chamber 40s., the yeomen ushers 20s., the grooms and pages 20s., the keeper of the great chamber door 6s.8d., the porters 20s., the yeomen of the cellars 10s., the yeomen of the buttery 10s.;[1] to William Edwyn bargeman for serving my lord mayor and aldermen with others in 3 barges to and from thence the same time 51s.8d.; summa £9.18s.4d.

[1] Identical fees were paid at the knighting of the lord mayor in 1563–64, save for the gentlemen ushers who received only 20s. (Chamber Accounts 1, f.110).

87. To Robert Smithe which he paid to Mr Eve of the crown office for the copy of a quo warranto brought against the city for certain liberties of London and Southwark, 3s.8d.

88. [f.54] 9 Dec. to Mr Christopher ⟨Osborn⟩ attorney accountant in the exchequer for the moiety of 2 bays 2 northern dozens marble and one double dozen blue being forfeit and due to the queen as in the 14th account of Mr George Eaton late chamberlain [1576–77] appears £3.17s.8d.; 10 Dec. by order of court [10 Dec. 1584, Rep.21, f.119b] to Roger Warffeild treasurer of Bridewell towards the conveying of all the Irish begging people in and near London to the city of Bristol (Bristowe) £5;[1] 15 Dec. by like order [15 Dec. 1584, Rep.21, f.123] to William Seager for writing and sealing 8 instruments of association with other charges thereof £3.6s.8d.;[2] 31 Dec. for a table for the entering of the names of all such persons as have protections from the queen or privy council for debt or otherwise 5s.; summa £12.9s.4d.

[1] By the same order payments of £5 each were also to be made by Christ's, St Bartholomew's and St Thomas's hospitals as well as the city.
[2] The Bond of Association, drawn up by the privy council in Oct. 1584, which pledged its signatories to prevent the succession of any person by whom, or in whose interest, any attempt should be made on the life of the queen, and to pursue any such person to the death.

89. [f.54v] 9 March [1586] to James Harman yeoman of the chamber for small coals, mending the lantern serving the Guildhall porch, herbs, flowers, rushes, beer, ale, wine, candles, mats, billets, making clean the Guildhall, carrying of books and records with other things for necessary business of the city, washing the city's damask napkins and table cloths, for one year ended at Michaelmas 1585 £9.11s.5d. as by 4 bills called quarter bills appears; 29 Jan. to Nicholas Smith merchant taylor for making John Luck's gown and coat[1] with furniture thereof 13s.6d.; more to him for stuff and workmanship bestowed in making his coat at Whitsuntide last past 5s.9d.; to Robert Durham skinner for furring the said gown with fox's skins 16s.; summa £11.6s.8d.

[1] See **26g** for other references to John Luck's liveries.

90. [f.55] To James Harman for horse hire for divers aldermen, Mr Recorder, Mr Town Clerk, Robert Smithe and others riding to the court and other places about the affairs of this city due for one quarter ended at Christmas 1584 £5.17s.; to him by order of court [6 May 1585, Rep.21, f.168] for horse hire with foot cloths for the Scottish ambassador in November 1584[1] £18.2s.10d.; 23 July by order of court [20 July 1585, Rep.21, f.192b] to John Tompson, John Forde and James Wheately hackney men for the hire of 38 horses by them and others lent by order from the council at the going away of Moivuser[2] out of England, and by Tompson, Forde and Wheteley to be repaid when the same shall be recovered by order from the council as by one obligation appears £15; [f.55v] 12 Nov. [1585] to James Harman for money laid out at sundry times for horse hire due for one quarter ended at Michaelmas 1585 9s.; summa £39.8s.10d.[3]

[1] Patrick, master of Gray, who came to London at this time (*Cal. SPF 1584–85*, 107, 161).
[2] Spelt 'Moivusyer' in the order in the repertory. Presumably Mauvissière, the French ambassador, who was recalled from England early in July 1585 (*Cal. SPF 1584–85*, 567).
[3] In the right margin '⟨8 pag' £73.6s.10d.⟩' which sum is the total of **86–90**. See **66** note 2.

91. 26 March to Edward Gillam waxchandler for 28 lb of red wax delivered to the city's use, due for one year ended at Michaelmas 1585 28s.; 27 March to James Larde ⟨serjeant of the chamber⟩ for charges ⟨in the law entering⟩[1] of 60 kerseys supposed to be foreign bought and sold 18s.4d.; 8 May by order of court ⟨27 April 1585, Rep.21, f.165⟩ to Mr Humfry Mosley, secondary in the compter (cownter) in Wood Street, which he lately disbursed in the court of exchequer for the discharge of the account of Sir James Hawes knight, late lord mayor [1574–75], for the office of escheatorship of this city £5.10s.4d.; summa £7.16s.8d.

[1] In substitution for 'for the condemning'.

92. [f.56] 8 April by commandment of my lord mayor to John Colebrand, Richard Buckley and Hugh Homes to every of them 6s.8d. for their pains in taking of flesh in Lent 20s., and to John Addys for his like pains 5s., and to William Harryson for his like pains 3s.4d., and to Mr Town Clerk's man for charges in putting the certificates for eating of flesh in Lent into the chancery 2s.; 16 April to Mr Owen and Mr Daniell to either of them 10s. for viewing the carpenter's yard ⟨late in the tenure of John Hyllyard carpenter⟩ at Cripplegate now in controversy ⟨and pretended to be concealed lands⟩ and consulting in the same 20s.; to Mr Daniell for viewing the city's tenements in the parish of St Clement's [Eastcheap] with back doors, jetties (jectes) and passage to and from the same through the churchyard there 10s.;[1] to Mr Dalbie for charges in law in a suit against Mr Bayerd clothworker for £20 by him due to this city 5s.10d.; summa £3.6s.[2d.][2]

[1] The parson, churchwardens and parishioners had closed up various doors and ways of free passage from the city's tenements through their churchyard into St Clement's Lane (Rep.21, ff.187, 246b. And see **213**).

[2] In the right margin '⟨9 pag' £11.2s.10d.⟩' which sum is the total of **91–2**. See **66** note 2.

93. [f.56v] 16 Dec. to Robert Smithe for money by him laid out in a suit against Robert Snagg for the portions of the orphans of John Easton grocer deceased 53s.4d.; to Mr Daniell and Mr Dalton to either of them 10s. for their pains taken severally at the chancery bar in the said suit 20s.; to Robert Smithe for his pains and charges in the suit 37s.8d.; 5 April to him which he gave to the master of the rolls' man 2s.6d.; to Mr Daniell for moving the court of chancery for the dismissing of a bill exhibited by Mr Snagg 10s.; to Robert Smithe for his charges and pains 12s.6d.; to Mr [f.57] Daniell for his pains taken sundry times at the chancery bar 20s.; to Robert Smithe for money by him laid out in Trinity term in the suit 16s.6d.; to Mr Daniell for his travail at the chancery bar for the said orphans 10s. [cf.**214**]. To Robert Smithe for money by him laid out in a suit prosecuted against the lord mayor and commonalty in the court of chancery by Robert Newditt and George Smedly for money supposed to be due unto them in the right of their wives, the daughters and orphans of Thomas Whitlock merchant taylor deceased, and from them detained 26s.6d.; to Mr Common Serjeant for so much by him paid for an abstract of a copy of Whitlock's inventory and search of his will 9s.4d.; to [f.57v] him for the search and copy of the particulars of Whitlock's debts sperate and desperate 2s.6d.; to Mr Daniell and Mr Owen for their pains therein 20s.; to Mr Daniell and Mr Owen to either of them 10s. for moving the court of chancery 20s.; to Robert Smithe for money by him laid out and for writing and engrossing divers things touching the matter 18s.6d.; to Mr Recorder for his counsel in a suit against John Bill for the portions of the said orphans 10s.; to Robert Smithe for money by him laid out in the said suit 11s. [cf.**228**]. To Mr Daniell for [f.58] penning an answer to a bill of complaint exhibited into the chancery against this accountant by Roger Rigby grocer touching the orphans of Anthony Hobson deceased 10s.; to Robert Smithe for money by him laid out and for his pains in the matter 16s. 25 Feb. by order of court to Mrs Alice Spencer, the wife of Mr John Spencer alderman, for the use of Judith Huson for allowance of £300 which remained in the chamber due for 15 months ended 21 Feb. 1585 £16.10s.9d.; 3 Sept. by like order to Robert Huson gentleman and Judith his wife, the daughter and orphan of William Cox haberdasher deceased, in satisfaction of £300 by them forfeited to the city for marrying without the consent of my lord mayor and court of aldermen £200 and for consideration thereof for half a year remaining in the chamber £5.[1] Summa £237.[17s.1d.]

[1] For references to Robert and Judith Huson (Hughson, Hewson), including the orders quoted above, see Rep.21, ff.6b–7, 82, 122b, 205 and *Remembrancia*, 307–8. Alice Spencer was Judith's mother.

94. [f.58v] 6 Nov. to Mr Mosley for the clerk of the crown in the chancery for filing the parliament's writ and the return of the same 12s.; 20 Nov. by order of court [19 Nov. 1584, Rep.21, f.112b] to Mr [John][1] Puckeringe serjeant at law and speaker of the parliament house as of the free gift of this city £6.13s.4d.; by like commandment to the gentlemen ushers, yeomen ushers and 5 porters of the higher house in reward 40s., and to Mr Boweyer serjeant of the lower house in like reward 20s.,[2] and for a book of statutes of the parliament 2s.; to Sir Nicholas Woodrooff, one of the knights of the parliament, for his livery gown of scarlet for the session of parliament holden in the 27th year of her majesty's reign[3] £6.13s.4d., [f.59] and for his fee for 83 days all which time the parliament continued at 4s. the day £16.12s., and for his boat hire at 12d. the day £4.3s., ⟨summa £27.8s.4d.⟩; to Mr Recorder, one other of the knights of the parliament, for his like livery gown £6.13s.4d., and for his fee for 83 days at 4s. the day £16.12s., and for his boat hire at 12d. the day £4.3s., ⟨summa £27.8s.4d.⟩; to Mr Walter Fishe merchant taylor, one of the burgesses of the parliament, for his like livery gown £6.13s.4d., and for his fee at like time ⟨at 2s. the day⟩ £8.6s., and for his like boat hire at 12d. the day £4.3s., ⟨summa £19.2s.4d.⟩; to Mr Thomas Aldersey haberdasher, one of the burgesses of the same parliament, for his like livery gown £6.13s.4d., and for his fee at like time at 2s. the day £8.6s., and for his boat hire at like time and rate £4.3s., summa £19.2s.4d.; to Mr Secretary's clerk for the charges of a new writ out of the chancery for the [f.59v] choosing of a burgess of the parliament in the place of Mr Walter Fishe deceased 8s.2d.; to Mr Secondary Mosley for filing the parliament writ and the return of the same for Mr Henry Billingsly haberdasher being chosen burgess of the parliament[4] 2s.; summa £103.18s.10d.[5]

[1] Blank in the Ms.
[2] Ralph Bowyer (P. Marsden, *Officers of the House of Commons*, 1966, 227).
[3] Sir Nicholas Woodroffe, alderman and lord mayor 1579–80, and his 3 fellow M.P.s were elected 20 Oct.1584 (Jor.21, f.390).
[4] Elected 29 Sept. 1585 (Jor.21, f.469).
[5] In the right margin '⟨pag' 10. £341.15s.11d.⟩' which sum is the total of **93–4.** See **66** note 2.

95. 7 Nov. to Mr Recorder, Mr Daniell and Mr Owen to every of them 10s. for his pains taken touching the indictment put up against my lord mayor and 25 aldermen by John Mellowes[1] 30s.; to Mr Fuller for his pains therein at the assizes in Sussex 20s.; to Mr John Eve attorney in the crown office for entering the answer of the lord mayor and aldermen to the indictment, for every of the aldermen 2s.8d., £3.9s.4d., and for other charges [f.60] in the suit 22s.4d., ⟨summa £4.11s.8d.⟩; to Mr Recorder, Mr Daniell, Mr Owen, Mr Fuller and Mr Cook to every of them 20s. for his pains taken at the king's bench bar the last day of the ⟨Michaelmas⟩ term to move the court that the matter might be dismissed as insufficient £5; to Robert Smithe ⟨the same term⟩ for money by him laid out and for his pains in the matter £5.19s.11d.; ⟨26 Jan.⟩ to Mr Recorder, Mr Daniell, Mr Owen, Mr Fuller and Mr Cooke for every of them 20s. for his pains at the king's bench bar £5; to Mr Daniell, Mr Owen, Mr Fuller and Mr Cook to every of them 10s. for their pains at the king's bench bar ⟨the 11th of February⟩ 40s.; [f.60v] to Robert Smithe for his pains and charges

⟨in Hilary term⟩ 50s.2d.; to Mr Recorder, Mr Daniell and Mr Cooke for every of them 10s. for their pains at the king's bench bar for the dismissing of the matter of the indictment ⟨in Easter term⟩ 30s.; ⟨the same term⟩ to Robert Smithe for money by him laid out and for writing divers copies touching the matter £3.8s.8d.; to him ⟨in Trinity term⟩ for money by him laid out in the same matter 15s.8d.; summa £33.6s.1d.[2]

[1] John Mellowes married Elizabeth, one of the daughters and orphans of Thomas Gilson grocer, who acknowledged satisfaction of her portion on attaining the age of 21 in 1576 (Rep.19, f.59). Nevertheless between 1579 and 1585 the court of aldermen appointed a number of committees to investigate matters complained of by Mellowes and his wife (Rep.20, ff.13, 115, 141; Rep.21, ff.187, 190b). In 1581 Mellowes was committed to Newgate for slanderous allegations against alderman Edward Osborne (Rep.20, f.221b). Reports of 2 committees give considerable detail of Mellowes' grievances: he alleged omissions from the inventory of Gilson's personal estate; complained of Sir Edward Osborne's receipt of the revenues of Gilson's lands and alleged that Osborne had forfeited a recognizance to bring in Elizabeth's orphanage money (Rep.20, ff.225b–227; Rep.21, f.251. And see **228**).

[2] In the right margin '⟨11 pag' *ut supra*⟩'. See **66** note 2.

96. 21 Nov. to Mr Waterbailiff for a search by him made on the River of Thames 34s.8d.; [f.61] 11 Jan. to him for like search, 7, 8 and 9 January 37s.8d.; 16 March for like search made 10, 11 and 12 March 38s.; 20 April for like search made 16, 17 and 18 April 42s.2d.; for like search made 15, 16 and 17 May 35s.6d.; 14 July for like search made 6, 7 and 8 July 38s.1d.; 21 Aug. for like search made 17, 18 and 19 [f.61v] August 35s.11d.; 11 Sept. to William Lathes under waterbailiff for 2 writs of attendance directed to the sheriffs of Surrey and Middlesex for the appearance of certain persons out of the said counties ⟨to appear⟩ before my lord mayor ⟨as well at Putney as at Fulham as conservator of the Thames sitting there to enquire for the conservancy of the same⟩[1] 15s., and for his charges riding for the obtaining and delivering and writs 17s.6d.; for the charges of a dinner at Putney for my lord mayor and ⟨certain⟩ aldermen sitting there 22 Sept. for the conservancy of the river £8.3s.4d.; to the sheriff of Surrey for making [f.62] warrants for summoning a jury to appear before my lord mayor there 10s., to 4 bailiffs for summoning 21 men which appeared to be of the jury 7s., to the said bailiffs for their dinners at 12d. the piece 4s., and to the said 21 men, whereof 18 only were sworn, for their dinners at 12d. the piece 21s.; for a dinner at Fulham for my lord mayor and aldermen sitting there 23 Sept. for the conservancy £8.11s.4d.; to the sheriff of Middlesex for summoning a jury to appear before my lord mayor there 10s., to 4 bailiffs for summoning 35 men which appeared [f.62v] to be of the jury, whereof 26 men only were sworn, 11s.8d., to the said bailiffs for their dinners at 12d. the piece 4s., to 34 men of the said 35 men for their dinners at 12d. the piece 34s., to Mr Chalenor's daughter by my lord mayor's commandment 6d.,[2] and to the poor there 3s.; to William Edwyn bargeman for stuff in trimming the great barge to serve my lord mayor and aldermen the same time 8s.9d.; to him for serving my lord mayor and aldermen to and from Fulham and Putney and for the carriage of the provision of the said 2 dinners to and from the said places for hire of divers wherries £3.16s., [f.63] and to the bargemen by my lord mayor's commandment 2s.; to Mr Waterbailiff for the charges of himself, the under waterbailiff's man with 12 watermen in 2 barges with the juries of Middlesex and Surrey ⟨passing with them⟩ from London Bridge to Blackwall and from thence back again to Colney Ditch to search out the annoyances of the river £6.12s.3d.; to the jury of Surrey in reward giving up their verdict in Southwark before my lord mayor presenting the annoyances of the river 20s., to the jury of Middlesex in reward giving up their verdict at Westminster before the lord mayor presenting also [f.63v] the annoyances of the river 20s., and to the keeper of the chancery court there in reward 2s.6d.; to William Edwyn for serving my lord mayor and aldermen to and from Westminster to take the verdict 13s.2d., and to the bargemen in reward 2s.; summa £50.10s.0d.[3]

[1] The conservancy jurisdiction at this date was being exercised only west of Blackwall, see p. xx.

[2] Probably John Chaloner, haberdasher and wealthy merchant, who occupied a house known as Goodriche's on the north side of Church Row, leading from the present Fulham High Street (C. J. Feret, *Fulham Old and New*, i, 1900, 137–8. I am indebted to Mr. C. J. Jeens, archivist to the London Borough of Hammersmith and Fulham, for this reference). The lord mayor usually dined at a local house or inn when holding the courts of conservancy.

[3] In the right margin '⟨12 pag' *ut supra*⟩'. See **66** note 2.

97. 13 May by order of court [4 May 1585, Rep.21, f.166b] to Richard Peirson draper in consideration of his extraordinary charges in hiring men to draw water at Dowgate when the same was scant within this city[1] 48s.; 22 May to Mr Town Clerk which he paid in the exchequer for a copy of the rates of the 15th and 10th for London 12d., and for a buckram bag for the city's books 10d.; [f.64] by the bequest of Mr Tailor alderman[2] deceased for the discharge of poor householders being assessed (sessed) at 12d. and under for the 15th granted to the queen in the 27th year of her reign, viz. 26 May for 22 in the parish of St Mary le Bow in Cordwainer ward 19s.10d. and 15 in [Holy] Trinity parish in the said ward 14s., 29 May for 26 persons in the parish of St Antholin 26s., 7 in the parish of St Benet Sherehog 7s., 16 in the parish of St John [the Baptist, Walbrook] 15s.2d., [f.64v] 29 in the parish of St Mary Aldermary 27s.10d., and 28 in the parish of St Thomas the Apostle 24s.; 1 June to Mr Duffeilde[3] for preaching at the new churchyard[4] on Whitsunday last past 13s.4d.; by order of court [10 June 1585, Rep.21, f.176b] to Robert Glover clerk to Mr Dalby for his pains in drawing the late act of common council for the election of the sheriffs [27 May 1585, Jor.21, ff.437–8] and for other business 20s.; summa £10.17s.0d.

[1] The shortage was due to the conduit pipes being under repair.

[2] Sir William Taillour, grocer, alderman 1458–83 and lord mayor 1468–69, died 1483 (Beaven ii, 11; Thrupp, 368–9). His will (PCC 10 Logge) left the residue of his personal estate to be disposed of at the discretion of his executors, William Heede and John Wattes, for the benefit of the poor and other charitable causes, and refers to the existence of another will concerning the disposition of his real property. On 13 June 1511 John Watts, grocer, delivered to the chamberlain documents of title concerning Taillour's lands in the parishes of St Mary Aldermary and St Antholin (Rep.2, f.91b). Curiously, neither this repertory, the Chamber Accounts, nor Stow (Stow, i, 253, ii, 176) in referring to this bequest in discharge of poor householders of Cordwainer ward, acknowledge Taillour's knighthood which he received in 1471 (*Cal. Letter Book L*, 98).

[3] John Duffield, prebendary of Hoxton in St Paul's?

[4] Constructed in 1569 near Bethlem without Bishopsgate. A sermon was to be preached every Whitsunday at the pulpit there. The lord mayor was to attend, if possible, and the preacher was to receive 13s.4d. (Rep.16, ff.491b,492).

98. [f.65] 29 Dec. for 4 oz 3½ dwt of silver to make 12 bosses and 2 clasps for the garnishing of a book of the new testament for the council chamber 20s.4d., and for the making of the bosses and clasps 4s.8d.; 17 July to Thomas Childe for the charges of putting in the certificate into the chancery for the rate of servants' wages 5s.; to James Lorde for arresting Mr Thomas Gore grocer for money by him due to this city 2s.; to Mr Town Clerk which he paid for the carriage of a letter into Buckinghamshire to Mr Recorder 2s.; summa £1.14s.0d.

99. [f.65v] 13 March to Mr Waterbailiff for horse hire and other charges for Mr Baites, Mr Huntlowe, the waterbailiff and John Bisshop, one of her majesty's servants, riding to Marlow lock and Temple lock to view the dangers thereof £3.3s.8d., and for a supper at Maidenhead for Sir Rowland Hayward, Mr Bond, Mr Martyn, Mr Webb, aldermen, with their servants and others and for their horse meat at what time they did ride to view the said lock[s] £3.0s.8d.; to James Harman for horse hire for the aldermen's servants and others the same time to the said places 56s.8d.; to Sir Rowland Heyword for money by him laid out in their journey ⟨as by the journal appears⟩ 34s.6d.; [f.66] 15 May by order of court ⟨13 May 1585, Rep.21, f.169] to John Bisshop ironmonger as well in respect of his travail about the said locks as ⟨for his relief⟩[1] of the free gift of the court £3; summa £13.15s.6d.

[1] He was then a prisoner in the Fleet prison.

100. 11 May by commandment of my lord mayor in reward to the queen's master gunner for making ready the way through the Artillery Yard for the passage of the lady [mayoress][1] and other aldermen's wives to and from the sermons at St Mary Spital in Easter holy days 20s., and to James Harman for rushes, flowers, strawings, faggots, coals, men's wages, carrying of cushions, perfumes, bread, ale, *aqua cum posita*, spent at the Spital the same time 31s.; summa £2.11s.0d.[2]

[1] The Ms has 'Ladyes marye' with the second word struck through.
[2] In the right margin '⟨13 pag' £28.17s.6d.⟩' which sum is the total of **97–100**. See **66** note 2.

101. [f.66v] To Mr Beale ⟨clerk of the council⟩ for writing and procuring 6 letters from the lords of the council,[1] viz. one to the archbishop of Canterbury touching the doctors and proctors of St Paul's, one to the Lord Thomas Heywarde[2] and Sir Francis Hinde for ⟨the inhabitants in⟩ Christ Church near Aldgate, one to the dean and chapter of Westminster for St Martin le Grand;[3] one to Sir George Carey and Sir William Moore for ⟨the inhabitants in⟩ the Blackfriars,[4] one to the Lord Delamare and Mr Morrys for ⟨the inhabitants in⟩ the Whitefriars, and one to the master of the rolls touching ⟨the clerks of the chancery, to join with the citizens in watch and musters pretended to be made at Midsummer and at St

James' tide [25 July] last past⟩[5] 40s., and to Mr Beale's clerk [for] the copies of all the said letters for my lord mayor and aldermen by the hands of Mr Sebright ⟨10s.⟩; [f.67] 28 May by order of my lord mayor to Thomas Wilbraham the elder for his travail in receiving £81.5s.10d. collected by the deputies of 12 wards towards the training up of 4,000 men mustered with pikes and gun shot 10s.10d., and to him for his clerk's pains therein 5s.; 5 June by commandment of my lord mayor and court to Mr Captain Shoott by him and Sir Robert Counstable knight to be delivered to 4 gentlemen for their pains in training and making show before the queen at Greenwich with the 4,000 men £10;[6] 9 June by order of court [9 June 1585, Rep.21, f.175] to Mr Wade clerk to the council for writing [f.67v] and procuring further letters for privileged places to be contributory to the said musters 40s.; 25 June by commandment of my lord mayor to 6 trumpeters for their pains on Midsummer Eve sounding their trumpets before my lord mayor through the city 30s.; to James Harman for 2½ dozen of straw hats for 24 cresset bearers and 6 bag (bagg) bearers standing in Cheapside with their lights in the watch on Midsummer Eve at night at 6d. the piece ⟨15s.⟩, for 36 badges with the city's arms to be set in the hats 3s., for the wages of the cresset bearers at 8d. the piece 16s., to 6 labourers of the chamber being bag [f.68] bearers 4s., to 3 men taken upon the streets to carry bags without hats 3s., to 4 rulers of the waterbearers looking to the cresset bearers and bag bearers 3s.4d., to 4 men looking to the cressets and lights 4s., to a poor man for taking the old cresset lights out of the storehouse in the bayhall 8d., and to one other poor man for fetching cresset lights from the Guildhall into Cheapside the same night 8d., summa 49s.8d.;[7] by commandment of my lord mayor to William Lathes, William Ravenscroft, Thomas Sympson, Robert Lyddus, Richard Dodd, and Philip Trehearne to every of them 5s. for his pains about the late musters 35s. [*sic*]; and to this accountant's clerk [f.68v] for his pains in receiving the money collected of foreigners and strangers towards the charges of the musters and for making acquittances for the receipt of the money 5s.; by warrant from my lord mayor to John Daie and John Benson for their pains about the collecting of the said money and the late soldiers 40s.; more laid out by his lordship on Midsummer Eve at night 16s.3d.; by order of court [28 Oct. 1585, Rep.21, f.228] to John Savidge the swordbearer's man, Thomas Sympson the common cryer's man and William Ravenscroft the common hunt's man to every of them 20s. for their pains about the musters and soldiers sent into the Low Countries £3; by like order [18 Nov. 1585, Rep.21, f.239] to Robert Lyddus, Richard Dodd, William Lathes and Philip Treherne to every of them 20s. for their like pains £4; summa £31.1s.9d.[8]

[1] 'concerning contributions towards the musters Midsummer and St James watches', struck through.

[2] Lord Thomas Howard, see **83**, note.

[3] St Martin le Grand had been appropriated to the use of Westminster Abbey in 1503.

[4] Carey and Moore (More) both left property in Blackfriars in their wills (*The House of Commons 1558–1603*, ed. P. W. Hasler, i, 547–8, iii, 86–9. And for Moore, see **233**).

[5] Written in substitution for 'the inhabitants of this city'. A letter from the queen dated 20 April 1585 confirmed orders for the levying of 4,000 men who were later to muster before her at Greenwich (cf. **11 l** note) and also directed the revival of the marching

watches formerly held on the eve of the feasts of St John the Baptist and St Peter the Apostle (Jor.21, f.421b).

[6] An order of 27 May 1585 provided for the payment of £10 to Sir Robert Constable to be bestowed by him upon such corporals, serjeants and other officers as had served under him in the late musters (Rep.21, f.172b).

[7] A book containing an elaborate 'manner and order' of the watch for Midsummer Eve and St Peter's Eve, written in 1585 by John Montgomery and presented to the lord mayor and aldermen, is extant (CLRO 36C). An earlier version written in the mayoralty of Sir Lionel Duckett, 1572–73, had not, the author complained, been put into practice. (And see Stow, i, 101–4, ii, 284). For the expenses of the Midsummer watch in 1570–71? see Chamber Accounts 1, f.34v.

[8] In the right margin '⟨14 pag' *ut supra*⟩'. See **66** note 2.

102. [f.69] 14 Aug. Paid by my lord mayor wherewith this accountant is charged to Edwin Babington draper for 56 pieces of Bridgewater reds containing 1,350 yards at 43s. the piece for the coats of 450 soldiers, parcel of 500 soldiers pressed in this city and sent into the Low Countries of Flanders for her majesty's service[1] £120.18s.9d., to [. . .][2] Rysley for 26 lb 12 oz of tape at sundry prices for the coats £5.1s.2d., and to [*blank*] Bothby for 97 pieces of tape for the coats at 13d. the piece £5.5s.2d., and more by my lord mayor to Edwin Babington for 104½ yards of stammell cloth for the coats of 50 soldiers being of the guard of Mr John Norrys general of the army at 9s. the yard £47.0s.6d., [f.69v] and for 33½ dozen of yellow silk ribbon (silck ribband) for the said coats at 2s.4d. the dozen £3.17s.8d., and for making the 500 coats at 14d. the piece £29.3s.4d.; summa ⟨£211.6s.8d.⟩[3]

[1] See p. xxviii.

[2] Ms mutilated.

[3] **102**, **103** and **104** were originally written as a single entry.

103. To Francis Covell skinner for ¾C of match at 3d. the pound 21s., 150 pound of corn powder at 11d. the pound £6.17s.6d., and 3 barrels for the powder (powther) 21d., summa £8.0s.3d., and by commandment of my lord mayor to Thomas Kyddy for C of lead for bullets 10s., being all for the use of 450 of the soldiers; more by order of court [14 Aug. 1585, Rep.21, f.202b] for powder, match and bullet for 50 of the soldiers being of the guard of [f.70] the said general 50s.; to my lord mayor to be paid to certain of his officers for their pains in the business 13s.5d.; to John Gibson for his pains taken in victualling the ships for 1,050 men 40s.; summa ⟨£13.13s.[8d].⟩

104. 17 Aug. to the several wards for the press (prest) money of 550 men at 12d. the piece, whereof 500 were sent into the Low Countries, viz. to Aldersgate 50s., Aldgate 14s., Bassishaw 4s., Billingsgate 21s., Bishopsgate 40s., Bread Street 15s., Bridge Within 15s., Broad Street 15s., Candlewick Street 15s., Castle Baynard 20s., Cheap 20s., [f.70v] Coleman Street 15s., Cordwainer Street 10s., Cornhill 10s., Cripplegate £3, Dowgate 10s., Farringdon Within 30s., Farringdon Without 50s., Langbourn 20s., Lime Street 6s., Portsoken 20s., Queenhithe 15s., Tower 21s., Walbrook 15s., and Vintry 40s.; by commandment of my lord mayor for 5 men out of Cornhill ward for that so many were misliked of the same ward 5s.; by like commandment for the hire of 2 drums into the field with the soldiers of divers companies 10s.; summa ⟨£28.6s.0d.⟩

105. [f.71] 10 July to James Harman[1] for malmsey, claret, wine, ale and other things when William Parry should have been arraigned at the Guildhall ⟨for treason⟩[2] 5s.3d.; by commandment of my lord mayor to William Shawe brewer towards an offering ⟨towards his maiden's marriage⟩[3] 2s.; to my lord mayor which he gave to a pursuivant for the delivery of a letter to the Lady Gressam 10s.; summa [17s.3d.]

[1] 'Harmeman' in Ms.

[2] Parry, accused of plotting to murder the queen, had been tried at Westminster and executed on 2 March 1585.

[3] Written over 'for the marriage of the said Shawe's maid', deleted.

106. To Sir Thomas Pullison knight, lord mayor, for the measuring of linen cloth due for one year ended at Michaelmas 1585, £50.0s.0d.[1] [cf. **7n**]

[1] In the right margin '⟨pag' 15 [£304.3s.7d.]⟩' which sum is the total of **102–6**. See **66** note 2.

107. By order of court to William Midleton vintner and Richard Tomkyns grocer to either of them 50s. for their pains in apprehending divers legers (lidggers)[1] which usually shoot coals and for their pains in measuring of coals £5; [f.71v] to Richard Grewe one of the common hunt's men for killing 515 dogs at 2d. the piece £4.5s.10d., and for killing 312 dogs at like rate 52s., and for killing 168 dogs at like rate 28s. [cf.**21**, **238**]; summa £13.5s.10d.

[1] On 29 July 1585 Tomkyns and Midleton had been instructed to bring legers (men who bought coals of country colliers and resold at a profit) before the lord mayor to be bound not to deal in the buying and selling of charcoals in or near the city; no remuneration was specified (Rep.21, f.200).

108. To John Dewell common hunt for his charges to and from the court to my lord of Leicester for warrants for bucks 3s.8d., to Mr Knevett's household servants[1] when my lord mayor rid on hunting in St James' park 5s., to the keeper of the park gate 12d., to William Edwyn for serving my lord mayor and aldermen by water the same time 14s.10d., and more by order of court [9 Sept. 1585, Rep.21, f.207] to John Devell for his further charges in obtaining the warrants £6.6s.; summa £7.10s.6d.

[1] Henry Knyvet of Charlton, Wilts., at this date M.P. for Malmesbury, and brother of Thomas Knyvet, M.P. for Westminster, had a house in St. James' Park (*The House of Commons 1558–1603*, ed. P. W. Hasler, ii, 420–3).

109. [f.72] To Mr Stephen Slany and Mr Henry Billingsly sheriffs for wax, herring and sturgeon wont to be paid by the Easterlings inhabiting the Steelyard £5.6s.8d. and for a petty toll wont also to be paid by the Easterlings 40s. due for one year ended at Michaelmas 1585, and to Sir Thomas Pullison knight, lord mayor, for wax, herring and sturgeon wont also to be paid by the Easterlings £5.6s.8d.; summa £12.13s.4d.[1]

[1] A confirmation by the city of the privileges of the merchants of the Hanse of Almaine

granted 20 Feb. 1427 made further provision that they should be quit of all custom etc. payable on merchandise on condition of the yearly payment of 40s. to the sheriffs and certain quantities of herring, sturgeon and wax to the mayor (*Cal. Letter Book K*, 46). The merchants of the Steelyard were greatly in arrears with these payments (see **139e**,**f**).

110. To Mr Chamberlain for his horse hire due for one year ended at Michaelmas 1585 40s. and for his boat hire for like time 30s., and to Mr William Dummer comptroller of the chamber for his horse hire for like time 40s., summa £5.10s.0d.

111. [f.72v] 19 Oct.1585 to Mr Dumer, Henry Woodwall, John Shawe, Richard Foster, Edward Lile, James Lorde and Leonard Largen, to every of them 6s.8d. for measuring and treading out the ground at Bartholomew (Barthelmew) Fair last past 46s.8d., to Foster, Lile and Lorde for weighing of cheese at the cheese beam 6s., for meat and drink for 6 days for the said officers with a dinner on the Fair Eve for Mr Chamberlain and others £7.11s.3d., to a poor man for breaking and making the ground with a pick axe 6d., for writing 2 copies of the particular profits of the fair 2s.6d., and spent by John Shawe at the toll booth 23s.11d.; summa £11.10s.10d.

112. [f.73] 27 Aug. to John Grafton and Oswald Bate serjeants to Mr Sheriffs for their pains taken as sticklers (stucklers) at the wrestling 6s.8d.; by commandment of my lord mayor to the 2 clerks of St Magnus' church for making ready the church when my lord mayor and aldermen rode into Southwark at Our Lady Fair there 2s., and by like commandment the same time to the prisoners of the Marshalsea and King's Bench 4s., and to my lord mayor which he gave to 6 waits and trumpeters at Our Lady Fair 5s.; 25 Sept. by order of my lord mayor to William Ravenscroft and Robert Lyddus to either of them 20s. for their pains in seeing bills set upon such houses as were infected with the plague 40s.; summa £2.17s.8d.[1]

[1] In the right margin '⟨pag'16. £53.8s. 2d.⟩' which sum is the total of **107–12**. See **66** note 2.

113. [f.73v] 28 June by a tally out of the exchequer to Robert Holmes one of the gentlemen porters to her majesty for her grace's moiety of such fines and penalties ⟨being the moiety of £41.18s.8d. received of John Fraye[?] of Durfeld[?] clothier and 78 others upon divers penalties charged upon divers acts of parliament for defaults upon divers woollen cloths by the same persons divers times made from⟩[1] Michaelmas ⟨1583 unto Michaelmas⟩ 1584 £20.19s.4d.; more into the exchequer for the moiety of like fines and penalties seized upon faulty woollen cloths put to sale as aforesaid ⟨being the moiety of £41.6s.8d.⟩ and is due for one year ended at Michaelmas 1585 £20.13s.4d., for a tally for the same 20d., for joining 2 tallies for the foresaid fines and penalties for the said 2 years 3s.4d., to Mr Fanshaw for putting his hand to the rolls of the said accounts 53s.4d., and to [*blank*] Luttick his clerk for engrossing the said accounts 53s.4d.; to Mr Gadbery for setting down the debts of the said two years' accounts 13s.4d., to Mr Morrys and his clerk for a warrant to Mr Peter for a tally of reward 2s., to Mr Peter for the same tally 3s.4d., and for joining the same 3s.4d., to Mr Morryson for allowing the said 3 tallies and for a *quietus est* for the same 36s. and to his clerk 4s.; to Mr Christopher Osborne attorney accountant in the exchequer for the sheriffs of London for the farm of the office of alnage of woollen cloths due to her majesty for one year ended at Michaelmas 1585 £60; summa £110.6s.4d.[2] [cf.**8h**]

[1] Written over 'for divers persons for putting certain woollen cloths to sale within the city contrary to the form of divers statutes and due for one year ended at', deleted. An insertion '⟨forfeited by Rowland Jenning[?] of Kendal and other clothiers⟩' is also struck through.

[2] In the right margin '⟨17 pag' *ut supra*⟩'. See **66** note 2.

114. ⟨Summa totalis of Foreign Charges £1,586.16s.1½d.⟩

115. [f.74] *Margin* New Year's Gifts

a. To Sir Thomas Bromely knight lord chancellor[1] £20.0s.0d. To Sir William Scicle[2] knight lord high treasurer £20.0s.0d. To Mr John Popham attorney general £10.0s.0d. For purses for the said new year's gifts 2s.8d.

[1] He had been the city's recorder 1566–69 before becoming solicitor general in 1569 and lord chancellor in 1579.

[2] Cecil.

b. 7 Oct. 1585 to Sir Thomas Pullison knight, lord mayor, in recompense of 4 tuns (tonnes) of wines towards the provision of his house allowed to every lord mayor, as well as by act of common council [7 Oct.1583, Jor.21, f.324] as by act of court of aldermen 2 July 1583 [Rep.20, f.442b], in consideration that by virtue of his office he should not make nor admit any man into the freedom or liberties of this city by redemption £40.0s.0d.[1]

[1] The mayor's ancient right to admit 6 persons to the freedom without fee was surrendered in return for an allowance of 4 tuns of wine by act of common council 23 Oct. 1434. From 1583 he received £40 in lieu of the wine.

c. Summa totalis £90.2s.8d.

116. [f.74v] *Margin* Winter Liveries

a. ⟨To Mr Richard Maye for 3 yards of broad fine marble cloth given to the Earl of Leicester at 22s. the yard, £3.8s.0d. [*sic*]⟩

b. To John Allington draper for 30 yards of London russet at 8s.4d. the yard £13.3s.4d. [*sic*], 32 yards at 10s. the yard £16.5s.[*sic*], 33 yards at 11s. the yard £18.3s., 19 yards at 12s.8d. the yard £12.0s.8d., 30 yards at 13s. the yard £19.10s., 36¼ yards at 14s. the yard £25.7s.6d., 20 yards at 14s. the yard £14, 32 yards at 15s.8d. the yard £25.1s.4d., and for 12 yards of cotton at 8d. the yard 8s.; summa ⟨£143.19s.10d.⟩

c. *Margin* John Luck's gown and coat[1]

To Stephen Mabb and Jeffery Hosier for 4½ yards of French tawny at 11s.4d. the yard 51s., 1¼ yards of pheasant colour (fesante collour) at 10s.8d. the yard 18s.8d. [*sic*], and 13 yards of blue bays at 14d. the yard 15s.2d.; summa ⟨£4.4s.10d.⟩

[1] See **26g** for other references to John Luck's liveries.

d. ⟨Summa of the winter liveries in cloth £152.12s.8d.⟩

117. *Margin* [Money paid instead of][1]
cloth for winter liveries

To Mr Chamberlain 53.4d., Mr Common Serjeant 53s.4d., Mr Kitchen 40s., Mr Dalton 40s., Mr Owen 40s., Mr Fuller 40s., Mr Common Cryer 53s.4d., Mr Waterbailiff 53s.4d., Mr Common Hunt 53s.4d., the renter general 32s., the renter of Mr Raynewell 31s., the steward of Finsbury 24s., the renter of Finsbury 24s., the bailiff of Finsbury 24s., *margin* ⟨the 6 waits⟩,[2] Anthony Tyndall 28s., Walter Lowman 28s., Robert Strachy 28s., Thomas Comyn 28s., Arthur Norton 28s., Thomas [*sic*][3] Blanckes 28s., [f.75] William Browne foreign taker 28s., John Evans mealweigher 28s., Mr Chamberlain's clerk 30s., Mr Common Serjeant's clerk 26s.8d., Mr Town Clerk's clerk 26s.8d., Peirson keeper of the star chamber 32s.
Summa £45.1s.0d.

[1] Ms mutilated.
[2] The next 6 names are bracketed.
[3] In error for Edward? (Woodfill, 248).

118. *Margin* Summer Liveries

a. To John Allyngton draper for 33 yards of sad new colour (coller) at 7s.6d. the yard £12.7s.6d., 32 yards at 7s.8d. the yard £12.5s.4d., 31 yards at 9s. the yard £13.19s., 32 yards at 9s. the yard £14.8s., 15 yards at 10s.6d. the yard £8.2s.9d. [*sic*], and 12 yards of black cotton at 8d. the yard 8s., ⟨summa £61.10s.7d.⟩

b. *Margin* John Luck

To Richard Mabb and Stephen Mabb for 1¾ yards of popinjay green (popingay grene) for John Luck's coat at 9s. the yard 16s.7d. and for 2½ yards of watchet bays to line the same 5s.5d.; summa 22s.

c. ⟨Summa totalis £62.12s.7d.⟩

119. *Margin* Money paid instead of cloth for summer liveries

To Mr Chamberlain 53s.4d., Mr Common Serjeant 53s.4d., Mr William Domer 53s.4d., Mr Common Cryer 53s.4d., Mr Common Hunt 53s.4d., Mr Waterbailiff 53s.4d., the renter general 32s., Edward Lile 32s., the renter of Mr Raynewell 31s., Henry Woodwall 32s., James Harman 32s., [f.75v] Humfry Wynnington 32s., the accountant's clerk 30s., Mr Town Clerk's clerk 30s., William Edwyn bargeman 26s.8d., Mr Common Serjeant's clerk 26s.8d.
Summa ⟨£31.4s.4d.⟩

120. ⟨Summa totalis of the winter and summer liveries and money paid instead thereof £291.10s.7d.
whereof to be deducted for the account of Mr Carpenter £5.14s.1½d., for the account of Mr Raynewell £3.2s.0d., for the account of Finsbury £3.12s.0d., summa £12.8s.1½d.
So to be allowed in the general account £279.2s.5½d.⟩

121. [f.76] *Margin* Allowances
First this accountant asks allowance of £10 to him given by act of court and of £10 more given at the audit, of 20s. paid to the comptroller and clerk of the chamber for examining this account, of £6.13s.4d. paid to the comptroller of the chamber for his reward at the audit, and for purses and counters for the examination and casting of this account ⟨19s.⟩, and of £300 delivered 16 November by order of court [20 Oct. 1584, Rep.21, f.96b] to the honourable Thomas Pullison lord mayor by way of loan ⟨for the repayment whereof Mr Pullyson and Mr William Thorowgood stand bound to this accountant⟩,[1] summa ⟨£328.12s.4d.⟩
Margin ⟨£300 debt⟩ [f.76v blank]

[1] The total loan to Pullison, authorised on 20 Oct. 1584 when he was lord mayor elect, was £500 of which £200 was to be provided by the bridgemasters who were later to be reimbursed by the chamberlain. Both Pullison and his surety, Thorowgood, were prominent members of the Drapers' Company.

122. [f.77] *Margin* Orphanage [Payments]
Paid to the use of divers orphans from Michaelmas 1584 unto Michaelmas 1585, as particularly appears by an account thereof kept by James Pele by two books, the one called the ledger, folio 44, and the other called the journal, folio [*blank*],[1] as also by the repertory kept in the inner chamber of the Guildhall, and acquittances made by the receivers thereof, £1,411.4s.7d.

[1] No longer extant, see p. xvi.

123. *Margin* Finding of Orphans
More paid within the time of this account to sundry persons for finding divers orphans whose portions remain in the chamber, as appears as well by the said journal kept by James Peele as also by sundry acquittances made by the parties receiving the same, £245.19s.0¼d.

124. Total of the discharge £6,189.1s.1¼d.

125. [f.77v blank, f.78] The account of the chamberlain for the lands and tenements late of Sir John Philpott knight for the year aforesaid.
[Receipts]
a. Arrearages by this accountant due upon the foot of the last account, £119.7s.1d.
b. Receipts of the lands late Sir John Philpott's, vacations and desperates allowed, as in the rental appears, ⟨£72.3s.4d.⟩
c. Of John Giles joiner for a fine for the lease of his house at Queenhithe late in the tenure of John Andrewe deceased, £35.0s.0d.
d. Of Robert Medley goldsmith in part of £120 for a fine for the lease of his house and shop in West Cheap late in the tenure of John Lonyson goldsmith deceased and also a back room late in the tenure of John Marsham deceased, £30.0s.0d.
Margin ⟨Rest £90⟩

[1] Grant of lease approved 12 Jan. 1585 (CCPR, Cheapside, 1584).

e. [f.78v] Of John Wilson goldsmith in part of £80 for a fine for a lease of

his shop in West Cheap in the parish of St Vedast late demised with other things to John Lonyson goldsmith deceased, £20.0s.0d.[1]
Margin ⟨Rest owing £60⟩

[1] Grant of lease in reversion approved 17 Dec. 1584 (CCPR, Cheapside, 1584).

f. Summa totalis of the charge ⟨£276.10s.5d.⟩

126. [f.79] The Discharge [Payments]
a. To the dean and chapter of St Paul's for quitrent out of tenements in the parish of St Vedast in Foster (Vaster) Lane for one year ended at Michaelmas 1585, 6s.6d.
b. To this accountant by the bequest of Sir John Philpott 13s.4d., to the rent gatherer for gathering the rents and potation money £3.6s.8d., and to Mr Dummer comptroller of the chamber by like bequest 3s.4d., summa £4.3s.4d.
c. In alms to 8 poor men and 5 poor women, to every of them 1d. by the day by the bequest of Sir John Philpott and due to them for 365 days, £19.15s.5d.[1]

[1] There follow 2 entries relating to materials and workmen's wages which have been deleted as nothing was charged this year upon the Philpott account in respect of these items.

d. Summa totalis ⟨£24.5s.3d.⟩

127. And so due to the city upon this account ⟨£252.5s.2d.⟩

128. [f.79v] The account of the chamberlain for the lands and tenements of Mr John Carpenter sometime common clerk of this city for the year aforesaid.

[Receipts]

a. Arrearages by this accountant due upon the foot of his last account, £19.2s.6d.
b. Receipts of the rents for the lands of Mr Carpenter as by the rental appears, vacations and desperates allowed, ⟨£34.0s.0d.⟩
c. Summa totalis of the whole charge ⟨£53.2s.6d.⟩

129. [f.80] The Discharge [Payments]
a. To the dean and chapter of Westminster for quitrent out of a tenement 'Dragon' in Bridge Street 4s. and for a quitrent out of the tenement 'Crowne' near St Magnus 4s., due for one year ended at Michaelmas 1585, as by the acquittances of Godfrey Goodman collector for the dean appears, 8s.0d.
b. To this accountant for overseeing 4 poor children being found at school and learning by the bequest of Mr Carpenter 6s.8d. and to the comptroller of the chamber for like consideration 6s.8d., summa 13s.4d.
c. To the rent gatherer for gathering the rents and potation money £1.3s.4d.
d. [f.80v] To the friends of the 4 children for barber, laundry (launder),

school, hose, shoes (shewes) and other necessaries for the children for one year ended at Michaelmas 1585, £4.0s.0d.
e. For the commons of the 4 children for 52 weeks ended at Michaelmas last past after the rate of 3s.6d. the week, £9.2s.0d.
f. For ⟨5½ yards⟩ of London russet for the coats of the 4 children against Christmas 1584 at ⟨10s.⟩ the yard ⟨55s.⟩, ⟨5¾⟩ yards of broad cloth of new colour for the coats of the 4 children against Whitsuntide 1585 at ⟨7s.6d.⟩ the yard ⟨43s.1½d.⟩, for ⟨24⟩ yards of black cotton for lining for the 8 coats ⟨at 8d. the yard 16s.⟩, and to James Harman yeoman of the chamber which he laid out for buttons and making of the 8 coats ⟨10s.4d.⟩,[1] summa ⟨£6.4s.5½d.⟩

[1] Two payments to Harman of 5s.2d., each for buttons and making of 4 coats, were entered at the foot of f.52v and struck through.

g. For wages of workmen and labourers for reparations done upon the tenements of Carpenter as by 2 bills appears ⟨£5.17s.11d.⟩ [cf.**29m**]
h. [f.81] For timber, lead, paving stone, brick, lime, sand, gravel, lead [*sic*] and other necessaries spent in repairing the tenements this year ⟨£5.0s.0d.⟩
i. 10 March to George Nicholles tailor, £5.19s.7d.[1]

[1] For the full entry see **27j** which is repeated here except for the insertion within angle-brackets at the end. The sum paid to Nicholles was charged half to the Carpenter account and half to the General account.

j. [f.81v] Summa totalis of the discharge ⟨£38.8s.7½d.⟩

130. And so due to the city upon this account ⟨£14.13s.10½d.⟩

131. [f.82] The account of the chamberlain for the lands and tenements sometime of Sir John Raynewell knight [*sic*] late lord mayor for the year aforesaid.

[Receipts]

a. Arrearages by this accountant due upon the foot of the last account, £179.6s.4d.
b. Receipts of the rents of the lands and tenements of Sir [*sic*] John Raynewell, vacations and desperates allowed, £125.3s.4d.
c. Summa totalis of the charge £304.9s.8d.

132. The Discharge [Payments]

a. To Nicholas Kennam to the use of the petty canons of St Paul's for Folliate's chantry,[1] £1.0s.0d.

[1] Gilbert Foliot, bishop of London 1163–87.

b. [f.82v] To the chamber of London for quitrent out of a vestry of St Botolph Billingsgate charged in the rental of the general lands in the title of Tower Street and Bridge Street[1] for one year ended at Michaelmas 1585, £1.0s.0d.

[1] The heading of a section of the general rental (Chamber Accounts 2, f.174v).

c. To Henry Bedles of Wootton (Wotton), Beds., gentleman for the rent of a barn and ground near Vauxhall (Fauxe hall) in Water Lambeth for one year ended at Michaelmas 1585, £1.6s.8d.
d. To the renter for gathering the rent and potation money £6.13s.4d. and for his liveries £3.2s., summa £9.15s.4d.
e. To Mr William Dummer comptroller of the chamber for overseeing this account, £2.0s.0d.
f. To Henrick Lamberte alias Gittens, who married the late wife of Thomas Kellye butcher deceased, for a quitrent out of Holy Rood Alley near Billingsgate for one year ended at Michaelmas 1584 [*sic*], 10s.0d.
g. To Mr Stephen Slany and Mr Henry Billingsly sheriffs for a discharge of a toll of London Bridge due for one year ended at Michaelmas 1585, £8.0s.0d.
h. To Christopher Osborne attorney, accountant in the exchequer for the sheriffs, for the farm of the borough of Southwark due to the queen for one year ended at Michaelmas 1585, £10.0s.0d.[1]

[1] There follow [f.83] two entries relating to workmen's wages and materials which have been deleted as nothing was charged this year upon the Reynwell account.

i. To William Garrawaye draper and Alexander Grey clothworker, high collectors of the first fifteenth granted to the queen to be paid within the city of London, by the bequest of Sir [*sic*] John Raynewell, viz. for the ward of Aldgate £5, Billingsgate £32 and Dowgate £28, being all for the discharge of all the inhabitants within the said wards, summa £65.0s.0d.
j. Summa totalis of the discharge ⟨£98.12s.0d.⟩

133. And so is due to the city upon this account ⟨£205.17s.8d.⟩

134. [f.84][1] The account of the chamberlain for the transportation and necessary provision of 2,420 soldiers into the Low Countries of Flanders for the service of her majesty.

[Receipts]

This accountant charges himself with £50 received 14 August of Mr Richard Huddleston, treasurer of the queen's wars in the Low Countries of Flanders, for the transportation of 500 soldiers at 2s. per poll and with £122 received of him 23 August for the transportation of 1,220 soldiers at the like rate, and with £30 received of him for the transportation of 300 soldiers after the same rate, [f.84v] and with £266.13s.4d. received of him for the furnishing of 400 vagrant and masterless men taken up as pioneers (pioners) from her majesty's service there at 13s.4d. the piece, summa £468.13s.4d.

Summa totalis of the charge £468.13s.4d.

[1] All entries on f.83v have been deleted and re-entered on ff.84v–85.

135. The Discharge [Payments]

a. 14 Aug. for the transportation of 500 soldiers into the Low Countries of Flanders at 2s. per poll, viz. in the ship called the 'Roberte Bonaventure' of Yarmouth 150 men, in the 'John' of Yarmouth 150 men, in the 'Thomas' of Yarmouth 50 men and in the 'Swallowe' of London 150 men, whereof there were under Mr John Norrys general of the [f.85] said wars 50 men, under [*blank*] Athrington captain 150 men, under Thomas Knowles captain 150 men, under Thomas Maria Winckfeild captain 150 men, summa £50.0s.0d.

b. 16 Aug. for the transportation of 300 men at 2s. per poll, viz. under Francis Carsey captain 150 men in the ship called the 'Mary Flower' of London, John Bennett master, and under Henry Norrys captain 150 men in the 'Guifte of God' of London, Thomas Stephens master, ⟨as by their 2 acquittances appears £30⟩; 17 Aug. for transporting 100 soldiers under John Robertes captain at like rate in the 'Daniell' of London, James Mortymer master, ⟨as by the acquittance of John Porter owner of the ship appears⟩ £10; 18 Aug. for transporting 310 men at like rate £31 ⟨as by 2 acquittances the one of £16 made by Clement Wylkynson and the other of £15 made by Peter Olyver appears⟩, viz. under Edward Huntley captain 160 men in the 'Rowe Buck' of Blakeney (Blackney), Clement Wilkinson master, and under Thomas Baskervilde captain 150 men in the 'Guifte of God' of London, Peter Olyver master; 19 Aug. for [f.85v] transporting 50 men at like rate in the 'Mary Katheryn' of London, Edward Owen master, and under John Sybthorpe captain ⟨as by the acquittance of Christopher Abdye appears⟩ £5; 20 Aug. for transporting 250 men at like rate ⟨as by the acquittance of John Love master of the 'Honde' of London appears⟩ £25, viz. under Mr Richard Huddleston treasurer of the queen's wars there 150 men in the 'Hounde' of Colchester, John Love master, and under the said John Sybthorpe 100 men in the said 'Hounde' of London, John Love master; 21 Aug. for transporting 210 men at like rate ⟨as by 2 acquittances the one of £15 made by William Bradley of Hull master and [the other of £6 made by][1] Thomas Langthorne salter appears⟩ £21, viz. under Francis Darcye captain 150 men in the 'Phenix' of Hull, William Bradley master, and under the said Edward Huntley captain 60 men in the 'Elizabeth' of London, William Noble master; summa £122.0s.0d.

[1] Omitted in error?

c. [f.86] 20 and 28 Sept. for the transportation of 300 men, viz. to Richard Buckley of London mariner for transporting 150 men under Edward Norrys captain in the 'Ann' of London, the said Richard Buckley master, at 2s. per poll ⟨as by the acquittance of [blank]⟩ £15, and to Francis Anthony for transporting 150 men under John Wotton captain in the 'Guifte of God' of London, James Church master, at like rate ⟨as by [the acquittance of][1] Charles Anthony goldsmith appears⟩ £15; summa £30.

[1] Omitted in error?

d. 26 Oct. [1585] to Sir Thomas Pullison knight lord mayor which he paid for the furnishing and transporting of 400 masterless men taken up within London, Middlesex and other places into the Low Countries as pioneers viz. for their coats at 4s. the coat £80, for their victuals to the sea £40, for their transportation at 2s. the piece £40, and to every of the 400 5s.4d. the piece £106.13s. 4d., of which 400 men 200 were under Jeffery Gates captain and shipped in the 'Flower of Comforte' of London, William Williams master, and 200 under [f.86v] John Potter captain and shipped in the 'Grace of God' of London, Samuel Spencer master; summa £266.13s.4d.

e. Summa totalis of the discharge £468.13s.4d.

[f.87] More owing to the City

136.a. 1. Hugh Stewkely gentleman for the rest of £13.6s.8d. towards reparations done in the house wherein he dwells in the Old Bailey,[1] as appears in the account of the year 5 & 6 Philip and Mary [1558], £3.6s.8d.

[1] He held two tenements by a lease for 31 years from Michaelmas 1556 (Rental, Chamber Accounts 2, f.158).

b. 2. Leonard Warcopp gentleman for a fine assessed (ceased) upon him by the court 5 April 1571 [Rep.17, f.134] for marrying Rebecca daughter and orphan of William Coxe haberdasher without licence, £10.0s.0d.

c. 3. Richard Mathewe cutler for money to him lent as by the third account of Mr George Heaton late chamberlain [1565–66] appears £100, for the payment whereof he has assured to the use of the city one messuage near Fleet Bridge, £100.0s.0d.[1]

[1] On 18 June 1566 the court approved articles (details not given) which gave Mathewe the custody of Fleet Ditch for 99 years (Rep.16, f.62).

d. 4. The master and governors of Christ's Hospital and St Bartholomew's Hospital for £50 paid by George Heaton late chamberlain to George Davies, as in his 4th account [1566–67] appears, for the redeeming of a lease which Davies had for marsh ground in Poplar and a wharf now in the tenure of William Dente whereof the hospitals took the benefit, £50.0s.0d.

e. 5. The master and governors of St Bartholomew's Hospital for reparations done upon the west part of Christ Church belonging to the hospital, as by the weeks' bills and emptions mentioned in the last account of the said late chamberlain [1576–77] appears, £74.8s.5d.[1]

[1] There follows [f.87v] a deleted entry: 'Thomas Wrighte for a fine of a messuage in Tower Street to him granted in reversion to begin at Christmas 1584 and then to pay £6.13s.4d.' This is annotated in the margin 'Received' and is probably one of the items missing from the beginning of the 'Debts received' section of the account, see **12a**. A grant in reversion of the Salutation in Tower Street to Wright had been approved 6 Sept. 1575 (CCPR, Tower Street, 1575).

137.a. 6. Richard Clifton leatherseller by obligation in the hands of the chamberlain in £40 for payment of £24 5 August 1577, £24.0s.0d.

b. 7. George Gunnes merchant taylor for the rest of £4 due for the fine of his house near Broken Wharf,[1] £2.0s.0d.

[1] Lease approved 24 July 1576 (Rep.19, f.104b).

c. 8. Peter Morrys stranger for the rest of £50 which was impressed to him upon a bargain to bring up water out of the Thames to the height of the steeple of St Magnus church and from thence to be conveyed further up into the city,[1] £25.0s.0d.

[1] For the London Bridge waterworks established by Peter Morris or Morice, a Dutchman, see G. Home, *Old London Bridge*, 1931, 193–5; *Remembrancia* 550–1, 553.

d. 9. Sir Edward Osborne knight and alderman, £400.0s.0d. [see **11x**]
e. 10. Edward Glover grocer for the rest of his fine of a tenement without Newgate now in the tenure of Gregory Newman respited till after the death of Newman,[1] £33.6s.8d.[2]

[1] Grant of lease in reversion approved 9 Jan. 1582 (CCPR, Newgate without, 1582).
[2] The rest of 87v is much amended. There follows an insertion, deleted, relating to the debt of Sir Thomas Pullyson for £300 which is entered later as debt 46 (**141b**); a deleted entry for 40s. owing by William Dent for the farm of the improvement of rushes, being parcel of £4 due for the quarter ended Michaelmas 1582, according to a new grant to him at £16 p.a. (15 May 1582, Rep.20, f.322b); an insertion, deleted, which repeats the entry for debt 10 (**137e**) and a deleted entry for Dent's debt for the aforesaid farm for 3 quarters of a year due at Michaelmas 1583. The entries below numbered 11–14 are written in the order 11, 14, 12, 13.

f. 11. ⟨William Dent for the rest of an obligation of £34 payable by 40s. a quarter, £32.0s.0d.⟩
g. 12. ⟨John Martyn now the master plumber to the chamber of London and his successors being the rest of £37 due by William Axe late master plumber deceased payable by order of court 17 March 1584 [Rep.21, f.40], £32.0s.0d.⟩[1]

[1] Axe died owing the city £37 which his widow, Margery, was too poor to pay. Martyn was admitted his successor but Margery was to have one fourth of the profits of office and to bear one fourth of the charges. Martyn was to pay to the chamberlain £5 p.a. until the £37 was paid off if he remained so long in office. This insertion is in substitution of a similar entry, deleted, on f.91.

h. 13. John Warter and Francis Brampton and their sureties being the rest of £1,000 by them due by divers obligations and payable by £100 yearly, £100.0s.0d. [see **12e**]

138.a. 14. George Heaton late chamberlain and his sureties, being parcel of the foot of his last account ⟨1576–77⟩ with £7 due by Edward Welton as by the same account appears, £1,463.0s.10¾d. and 28 peppercorns.
b. [f.88] 15. George Heaton and his sureties for £10 to him allowed in his last account [1576–77] for the lands, revenues and profits of Mr Raynewell for money paid to Gilbert Hill attorney, accountant to the then sheriffs, for the fee farm of Southwark when in deed the same remained unpaid, and since paid by Mr Mabb late chamberlain and to him allowed in his first account for Mr Raynewell [1577–78], £10.0s.0d.
c. 16. George Heton and his sureties for plate remaining in his custody for the use of the orphans of Thomas Rundell, wherewith he was not at any time charged in any account but remained a pawn for the payment of £20 due to the said orphans and by him laid to gage and now redeemed by the late chamberlain [Mabbe] as by his first account [1577–78] appears, £20.0s.0d.

d. 17. John Johnson basketmaker for the rest of his fine of £3 for his admission into the liberties of this city, £1.10s.0d.
e. 18. The aforesaid Peter Morrys for £25 paid by order of court 16 Feb. 1581 [Rep.20, f.170b] to John Martyn plumber for Morrys' debt,[1] £25.0s.0d.

[1] Martin had paid £25 into the chamber on Morris's behalf.

f. 19. The said Morrys for the which George Carleton and Humfry Michell esquires stand bound by obligation to the chamberlain in £200 for payment of £100 at the end of one year which expired in February 1582 by the said order [Rep.20, f.170b],[1] £100.0s.0d.

[1] Morris and his sureties were bound for the repayment at the end of a year of an interest free loan of £100. Repayment was deferred for another year in both March 1582 and March 1583 (Rep.20, ff.303b, 409b).

g. [f.88v] 20. Nicholas Willye late waterbailie for the rent of the tenement within Bishopsgate called the 'Ancres House'[1] due for 2¾ years ended at Midsummer 1580, £7.10s.0d.

[1] For the anchorites of London Wall, see C. Welch, *Churchwardens' accounts of the parish of All Hallows on the Wall 1455–1536* (1912), xxviii–xxxiv.

139.a. 21. The executors of Mr William Boxe late alderman deceased for his fine to be discharged of the mayoralty, £200.0s.0d.[1]

[1] Boxe was excused the mayoralty for the time being on health grounds on 24 Sept. 1579 and agreed to pay £200. He surrendered his aldermanry on 1 June 1581 (Rep.19, f.490b; Rep.20, f.202).

b. 22. Thomas Skynner clothworker for a fine upon him assessed (seaced) by the lord mayor and court of aldermen for certain unreverent speeches by him spoken against the lord mayor,[1] £66.13s.4d.

[1] 'He that had that Crochett in his heade to chose me Sheryve of London had byn better to have lent me one hundred Poundes', spoken on 21 July 1580 after Skynner had been nominated as sheriff by the lord mayor. He was forthwith committed to Newgate but discharged on condition of payment of a fine of 100 marks (Rep.20, ff.95b–96).

c. [23] The said Skynner for the rest of his fine of £200 for that he refused to take the office of shrievalty, £140.0s.0d. [see **12f**]
d. 24. Cuthbert Buckle vintner for the rest of his fine of £200 for that he refused to be sheriff [6 Aug. 1580, Jor.21, f.60], £50.0s.0d.[1]

[1] Buckle in fact paid his fine but in Oct. 1583 asked that it might be given him again (Rep.20, f.470).

e. 25. The merchants of the Steelyard for that the chamberlain has paid yearly by the space of 24[1] years to the lord mayor and sheriffs for the time being, in consideration as well of wax, herring and sturgeon wont yearly to be paid to them by the merchants as also 40s. yearly [f.89] for a petty toll due by them to the sheriffs, as by divers accounts as well of John Sturgeon late chamberlain as by all the accounts of George Heton also late chamberlain appears, amounting in the whole, over and above the charges which the city has been at for the repairing of Bishopsgate which should have been borne by them, to the sum of [*blank*][2]

[1] *Recte* 23? [See note 2.]
[2] In the next year's account this debt is given as £291.6s.8d., (see **275e**) which is 23 years at £12.13s.4d., the sum paid annually by the chamberlain (see **109**). The Hanse merchants had had an obligation since 1282 to keep Bishopsgate in repair (*Liber Albus*, transl. H. T. Riley, 417–18).

f. 26. The merchants of the Steelyard for like consideration for 6[1] years ended at Michaelmas last past [blank][2]

[1] *Recte* 8 years, i.e. from the beginning of John Mabbe's chamberlainship.
[2] This figure should be £101.6s.8d., i.e. 8 years at £12.13s.4d. The next year's account has £114 for 9 years, see **275f**.
There follows a deleted entry: 'William Dante improver of rushes for the rest of £25.8s.8d. by him due, as by the foot of the 4th account of Mr Mabb late chamberlain [1580–81] appears, and for which he stands bound in 4 obligations to be paid at 4 several terms of the year, the first payment at Michaelmas 1582 according to an order of 15 May 1582 [Rep.20, f.322b], by which order he was remitted of £5.8s.8d. being the rest of his debt'.

140.a. [f.89v] 27. Christopher Lightfoote for the rest of £20 for a messuage in the Old Bailey to him demised and to be paid at the commencement of his lease, £10.0s.0d.[1]

[1] Grant of lease in reversion approved 5 March 1583 (CCPR, Old Bailey, 1583).

b. 28. Thomas Bayarde clothworker in full discharge of £200 of which he is to pay by order of court 15 Feb. 24 Elizabeth [1582] £100 by £20 yearly, the first payment to begin at Christmas 1583, for which he stands bound by 5 obligations of £20 the piece, £60.0s.0d. [see **12g**][1]

[1] There follows a deleted entry: 'Sir Edward Osborne knight now lord mayor for a lease for 30 years beginning at the Annunciation 1584 for a garden without Aldgate against the Minories'. This was paid within the time of this account, see **12b**.

c. 29. Thomas Evely haberdasher for £10, parcel of £50 for the farm of measurage of linen cloth due at Michaelmas 1583, £10.0s.0d.
d. [f.91][1] 30. William Phillips for a garden ⟨against the Minories⟩, £5.0s.0d.[2]

[1] An instruction in the margin at the foot of f.89v, 'Here follow the debts due to the city in folio 65 [now 91] no.30', has been followed in the order of calendaring.
[2] CCPR, Aldgate without, 1578.

e. 31. John Porter for a garden there, £5.0s.0d.[1]

[1] CCPR, Aldgate without, 1578.

f. 32. John Skynner for a garden against the ⟨Minories⟩, £5.0s.0d.
g. 33. John Talbott for a garden at Houndsditch, £4.0s.0d.[1]

[1] CCPR, Houndsditch, 1580.

h. 34. William Henbyry for a garden at Bevis Marks (Bevy Merckes), £5.0s.0d.[1]

[1] CCPR, Bevis Marks, 1580.

i. 35. Thomas Newby for a garden there, £1.10s.0d.
j. 36. William Huckle for a garden there, £2.8s.0d.[1]

[1] CCPR, Houndsditch without Bishopsgate, 1581.

k. 37. John Prynne[1] for a garden there, £2.4s.0d.[2]

[1] Ms has 'Pryme' but 'Prynn(e)' in other entries and in the repertory.
[2] CCPR, Houndsditch without Bishopsgate, 1581.

l. 38. Richard Bushe for a tenement at St Mary Axe, £5.0s.0d.[1]

[1] Grant of lease in reversion approved 9 Jan.1582 (CCPR, St Andrew Undershaft, 1582).

m. 39. John Nicholas for a house in the Old Bailey, £20.0s.0d.[1]

[1] Grant of lease in reversion approved 5 March 1583 (CCPR, Old Bailey, 1583).

n. 40. William Lowe for a tenement in the Old Bailey, £10.0s.0d.[1]

[1] Extension of lease, fine £10, approved 16 Jan. 1584 (CCPR, Old Bailey, 1572).

o. 41. Thomas Westmerland for the rest of £20 due for his fine for his house in the Old Bailey, £6.0s.0d. [see **12c**]
p. 42. Thomas Davies cutler for the rest of £100 for a fine of a house over and on both sides of the gate of Temple Bar, £80.0s.0d.[1]

[1] Grant of lease approved 10 Sept. 1584 (CCPR, Temple Bar, 1584).

q. 43. Elizabeth Cann widow for the rest of £57 due by Martin Cann her late husband, £43.13s.4d. [see **12d**]
r. 44. William Crowther clothworker for the rest of £50 to him lent out of the chamber by order of court, £5.0s.0d. [see **12h**][1]

[1] The next entry is deleted and has been inserted above, see **137g**.

141.a. [f.91v] 45. Mr Thomas Gore grocer for his fine for that he refused to be sheriff [6 Aug. 1584, Jor.21, f.371b], £200.0s.0d.[1]

[1] On 21 July 1585 it was agreed that this fine should also discharge him from the office of alderman (Jor 21, f.454).

b. 46. Sir Thomas Pullison knight to him delivered by order of court 20 Oct. 1584, £300.0s.0d. [see **12l**]
c. 47. Mr Richard Gurney haberdasher for the rest of his fine of £200 for that he refused the office of shrievalty, £100.0s.0d. [see **11s**]
d. 48. Mr Thomas Bressey haberdasher for the rest of his fine of £200 for that he refused the office of shrievalty, £100.0s.0d. [see **11t**]
e. 49. Mr Robert Withens vintner for the rest of his fine of £200 for that he refused the office of shrievalty, £100.0s.0d. [see **11v**]
f. 50. Mr Richard Morrys for the rest of his fine of £200 for that he refused the office of shrievalty, £133.13s.4d. [see **11u**]
g. 51. Mr William Elkyn mercer for his like fine for refusing the office of shrievalty [14 June 1585, Rep.21, ff.176b–177], £200.0s.0d.

h. 52. Mr John Ketcher pewterer for his like fine for refusing the office of shrievalty [15 June 1585, Rep.21, ff.177, 178b], £200.0s.0d.
i. 53. Mr John Lacy clothworker for his like fine for refusing the office of shrievalty [24 June 1585, Jor.21, f.457; Rep.21, ff.185b–186], £200.0s.0d.
j. 54. Mr Edward Elmer grocer for his like fine for refusing the office of shrievalty [8 June 1585, Rep.21, f.173b], £200.0s.0d.
k. 55. Mr John Taylor haberdasher in discharge of all offices by order of court 2 Sept. 1585 [Rep.21, f.204b],[1] £333.6s.8d.

[1] Confirmed by common council 21 Oct. 1585 (Jor.21, f.475b). He had refused on 18 June 1585 to serve as sheriff (Rep.21, f.180).

l. 56. Mr William Gardyner leatherseller for his fine for refusing the office of shrievalty [25 June 1585, Rep.21, f.184], £200.0s.0d.
m. 57. Mr Richard Barne mercer for his discharge of the rooms of alderman and shrievalty by order of court 22 July 1585 [Rep.21, f.196], £133.6s.8d.[1]

[1] Common council consented to Barne's discharge on 12 July 1585 in consideration of his age and infirmity and payment of 200 marks (Jor.21, f.453b). The court of aldermen's order permitted him to pay by 3 six-monthly instalments.

142.a. 58. Thomas Lutwich joiner, keeper of the gaol of Ludgate, by his own agreement being the debt which Robert Thrower waxchandler, late keeper, did owe to this city, by order of court 26 Jan. 1585, £66.13s.4d. [see **11d**]
b. 59. William Hichecock fishmonger for the rest of £100 for the lease of his house, £70.0s.0d. [see **10c**]
c. 60. Robert Medley goldsmith for the rest of £120 for the lease of his house in Westcheap,[1] £90.0s.0d.

[1] Part of the Philipot estate, see **125d**.

d. 61. John Wilson goldsmith for the rest of £80 for the lease of his shop in Westcheap,[1] £60.0s.0d.

[1] Part of the Philipot estate, see **125e**.

e. [62] [*blank*] Ishame gentleman for paving work by the city done at his house at St Mary Spital at Easter 1584 £5.7s.2d. towards which there rests in the hands of Mr Chamberlain one tablet of gold supposed to be worth 40s. or thereabouts [see **35**].

143. [f.92] Plate and jewels remaining in the hands of the now chamberlain[1]

First 2 great gilt pots parcel of the fine of Mr John Browne sometime alderman for his discharge of aldermanship and mayoralty weighing 268 oz.

Also a standing cup with a cover antique work all gilt weighing 65 oz., one other standing cup with a cover with a crown imperial all gilt and weighing 40 oz., one dozen of spoons all gilt weighing 32 oz., 2 dozen of trenchers parcel gilt being late burnished and gilded weighing 205½ oz., and a basin and ewer all gilt antique work chased with the arms of this city weighing 129½ oz., [all] of the gift of William Denham knight and alderman for his fine of his discharge of aldermanship and mayoralty.

Also the collar of fine gold with the letter SS of the gift of Sir John Allen knight and alderman, deceased, lately enlarged and now weighing 39¼ oz.; a jewel of fine gold given by Sir Martin Boyes knight, with fair raised work and enamelled, with some gold added thereunto, having a great emerald and 12[2] sapphires moyen (moyne) fashion with a great balas (balist), 3 pointed diamonds and 4 great pearls, which stones and pearls were also given by Sir Martin Bowes late lord mayor, [with] also one fair sapphire of the gift of Sir Roger Martyn knight also late lord mayor, whereunto is also lately added one pearl which cost £8 as in the 9th account of Mr Heaton late chamberlain [1571–72] appears; also 2 livery pots which heretofore remained in the chamber white and now lately gilded and appointed now and henceforth [f.92v] to serve the lord mayor, the one weighing 49¼ oz. and the other 47½ oz.; also a fair basin and ewer of silver all gilt of the gift of Dame Margaret North, widow of Sir Edward North knight Lord North deceased, to the intent that they shall be yearly occupied at the lord mayor's feast and also at his house so long as the same shall endure weighing 140 oz.; also one great gilt bowl with a cover with the arms of the city weighing 43½ oz. of the gift of Robert Cristofer clothworker and one of the secondaries of the compter (counter); also 2 dozen of trenchers of silver parcel gilt with the arms of this city weighing 137¼ oz. which were provided at the charge of the city and appointed to pass from lord mayor to lord mayor yearly to be occupied in their houses according to an order of court 25 Feb. [*recte* Oct.] 1580 [Rep.20, f.127b].

[1] For notes on the history of the following pieces of plate, see Masters.
[2] Presumably an error since there were only 2 in the next year's account (**279**) and in other, later, inventories.

144. [f.90][1] For the which the City owes

[1] A marginal instruction, 'After the city's debts and plate enter the debts owing by the city as follows', has been followed in the order of calendaring.

a. There remains due for the captives by several collections as by the last account and this account appears, £193.18s.3¼d.[1]

[1] £100.8s.9½d. had been collected this year (see **11k**). Accounts of redemption money at 12 Nov. 1585 are set out in Rep.21, f.237. The amount then remaining in the chamber from earlier collections was £63.9s.5½d. but £30 had been paid out in October to Sir Edward Osborne (see **208**).

b. To the dean and chapter of Canterbury for lands of them purchased and left to the soil of the Royal Exchange now builded to be paid upon 6 months warning £600, and the city is charged to pay yearly to the dean and chapter over and above the debt aforesaid so long as the £600 shall be unpaid £30 yearly, £600.0s.0d. [see **16 l**][1]

[1] There follows a deleted entry: 'To Elizabeth Hilles widow for her interest in her house, parcel of premises taken into the soil of the Royal Exchange, to be paid yearly 31s. until £29 be fully paid, whereof she has received £21.16s.9d.' [see **16n**]

c. To divers orphans as appears in the book called the journal kept by James Poell, £5,493.17s.10½d.[1]

[1] There follows [f.90v] a deleted entry: 'To the children of George Lauson cooper deceased and unto Alice, one of the children and orphans of Robert Fisher haberdasher deceased, being given unto them by the legacy of Alice Smarte widow deceased for their interest in certain gardens and tenements in Chancery Lane, being the rest of £37.11s.8d. to them due'. [see **27j**]

d. To Elizabeth Jaques widow and her children to be paid when the children come to their age, over and above £3.6s.8d. yearly to be paid to her during the nonage of the children for their finding, in consideration of 100 marks to them also due for part of a house to them belonging taken in the said soil [of the Royal Exchange], 100 marks.[1]

[1] Elizabeth, widow of John Jaques (Jakes), agreed in 1566 that the city should have a little old house in Cornhill, late her husband's, for 100 marks. This sum was retained in the chamber, Elizabeth receiving 5 marks annually during her life, and was to be paid to her husband's eldest son in the event of her death (Rep.16, ff.45, 79b).

e. [f.91] And the commonalty of this city remains in debt for the foot of the account, viz. Philpott, Carpenter, Raynewell and Finsbury as appears in anno 1582 £745.18s.5½d. and more for this year £166.14s.10d.[1]

[1] This entry is not clear. The first figure possibly refers to a debt due to the estate of the former chamberlain, John Mabbe, who died in office during the financial year 1582–83, Robert Brandon being elected on 8 Jan. 1583. The second sum is possibly due upon the Finsbury account for 1584–85 for which no particulars survive. All other accounts for 1584–85 show the chamberlain a debtor to the city (see **146**). The excess of expenditure over income upon the Finsbury account would have had to be the unlikely figure of nearly £700 for the second sum to represent a balance due to the chamberlain upon a totalling of all the accounts. Neither debt is listed following the account for 1585–86.

145. [f.93 blank, f.93v] Foreign Charge 1585[1]

[1] Written in a bold hand. This leaf presumably served as the outer cover of that portion of the account which begins with the Foreign Charge and continues to the end of the account and which originally had its own separate foliation, 1–66.

146. [This draft account lacks the final totals and particulars of the audit such as are to be found in the account for 1585–86 (see **270** and **281**). The figures can be partially reconstructed as follows:
The chamberlain owes upon the general account £55.13s.4¾d. [**14**, **124**]
Also he owes upon the account of Sir John Philpott, £252.5s.2d. [**127**]
Also he owes upon the account of Mr John Carpenter, £14.13s.10½d. [**130**]
Also he owes upon the account of John Raynewell, £205.17s.8d. [**133**]
The Finsbury account [not known].
Also the chamberlain owes upon the Finsbury account, 3 red roses.[2]
Also he owes upon the general account, 12 peppercorns. [**14**]]

[1] This is Robert Brandon's third account as chamberlain. Four roses were due in the next account see **270**).

CHAMBERLAIN'S ACCOUNT 1585–86

147. [The fourth account of Robert Brandon chamberlain of the city of London from Michaelmas 1585 unto Michaelmas last past 1586][1]

[1] The first folio of the account for 1585–86 is missing. The recto would have contained the heading and the first 4 items of the charge which are partially reconstructed in **148–52**.

[The Charge]

148. [Money due to the city by this accountant as by the foot of his last account appears, £55.13s.4$\frac{3}{4}$d. and 12 peppercorns.][1]

[1] A known sum (see **14**, **124** and **146**).

149. [The receipts of the city's general lands and Blanchappleton lands, vacations and desperates allowed, approx. £837[1] and 4 peppercorns.]

[1] £836.18s.8d. in 1584–85 (**3**); £837.0s.8d. in 1586–87 (Rental, Chamber Accounts 2, f.190v).

150. [The receipts of enrolments of apprentices
151. [The receipts of admission of freemen
} approx. £642.][1]

[1] The contribution of apprenticeship and freedom fees cannot be distinguished but see **4–5** for the relative amounts in 1584–85.

152. [Summa £1,535.7s.6$\frac{1}{4}$d. and 16 peppercorns.][1]

[1] This total is required for the first 4 items of the charge if the sum of the surviving sectional totals of receipts is deducted from the grand total of receipts.

153. [Rent Farms [Receipts]][1]

[1] The verso of the missing folio would have contained the beginning of the Rent Farms. The missing items undoubtedly correspond closely to **7a–f** in 1584–85 and are summarised in **153a–f**.

a. [The rent farm of Blackwell Hall of the treasurer of St Bartholomew's Hospital, £33.6s.8d.]
b. [The rent farm of measurage of woollen cloths, cotton and friezes, £10.0s.0d.]
c. [The rent farm of custom of rushes at Broken Wharf for a half year, £7.0s.0d.][1]

[1] A new lease of the custom of rushes at £14 p.a. was granted to John Arderne bricklayer from Midsummer 1586 (Rep.21, f.312b). The former lessees were still owing their rent (see **278g**). A sum of £7 in respect of this entry satisfies the total of the Rent Farms.

d. [For the sealing of tanned leather at Leadenhall, £10.0s.0d.]
e. [For rent reserved for passing of barges to and from Gravesend, £30.0s.0d.]
f. [For wharfage of strangers at Billingsgate and for Romeland, £20.0s.0d.]
g. [f.94] As **7g**, £50.0s.0d.
h. As **7h**, £66.13s.4d.
i. As **7i** with these variations: received for sealing weights and measures £3.1s.4d. and for unsealed wine pots weighing 6 lb 2s., summa, £3.3s.4d.
j. As **7j**, £40.0s.0d.
k. As **7k**, 6s.8d.
l. As **7l** with this variation: sum received £19.19s.10½d.
m. As **7m**, £20.0s.0d.
n. [f.94v] As **7n**, £50.0s.0d.
o. As **7o**, £4.0s.0d.
p. As **7p**, £26.13s.4d.
q. Summa £391.3s.2½d.

154. [f.95] Casual Receipts Ordinary
a. As **8a**[1] with this variation: sum received £10.12s.8d.

[1] Save that 'brewers' is written over 'beerbrewers' struck through.

b. As **8b**, nil.
c. As **8c**, 13s.4d.
d. As **8d**, 4s.0d.
e. For standing of butchers at Leadenhall for half a year ended at the Annunciation 1586 as by the particulars may appear £36.15s.8d., and for the farm of the standing of the butchers there by order of court [28 April 1586, Rep.21, ff.292b–293b] for one half year ended at Michaelmas 1586 by Robert Aske and Richard Wistowe £38.6s.8d.[1] summa £75.2s.4d.

[1] To resolve a dispute between Robert Aske goldsmith, who held the profits of the Greenyard by grant of court, and Richard Wistowe barber surgeon, keeper of the Leadenhall, who claimed them as part of the perquisites of his office, the order specified that they should enjoy the keepership of Leadenhall and the Greenyard jointly without rendering any account of the profits of the stalls and standings but paying yearly £76.13s.4d.

f. As **8f** with these variations: 60 apprentices set over; sum received £6.0s.0d.
g. As **8g**, 8s.0d.
h. [f.95v] As **8h** with these variations: received of the same searchers of woollen cloths £16.2s.6d. for profits due to the queen, £71.7s.2¼d. for profits due to the chamber, and £60, as before, for farm of the office of alnage due to the queen, summa £147.9s.8¼d.
i. As **8i** with this variation: sum received £2.13s.4d.
j. As **8j** with this variation: sum received £23.11s.1d.
k. As **8k** with these variations: 'fourth part of the profits' amended to read 'third part'; sum received £19.12s.0½d.
l. As **8l**, £6.13s.4d.
m. Summa £292.19s.9¾d.

155. [f.96] Fines [Receipts]
As **9** with this variation: sum received £37.8s.4¾d.[1]

[1] For particulars, see the Book of Fines, ff.203r–204v.

156.[f.96v] Leases, Incomes, Arrearages of Rents, Venditions [Receipts]
a. 19 May. Of William Henbery baker for a fine for the lease of a garden near Bevis Marks within Aldgate, £5.0s.0d.[1]

[1] CCPR, Bevis Marks, 1586.

b. 27 April. Of John Beste cutler in part of £20 due for a fine for the lease of a house in the Old Bailey £10.0s.0d.[1]

[1] Grant of lease approved 5 March 1583 and fine of £20 payable when the chamberlain agrees with him over it (CCPR, Old Bailey, 1583).

c. 16 June. Of Henry Nayler clothworker for a fine for a lease of a house at Billingsgate for the use of the children of Jeffery Crome, fishmonger, the same tenement being in the tenure of Jeffry Crome, £100.0s.0d.[1]

[1] Grant of a lease to Geoffrey Crome and his sons, Arthur and Henry, of the tenement called the George, occupied by Geoffrey, was approved 2 June 1586. On 10 Oct. 1587, the fine of £100 having been already paid by Nayler, a new lease was made to Nayler and Crome's two sons (CCPR, Billingsgate, 1586).

d. 4 July. Of John Prynn grocer for a fine for the lease of a garden in Houndsditch without Bishopsgate, £2.4s.0d.
e. 20 July. Of Thomas Newby clothworker for a fine for the lease of a garden in Houndsditch, £1.10s.0d.
f. 27 July. Of William Phillippes merchant taylor for a fine for the lease of a garden without Aldgate over against the Minories there, £5.0s.0d.[1]

[1] CCPR, Aldgate Without, 1586.

g. 5 Aug. Of John Skynner armourer for a fine for the lease of a garden without Aldgate over against the Minories there, £5.0s.0d.[1]

[1] CCPR, Minories, 1586.

h. 21 Oct. [1586] Of William Lucas for the arrearages of rent due (for a garden without Aldgate over against the Minories) at Michaelmas 1585, 6s.8d.
i. 7 Nov. [1586] Of John Hetinge dyer towards the charges of a chimney set up at his house at St Lawrence Pountney, £1.0s.0d.
j. Summa £130.0s.8d.

157. [Receipts Extraordinary]
a. [The first folio of this section, no.5 in the original numeration, is missing. The missing entries should total £117.8s.6¾d.]
b. [f.97] 18 March and 17 June. Of the wards towards the payment of one fifteenth granted to this city by act of common council [23 Dec. 1585,

Jor.22, f.9b] for the affairs of the city,[1] viz. Aldersgate £7, Aldgate £5, Baynard Castle £12, Bassishaw £7, Bishopsgate £13, Billingsgate £32, Bridge Within £47, Bread Street £37, Broad Street £27, Candlewick Street £16, Coleman Street £16, Cordwainer Street £52.16s., Cornhill £16, Cheap [£52.16s.],[2] Cripplegate £40, Dowgate £28, Farringdon Within £50, Farringdon Without £35.1s., Langbourn £21.3s.4d., Lime Street £1.19s.11¾d., Portsoken £6, Queenhithe £20, Tower Ward £26, Vintry £16.13s.4d., Walbrook £33.6s.8d., summa £618.16s.3¾d.

[1] The money was raised for the payment of the 1,000 marks which it was agreed should be paid to Sir James Croft upon settlement of the dispute between him and the city concerning the office of garbling (see **79**, **226**). For an allowance to the chamberlain upon this assessment, see **251**.
[2] Ms mutilated.

c. 4 Aug. Of the rulers of the waterbearers for the city's moiety of £4.18s.1d. for the admission of 13 freemen at 12d. and 7 foreigners at 2s. in their fraternity and for fines levied upon offenders in their fraternity, £2.9s.0½d.
d. 19 Aug. Of John Barker of Ipswich, Suffolk, esquire by imprest to be repaid on 21 Nov. 1586, £100.0s.0d.[1]
Margin Debt

[1] Followed by a deleted entry: '14 Sept. Of Richard Martyn alderman by the appointment of this accountant to supply the city's want, £100'.

e. Summa £838.13s.11d.

158. [f.97v] Debts mentioned in the last account and other accounts and since received now being charged*
a. 24 Nov. Of Thomas Skynner clothworker in part of a fine for that he refused to be sheriff, £20.0s.0d. [see **139c**]
b. 25 Jan. Of Thomas Lutwitch joiner, keeper of the gaol of Ludgate, in part of a more sum by him due, £33.6s.8d. [see **142a**]
c. 7 Feb. Of Catherine Crowther widow in full of £50 due by William Crowther clothworker, her late husband, £5.0s.0d. [see **140r**]
d. 25 Feb. Of Thomas Gore grocer by act of common council as well for his discharge from the office of shrievalty as from all other offices of charge within this city, £200.0s.0d. [see **141a**]
e. 26 Feb. Of Richard Barnes mercer in part of 200 marks due for his discharge from the office of shrievalty and other offices of charge within this city, £44.8s.10d. [see **141m**]
f. 1 March. Of John Lacye clothworker for his fine for that he refused to be sheriff, £200.0s.0d. [see **141i**]
g. [f.98] 24 March. Of Christopher Lightfoote barber surgeon in full of £20 due for a fine for a lease of a house in the Old Bailey late in the tenure of [*blank*] Mount deceased, £10.0s.0d. [see **140a**]
h. The same day. Of Thomas Davys cutler in part of £80 parcel of £100

*See **136–42**. References to court orders which have already been quoted in earlier entries respecting the debts listed below are not repeated here.

due for a fine for a lease of a house over and on both the sides of the Temple Bar, £40.0s.0d. [see **140p**]
i. 26 March and 28 Sept. Of Richard Morrys ironmonger for a fine for his refusal to take upon him the office of sheriffwick, £133.6s.8d. [see **141f**]
j. 29 March. Of Robert Withens vintner in full of a fine for that he refused to be sheriff, £100.0s.0d. [see **141e**]
k. 1 Oct. Of Edward Elmer grocer for a fine for that he refused to be sheriff, £200.0s.0d. [see **141j**]
l. 10 Nov. Of John Taylor haberdasher in part of £333.6s.8d. due by act of common council for that he is discharged from all offices within this city, £33.6s.8d. [see **141k**]
m. 7 April. Of Thomas Bressy haberdasher in full of £200 for his fine for that he refused to be sheriff, £100.0s.0d. [see **141d**]
n. 8 April. Of Thomas Bayarde clothworker in part of a more sum due for his fine for that he refused to be sheriff, £20.0s.0d. [see **140b**]
o. 18 April. Of Richard Gourney haberdasher in full of £200 for his fine for that he refused to be sheriff, £100.0s.0d. [see **141c**]
p. [f.98v] 19 April. Of Elizabeth Cann widow in part of a more sum by her due to this city, £6.13s.4d. [see **140q**]
q. 30 April. Of John Warter and Francis Brampton merchant taylors being the full and last payment of £1,000 by them and others due by £100 yearly, £100.0s.0d. [see **137h**]
r. 2 May. Of William Hitchcocke fishmonger in part of a more sum due for a fine for a lease of a house at Billingsgate, £20.0s.0d. [see **142b**]
s. 23 June. Of John Martyn plumber in part of a more sum due for the debt of William Axe deceased, £5.0s.0d. [see **137g**]
t. 25 June. Of Thomas Westmerland cordwainer in full of £20 for a fine for the lease of a house [in the][1] Old [Bailey][1] £6.0s.0d. [see **140o**]

[1] Ms holed.

u. Summa totalis £1,377.2s.2d.

159. [f.99] Orphanage [Receipts]
Money received from Michaelmas 1585 unto Michaelmas 1586 to the use of divers orphans, as particularly appears by an account thereof kept by John Benson in two books called the journal, folio 41, and the ledger, folio 47, £2,635.8s.4d.

160. Summa totalis of the Charge general £7,238.4s.0¼d. and [16] pe[ppercorns].

[f.99v] The Discharge

161. Salaries of Ministers[1]

[1] 'Ministers' written against 'Priests' struck through.

a. As **15a**, £6.0s.0d.
b. As **15b**,[1] £5.0s.0d.

[1] Save that 'serve' is written over 'say service' struck through.

c. To the vicar of St Lawrence [Jewry] for offering money out of the Guildhall 15s. and out of the Guildhall Chapel 10s. due for three years ended at Michaelmas 1586, as by the acquittance of Gilbert Wakering gentleman, collector for Balliol (Bayhall) College in Oxford appears, £1.5s.0d.[1]

[1] The advowson and vicarage of St Lawrence Jewry belonged to Balliol College (see Caroline Barron, *The Medieval Guildhall of London*, 1974, 17 and note 21).

d. Summa £12.5s.0d.

162. [f.100] Rents and Quitrents [Payments][1]

[1] Unless stated otherwise these were paid in respect of the year ending Michaelmas 1586.

a. As **16a** save that no money is entered as having been paid.[1]

[1] Ms torn but the total at **162r** is correct. The period of arrears, one year, is left blank.

b. As **16b**, £6.0s.0d.
c. As **16c**, 3s.0d.
d. As **16d**, £4.0s.0d.
e. As **16e**, £4.0s.0d.
f. [f.100v] As **16f** with this addition inserted at the end: '⟨for overseeing the lands of the compter in the Poultry⟩', 10s.0d.
g. As **16g**, £4.0s.0d.
h. As **16h**, 10s.0d.
i. As **16i** with this variation: payment for one year only, £2.10s.0d.
j. [f.101] As **16j**, £2.6s.8d.
k. As **16k**, 13s.8d.
l. As **16 l**, £30.0s.0d.
m. [f.101v] As **16m**,[1] £3.6s.8d.

[1] Save that Helen Romforde (Rumford) is now described as 'late' wife of Stephen.

n. As **16 o**,[1] £3.6s.8d.

[1] Save that 'Robert Maskall' is struck through and 'Stephen Barton' written over.

o. As **16p** with this variation: payment for three quarters of a year only ended at Michaelmas [*sic*] 1586, 15s.0d.
p. [f.102] As **16q**, £5.0s.0d.
q. As **16r**,[1] £1.14s.4d.

[1] The acquittance is here given by William Weekes deputy to William Dalby.

r. Summa £68.16s.0d.

[f.102v] Inward Fees from Michaelmas 1585 unto Michaelmas 1586 [Payments]

163.a. As **17a**, £80.0s.0d.
b. As **17b**, £23.6s.8d.
c. As **17c**, £20.0s.0d.

d. As **17d**, £20.0s.0d.
e. As **17e**, £30.0s.0d.
f. As **17f**, £40.0s.0d.
g. As **17g**, £1.0s.0d.
h. To James Smithe for keeping the journal in parchment[1] and engrossing therein as well all acts of common council as also recognizances for orphanage and other orders, decrees and other things out of the paper journal and repertory due for one year, £10.0s.0d.

[1] The Letter Book. This entry was first identical to **17h** but was then amended to what is a more accurate description of contents.

164.a. As **18a**,[1] £26.6s.8d.

[1] The tenement over Aldersgate is now described as being late in the tenure of John Day's widow.

b. [f.103] As **18b**, £25.13s.4d.
c. As **18c** with these variations: John Northage's reward at the audit now '40s.' written over '£3.6s.8d.' struck through; total sum paid £5.0s.0d.
d. As **18d**, £13.6s.8d.
e. As **18e**, £27.6s.8d.
f. [f.103v] As **18f**, £17.0s.0d.

165.a. As **19a**, £14.3s.4d.
b. As **19b** except that the fee and reward are both paid to John Shawe, £12.6s.8d.
c. To Hugh Mantell late keeper of the reparation stuff and clerk of the works for his fee, £10.0s.0d.

166.a. As **20a**, £5.3s.4d.
b. [f.104] As **20b**, £2.6s.8d.
c. As **20c**, £4.13s.4d.
d. As **20d**, £2.13s.4d.
e. As **20e**, £5.3s.4d.
f. As **20f**, £21.6s.8d.
g. [f.104v] As **20g**, £4.0s.0d.
h. As **20h**, £4.0s.0d.
i. As **20i** with this variation: the fee paid to Robert Lyddys for the quarter ended at Christmas 1585 only, 10s.; to Richard Dod for the whole year 40s.; summa £2.10s.0d.
j. As **20j**, £2.0s.0d.

167. As **21** save that all payments to John Smithe are made in respect of ten months only ended 2 July 1586, summa £6.4s.3d. (And cf.**217**).

168. [f.105] Summa £435.10s.11d.

[f.105v] Outward Fees [Payments]

169.a. To Mr Richard Shuttleworth serjeant at law, Mr William Danyell, Mr Thomas Owen, Mr Thomas Bowyer, Mr Mathew Dale,[1] Mr James

Morice, Mr Edward Cooke and Mr John Cowper, to every of them for his year's fee 40s. due at Michaelmas 1586 £18, and to Mr John Kytchin ancient pleader for his year's fee 20s., summa £19.0s.0d.

[1] 'Mr Robert Clarke' deleted. His fee is still included in the total.

b. To Mr William Butler attorney in the exchequer and to Mr George Kempe attorney in the king's bench and to Mr [*blank*] Nelson attorney in the common pleas[1] to every of them 20s. for his year's fee 40s., and to the keeper of the star chamber for his year's fee, 6s.8d., summa £2.6s.8d.

[1] William Nelson was appointed attorney for the city 28 Sept. 1585 (Rep.21, f.211). The reference to him is inserted above the line and his fee has not been added to the total. As Clarke's fee had not been deducted from **a** above, the sum of **a** and **b** remains correct.

c. As **23c**, £10.0s.0d.
d. [f.106] As **23d**, £75.0s.0d.
e. As **23e**, £3.6s.8d.
f. As **23f**, £1.0s.0d.
g. As **23g**, £1.6s.8d.
h. As **23h**, £2.0s.0d.
i. As **23i** with this variation: the sum of £5 has been struck through and the entry annotated 'Nihil quia allocatur in suo tempore pro lanis etc.'

170.a. As **24a** with these variations: William Perryn in place of Elizabeth Ball as keeper of the grate near St Bartholomew's; Daniel Wauden is paid the fees for the whole year for keeping the grate in Walbrook (20s.) and the watergate at Dowgate (reduced fee of 40s.); total of whole entry £15.15s.0d.
b. [f.107] As **24b**, £5.6s.8d.

171.a. To William Browne foreign taker by order of court for his fee [see **25a**] for one year and a half ending at the Annunciaton 1587, £3.0s.0d.
b. [f.107v] As **25b**, £10.8s.0d.[1]

[1] Followed by an entry, as **25c**, deleted.

c. As **25d** but annotated 'stayed by the auditors' and the total '13s.4d.', struck through.
d. As **25e**, £1.0s.0d.
e. As **25f**,[1] £8.0s.0d.

[1] Save that the description of the office held by David Manninge and Thomas Redknighte given therein has been struck through and 'yeoman of the woodwharves' written over.

f. As **25g**, 6s.8d.
g. [f.108] As **25h**, £1.0s.0d.
h. As **25i**, £2.0s.0d.
i. As **25j**, £8.0s.0d.

172.a. As **26a**, £1.0s.0d.
b. As **26b** with this variation: Richard Darrell (Dorrell) is deceased and

his pension is paid for the half year ended at the Annunciation 1586 only, £1.6s.8d.
c. As **26c**, but annotated 'stayed by the auditors' and the total, '£1.6s.8d.', struck through.
d. [f.108v] As **26d**, £4.6s.8d.
e. As **26e**, £4.0s.0d.
f. As **26f**, £6.1s.8d.
g. As **26g**,[1] £2.0s.0d.

[1] With the addition that this sum is here specifically stated to be Luck's 'fee'.

h. As **26h**, £1.6s.8d.
i. As **26i**,[1] £1.14s.8d.

[1] Save the widow Cottrell's name is here given as 'Agnes'.

j. [f.109] As **26j**, £4.0s.0d.
k. As **26k**, £2.0s.0d.
l. As **26 l**,[1] £1.0s.0d.

[1] The date of the court order is given in the text.

m. As **26m** with this variation: William Crowther is deceased and his annuity is paid for the quarter ended at Christmas 1585 only, £10.0s.0d.

173.a. [f.109v] As **27a**, £13.6s.8d.
b. As **27b**, £26.13s.4d. but annotated 'disliked by the auditors'.
c. [f.110] As **27c** with this variation: Christopher Fowlkes is deceased and all payments to him are made in respect of the half year ended at the Annunciation 1586 only, £10.0s.0d.
d. As **27e**, £6.1s.8d.
e. As **27f**, £2.0s.0d.
f. [f.110v] As **27h**, £20.0s.0d.
g. As **27i** with this variation: Vincent Hill[1] is paid his annuity for a full year, £2.13s.4d.

[1] Now described as 'late one of the sheriffs' serjeants'.

174.a. To John Watson alias Jocky a poor porter for one annuity of 26s.8d. granted by order of court 26 Oct. 1585 [Rep.21, f.226] for life, £1.6s.8d.
b. To Joan White widow for one annuity of £40 to her due by Mr Richard Maye and Mr Anthony Ratclyffe merchant taylors and William Elkyn mercer during her life, [f.111] and after her decease one annuity of £20 due to her executors and administrators during the term of years which shall be to come in a patent from the queen of the office of garbling of spices and drugs throughout England ⟨London only excepted⟩, by order of court 21 June 28 Elizabeth [1586 Rep.21, f.309][1] and to her due for 3 quarters of a year ended at Michaelmas 1586, £30.0s.0d.

[1] This was part of the settlement of the law suit about the office of garbling, see **79** note. By this order it was agreed that the city should be responsible for the sum for which

Maye, Ratcliffe and Elkyn stood bound and a bond had been entered into to save them harmless. The chamberlain was to be allowed in his account the £666.13s.4d. which he had already paid to Sir James Croft for his interest in the office of garbling.

c. To John de Cardenas for one annuity of £5 granted by order of court Michaelmas 1585 [Rep.21, f.212] to continue during his life if he shall well and honestly use and demean himself towards the state of this city, and to him due for one year ended at Midsummer 1586, £5.0s.0d.[1]

[1] Cardenas, servant to Sir Francis Walsingham, was also granted a freedom without fee and the first reversion of one of several offices.

d. [f.111v] To Robert Lyddus[1] now remaining lunatic in Bethlem for a weekly pension of 16d. granted by order of court 1 [*recte* 3] Feb. 1586 [Rep.21, f.261b] and due for 33 weeks ended at Michaelmas 1586, £2.4s.0d.

[1] One of the waterbailiff's men, see **20i** and **166i**.

e. To Richard Pegrem haberdasher, now keeper of the reparation stuff, for one annuity of 40s. granted by order of court 17 March 1586 [Rep.21, f.276][1] to continue for so long as he shall execute the office and as Hugh Mantell late keeper shall live, due for half a year ended at Michaelmas 1586, £1.0s.0d.

[1] This payment was in respect of a labourer's room and a clerk's wages.

175. Summa £329.18s.4d.[1]

[1] This total includes the 3 sums marked 'stayed' or 'disliked' by the auditors, **171c**, **172c** and **173b**.

176. [f.112] Paid for the weekly wages of masons, carpenters, sawyers, bricklayers, plumbers, paviours, labourers and others working at Ludgate, Guildhall, Blackfriars, conduit heads, Leadenhall and other places decayed, repairing sundry of the city's tenements, making ladders, amending conduit pipes, cleansing sewers, carriages to and from sundry places, for drawing of water at Dowgate and other works done at divers other places, and also for the weekly wages of the clerk of the works and of Francis Barnard as by the weekly bills particularly may appear. The total sums of which bills hereunder appear.[1]

[1] This is the final version of a much amended heading.

a. 2 Oct. £5.6s.7½d., 9 Oct. £5.8s.8d., 16 Oct. £7.11s.10d., 23 Oct. £8.13s.4½d., 30 Oct. £5.5s.4d. Summa £32.5s.10d.
Margin ⟨Carpenters, bricklayers, masons, plasterers, plumbers, carters, working at the great house near Leadenhall leased to George Stonehowse,[1] and at the Guildhall kitchens and other offices there⟩

[1] For the lease, see CCPR, Leadenhall, 1573. In 1584 the rent of £12 p.a. under this lease was being paid by Richard Kingswell, esq. (Rental, Chamber Accounts 2, f.177).

b. 6 Nov. £5.10s.5d., 13 Nov. £6.14s.2d., 20 Nov. £6.3s.0d., 27 Nov. £6.7s.5d. Summa £24.15s.0d.

Margin ⟨Work done at the said great house; at the Guildhall kitchen and other offices there; at the house at Leadenhall in the tenure of Thomas[1] Wroth; about Aldermanbury pipe in St James Field; at the Blackfriars stairs near Bridewell; in searching in the pipes in the deep ditch near unto St James Field; mending the walls of the storehouse at Leadenhall; at the conduit heads and Banqueting House⟩

[1] 'William' in the rental (Chamber Accounts 2, f.177v).

c. 4 Dec. £5.4s.3d., 11 Dec. £8.10s.4d., 18 Dec. £9.0s.10d., 24 Dec. £4.6s.5d., 31 Dec. £2.12s.7d. Summa £29.14s.5d.
Margin ⟨Work done for the bridge and building betwixt the Blackfriars and Bridewell; at the Sessions House; at the Guildhall kitchen; about Aldermanbury pipe in the deep ditch near St James Field; at the Blackfriars bridge and about the building there; at the conduit heads and the Banqueting House, searching and venting the pipes at the Banqueting House; at the Guildhall kitchen; making a door for the way near St Clement's church by Candlewick street to the city's tenants' houses there; at the vault for the pipes at Ivy bridge and soldering a pipe at the putgalley at Broken Wharf⟩

d. [f.112v] 8 Jan. £4.4s.8d., 15 Jan. £5.10s.10d., 22 Jan. £5.16s.4d., 29 Jan. £5.14s.8d. Summa £21.6s.6d.
Margin ⟨Work done at the bridge and building betwixt the Blackfriars and Bridewell; at the conduit heads and Banqueting House; taking down the city's wall in the Blackfriars for a way to pass into Fleet Street during the time that Ludgate was in building; setting up a new gate there⟩

e. 5 Feb. £4.15s.3d., 12 Feb. £7.4s.9d., 19 Feb. £5.11s.8d., 26 Feb. £4.15s.5½d. Summa £22.7s.1½d.
Margin ⟨Work at the said stairs and at the said wall in the Blackfriars; at the house of Hugh Overend next Ludgate;[1] about a frame for a cistern in Ludgate; at the wall near Lord Aburgeyny's garden;[2] a new wall in the vault at Ludgate; work at the bridge betwixt the Blackfriars and Bridewell; lining the stairs at Billingsgate; at the house in Bassishaw leased to William Hobbes;[3] at the receipt of the water in the Old Bailey from Ludgate; at Ludgate; at the house of James Harman keeper of the Guildhall; weighing new pipes, mending a pipe by the Stocks, mending a cistern at the little conduit⟩

[1] In 1586 a great part of this house without Ludgate belonging to the city was pulled down for the rebuilding of the gate and the property was empty for a year (CCPR, Ludgate, 1583 and Rental, Chamber Accounts 2, f.157).
[2] The 'Lord of Burgaveny' held two parcels of common ground within Ludgate of the city (Rental, Chamber Accounts 2, f.161).
[3] The rent of £10 p.a. for this property was paid by Mr Robert Levery, who had married the widow of William Hobbs, draper (Rental, Chamber Accounts 2, f.184).

f. 5 March £5.14s.0½d., 12 March £7.2s.11d., 19 March £8.8s.11d., 26 March £7.15s.0d. Summa £29.0s.10½d.
Margin ⟨Work at the conduit heads; at Ludgate; at the privy in the garden in the Sessions House; at [. . .][1] Fryth's house without Ludgate;[2] mending a pipe at [the] Strand and another serving Aldgate conduit; at

the conduit heads setting up a field gate; mending Fleet Street pipe in St James Field; at the said stairs betwixt Blackfriars and Bridewell; mending pipes at the Stocks; setting up rails in Smithfield; a pair of gates at Bishopsgate; conveyance of water near the Banqueting House⟩

[1] Ms mutilated.
[2] William Frythe was paid £10 for hindrance caused through loss of his shop near Ludgate during the rebuilding of the gaol (CCPR, Ludgate, 1587).

g. 2 April £7.13s.1d., 9 April £3.11s.2d., 16 April £9.0s.1d., 23 April £6.7s.6d., 30 April £6.3s.9d. Summa £32.15s.7d.
Margin ⟨Work about mending a gate at Leadenhall; framing a cage at Bridewell; making 2 suspirals at the conduit heads; at the Guildhall mending the roof; making a wall at the 'Green Dragon' in Fish Street [Hill]; mending pipes for Aldermanbury, Fleet Street and Bishopsgate conduits; the cage at Bridewell, for mending Aldermanbury pipe; tiling over the conduit at Bishopsgate; mending a pipe at Dowgate; tiling Mr Heton's house in St Lawrence Lane;[1] carriage of pipes etc.⟩

[1] Thomas Heton, mercer, was the city's tenant for a great messuage in St Lawrence Lane under a lease to Richard Springham for 40 years from 1550 with a reversionary lease to follow (CCPR, Lawrence Lane, 1571; Rental, Chamber Accounts 2, f.183. And see **h** note).

h. 7 May £5.7s.1d., 14 May £4.19s.3d., 21 May £4.10s.8d., 28 May £2.10s.4d. Summa £17.7s.4d.
Margin ⟨Conduit pipes laying and carriage etc.; work at the house of John Crowch in St Lawrence Lane;[1] working about the common stairs; in St Lawrence Lane; at the 'Green Dragon' in Fleet Street; digging gravel; soldering gutters at Mr Crowch's; post at St Magnus corner; at the Guildhall kitchen; at the grate at Bridewell⟩

[1] Formerly in the tenure of Thomas Heton, see **g** note (Rental, Chamber Accounts 2, f.183).

i. [f.113] 4 June £2.17s.2d., 11 June £5.0s.2½d., 18 June £3.8s.4d., 25 June £3.8s.10d. Summa £14.14s.6½d.
Margin ⟨Working at Mr Crowch's house in St Lawrence Lane; pumps at Bishopsgate and St Antholin's; work at the conduit heads etc.; setting up suspiral doors; at the common sewers; about a vent for the common sewer leading from Aldersgate⟩
j. 2 July £4.2s.8d., 9 July £4.5s.4d., 15 July £4.15s.7d., 23 July £3.14s.2d., 30 July £3.16s.7d. Summa £20.14s.4d.
Margin ⟨Work at the city's house near Ludgate; at the conduit house at Ivy bridge; at Ludgate; at the sewer at Aldersgate; at the house of William Lathes at St Lawrence Pountney;[1] at the common sewer in Finsbury; at the common sewer; at Fissher's house in St Lawrence Lane; at the common sewer in Finsbury Field for the conduit heads; at Dowgate a broken pipe⟩

[1] In the rental William Lathes is shown as a new tenant of 2 tenements in 'Candlewick' formerly in the tenure of the widow of Henry Duxsell (Chamber Accounts 2, f.180).

k. 6 Aug. £3.1s.7d., 13 Aug. £4.10s.10d., 20 Aug. £4.7s.4d., 27 Aug. £3.17s.9d. Summa £15.17s.6d.
Margin ⟨Work at Ludgate; at the gravel pits; at the water house at Dowgate; at the conduit heads; in the Old Bailey; at Queenhithe, at the conduit heads in Finsbury Fields; at the conduit heads near the Banqueting House; at the rails in Smithfield; at the wrestling and shooting at Barth[olomew] tide⟩
l. 3 Sept. £5.0s.3d., 10 Sept. £4.4s.2d., 17 Sept. £7.1s.5d., 24 Sept. £4.18s.5d. Summa £21.4s.3d.
Margin ⟨At the house next Ludgate; at Newgate mending the gate; at Ludgate; mending pipes at Fleet Street and Charing Cross, at the conduit heads; scaffold, gallows, rails and sleds for execution of traitors⟩
m. Summa £282.3s.3½d.
whereof to be allowed to the account of Mr Philpott 2s.2d., to the account of Mr Carpenter 34s.10d., to the account of Mr Raynewell nil, and to the account of Finsbury nil, summa 37s.0d.
And so to be allowed to the general lands £280.6s.3½d. [f.113v blank]

[f.114] Emptions of reparation stuff and other necessary things bought and provided this year needful for the service of the city whereof part is spent about the buildings and necessary reparations before mentioned in the weeks' bills and the rest remaining in store*

177. 2 Oct. to Robert Maskall carpenter for leather for 12 shoes for the pump at Milk Street end and the pumps at Dowgate and for other things appertaining, £2.3s.10d.

178. 9 Oct. to John Alenson blacksmith for mending 3 great beams to weigh meal in Newgate Market and for a new iron beam to weigh bags withal and for mending 5 beams to weigh meal in Leadenhall Market 30s.; 10 Feb. to John Evans for one pair of new scales and for mending old scales for weighing of meal at Leadenhall, 5s.10d.; summa £1.15s.10d.

179. 6 Nov. to William Kyrwyn freemason for 100 foot purbeck paving stone at 5d. the foot 41s.8d., 1½ foot of purbeck stone 7½d., 40 foot purbeck (purpick) stone at like rate 16s.8d., 10 foot hollow channel at 6d. the foot 5s., 89 foot free stone paving at 6d. the foot 44s.6d., 5½ foot of ashlar at 8d. the foot 3s.8d., summa £5.12s.1½d.

180. [f.114v] 12 Nov. to Randolph Bull goldsmith for stuff and workmanship bestowed in mending the clock in the council chamber 5s.; 24 March to Peter Meadcalfe for stuff and workmanship bestowed in mending the clock in the orphans' court 17s.4d.; 19 Aug. to Randolph Bull for stuff and workmanship bestowed in mending the clock in the council chamber 8s.4d.; summa £1.10s.8d.

181. At sundry times to William Kyrwyne freemason for the new building

*With the exception of **181** and **201** the following payments were made against bills.

of the gate and part of the gaol of Ludgate, over and above £421.11s.11d. (whereof £100 paid out of the Bridgehouse) to him paid in the last account, according to one pair of indentures between the mayor, commonalty and citizens on the one part and William Kyrwyn on the other, £1,000.0s.0d. [cf.**38**]
Margin A. Ludgate newly built. After this entry follow as in folio 29 at B.[1]

[1] See **201**, entered on the original folio 29 of this year's account, for further expenditure on Ludgate. This instruction would presumably have been followed in the writing of the engrossed account.

182. 24 Dec. to Joseph Estracke stranger for 2 new panes of drawn glass work and one other old pane set in new lead and 7 pieces new drawn and made in the great glass window in the west end of the Guildhall 35s.; 26 Jan. to Miles Mason glazier for new making the glass lighthorn serving at the little conduit in Cheap 5s.10d.; 31 May to Miles Mason for glass and other stuff and workmanship in the mayor's court, [f.115] orphans' court, the louvres (lovers) over the Guildhall, St Mary Spital and the chambers where Richard Pegrem[1] dwells 15s.3d.; summa £2.16s.1d.

[1] Recently appointed clerk of the city's works (Rep.21, ff.257b, 276).

183. 25 Nov. to Edward Nashe paviour for paving work done at Widow Cudner's house in the Poultry,[1] at the conduit in Aldermanbury, under Temple Bar, Holborn Bridge, and at Sir Francis Walsyngham's house in Seething Lane,[2] containing 29 'tesse' at 8d. the 'tesse' 19s.4d., and for 7 loads of gravel 7s., and for carriage of 9 loads of stones 5s., and for a labourer's wages for 7 days after the rate of 4 'tesse' for every day's work at 9d. the day 8s.3d.[3] and for links and candles spent at Temple Bar 2s.3d., summa 41s.10d.; 24 Dec. to Nash for paving work done in the yard of the house late Sir William Damsell's, at Ivy Bridge, and the scullery in Guildhall, containing 20 'tesse' at 8d. the 'tesse' 13s.4d., and for carrying of stones 20d., for 13 loads of gravel at 8d. the load 8s.8d., and for a labourer's wages at 9d. for every 4 'tesse' 3s.9d., and more given to the owner of the field where the gravel was dug 12d., summa 28s.5d.; 14 March to Nash for paving work done over the pipe serving the tenement 'Unicorne' near Broken Wharf (*margin* Philpott 12d.),[4] at the new gate in the Blackfriars and at the new stairs below there, over the pipe at the Stocks, at the pipe over against the Lord of Leicester's house,[5] over the pipe that leads from Ludgate to the Old Bailey, and between James Harman's house[6] and the Guildhall, containing in all 30½ 'tesse' [f.115v] at 8d. the 'tesse' 20s.4d., for rubbish 16d., for a labourer's wages for 7 days accounting every 4 'tesse' for a day's work at 9d. the day 5s.3d., summa 26s.11d.; 21 April to Nash for paving work done at Bishopsgate within and without and against the east side of St Lawrence church in the Jewry, containing 34½ 'tesse' at 8d. the 'tesse' 23s., and for 10 loads of gravel 10s., for carriage of stones 2s.10d., for carrying of rubbish 8d., for a labourer's wages for 8½ days at 9d. the day accounting 4 'tesse' every day 6s.4½d., summa 42s.10½d.; 12 July to Nash for paving work done at the Aldersgate, the cage at Bridewell, at Holborn Bars, at Fleet Street conduit, about the well at St Antholin's and the grate in Houndsditch, containing 37½ 'tesse' at 8d. the 'tesse' 25s., and for a labourer's wages for 9 days accounting 4 'tesse' for every day 6s.9d., for gravel 4s., for carriage of stone 9s.4d., and for carrying of rubbish 8d., summa 45s.9d.; 10 Sept. to Nash for paving work done before the conduit at Moorgate, against the meal house in Newgate Market, under Newgate and in the yard at the cistern there and from Newgate down the Old Bailey to Ludgate over the new pipes [f.116] laid [there?],[7] and over the pipes down towards Fleet Bridge, at the Sessions House, within the bars there and before the gate, covering a pipe at Dowgate and covering a pipe at Holborn Bridge, containing in all 150 'tesse' at 8d. the 'tesse' £5, and for a labourer's wages for 37½ days accounting for every day 4 'tesse' at 9d. the day 28s.1½d., and for 57 loads of gravel 57s., and for carriage of stone and rubbish to and from the same works 18s.10d., summa £10.3s.9d. [*sic*].[8] Summa totalis £19.9s.6½d.

[1] Agnes Cudner, a tenant of the city (Rental, Chamber Accounts 2, f.185; CCPR, Poultry Compter, 1587).
[2] See Stow i, 132.
[3] Written over '5s.3d.', which is correct, struck through.
[4] i.e. 12d. to be charged to the Philipot estate to which the 'Unicorne' belonged.
[5] Leicester House, later Essex House, on the south side of the Strand, a little outside Temple Bar. In 1601 Essex House was being supplied by the city with a pipe of water (*Remembrancia*, 554).
[6] Keeper of the Guildhall, see **7i**, note.
[7] Paper torn away.
[8] '9d.' written over '11½d.' which is correct, struck through.

184. To George Michell limeman for 57C of lime delivered at Leadenhall, Guildhall, the conduit heads and other places for three quarters [of a year] due at Midsummer 1586 £17.2s.0d.; 11 Oct. [1586] to Robert Noble limeman for 8C of lime likewise delivered at 6s. the C due for one quarter ended at Michaelmas 1586 42s. [*sic*]; summa £19.4s.0d.

185. 4 Jan. to Mr Waterbailiff for 18 yards of tilt for a wherry for the waterbailiff at 9d. the yard 13s.6d. and for hoops for the same wherry 2s.6d., summa 16s.0d.

186. [f.116v] 10 Jan. to Robert Northe of Hampstead, Middlesex, yeoman for 32,000 of plain tiles at 11s. the thousand, £16.10s.0d.

187. To Richard Awsten of Hoxton (Hogsdon), Middlesex, yeoman for 26,500 of bricks delivered at Leadenhall, the Guildhall and other places for one year ended at Michaelmas 1586 at 11s. the thousand, £14.11s.6d.

188. 18 Jan. to John Cox merchant taylor for two ropes for the crane at Queenhithe weighing 78 lb at 4d. the lb 26s.; 14 April to him for a counter line for the said cranes weighing 35 lb at 4d. the pound 11s.8d.; summa £1.17s.8d.

189. 18 Feb. to Richard Wyate carpenter for 1,000 of quarter boards at 4s.8d. the hundred 46s.8d. and for carriage of the same 10d., 47s.6d.; 6 July to [f.117] Richard Pegrem for the use of Nicholas Dendye for 805½ foot of quarter boards and eaves boards at 4s.6d. the hundred 36s.3d.; summa £4.3s.9d.

190. 12 March to Edward Downes nightman for cleansing a vault in the garden at the Sessions House containing 12 tuns (tonns) at 23d. the tun 23s., and for cleansing the common vault at Leadenhall containing 18 tuns at like rate 24s.6d. [*sic*] and the vault in the Greenyard there containing 15 tuns at like rate 28s.9d., and for candle for the same purpose 2s.6d., and for 2 labourers for 7 nights seeing the same tuns filled 3s.6d., summa £4.12s.3d.; 31 March to Downes for cleansing a vault at the house at St Mary Spital containing 8 tuns at 14d. the tun 9s.4d. and for digging a pit in a garden to bury the same in 10d., for candle 4d. and to a labourer seeing the same tuns filled 6d., summa 11s.0d.; 29 April to him for so much allowed towards the cleansing of a vault at the tenement 'Green Dragon' in New Fish Street 4s.8d. (*margin* Carpenter 4s.8d.);[1] summa totalis £5.7s.11d.

[1] i.e. 4s.8d. to be charged to the Carpenter account to which the Green Dragon belonged.

191. [f.117v] At sundry times to John Martyn plumber for 31 fother (fodder),[1] 9½C 6 lb of burnt pipes of lead delivered to supply to broken pipes serving the conduit in Aldermanbury at £16 the fother £503.13s. and for 31¾C 8 lb of solder delivered for the said pipes at 56s. the C £89.2s., and for wood and for digging 1,280 yards of ground to lay the said pipes in at 12d. the yard £64, summa £656.15s., whereof due by John Martyn for 20 fother 16¾C 24 lb of old lead to him delivered at £10 the fother £208.9s.7d., so paid clear to him in ready money £448.5s.5d.; to John Martyn for 5 fother 17½C 2 lb of burnt pipes for the conduits at Newgate and Ludgate at £16 the fother £94.0s.4d., and for 4½C 14 lb of solder for the same pipes at 56s. the C £12.19s., and for wood and digging 222 yards of ground for the laying of the pipes at 12d. the yard £11.2s., summa £118.1s.4d., whereof due by John Martyn for 5 fother 8½C of old lead to him delivered at £10 the fother £54.5s., so paid clear to him in ready money £63.16s.4d.; [f.118] to John Martyn for 50¼C 15 lb of cast and burnt pipes at 16s. the C £40.6s.2d. (*margin* Carpenter 12d., Philpott £3.9s.9½d.),[2] and for 4 fother 6C 25 lb of sheet lead and casting the same at £11 the fother, viz. 11s. the C, £47.6s.5d., and for 7½C 14 lb of solder at 56s. the C £21.7s., summa £108.19s.7d., whereof due by John Martyn for 4 fother 7C 5 lb of old lead to him delivered at £9 the fother £39.3s.5d., so paid clear to him in ready money £69.15s.5d.; to John Martyn for 10C 21 lb of sheet lead delivered for Redknighte's house at Queenhithe (*margin* Philpott 41s.5d.),[3] for the tenement 'Green Dragon' in New Fish Street (*margin* Carpenter 4s.4d.),[4] for Ludgate, for the cistern at Newgate, for square pipes for the Guildhall, and for two half C, one 14 lb, two 4 lb, two 2 lb and one 1 lb weights to weigh flesh at Leadenhall, and for 32¼C 4 lb of old lead delivered to William Kirwyn free mason for so much borrowed of him from Ludgate to the city's use, the whole received of John Martyn is 2 fother 2¼C 25 lb at £10 the fodder £21.4s.7d. and for casting 10C 2 lb of new lead at 2s. the C 20s.4d. and ½C 23 lb of solder by him delivered to the same work at 6d. the pound 39s.6d., summa £24.4s.5d., whereof received of John Martyn for 4½C 9 lb of old lead to him delivered at 10s. the C 45s.9d., so rest clearly paid to him £21.18s.8d.; Summa totalis £[6]03.15s.10d.[5]

[1] Here equivalent to 20 cwt.
[2] i.e. to be charged to these accounts.
[3] i.e. to be charged to the Philipot estate. Thomas Redknight, a yeoman of the woodwharf (**171e**), was tenant of a house at Queenhithe belonging to the estate (Rental, Chamber Accounts 2, f.191v; CCPR, Queenhithe, 1587).
[4] i.e. to be charged to the Carpenter estate.
[5] Ms holed.

192. [118v] To Thomas Bennet ironmonger for locks, staples, hooks, spikings and nails of sundry sorts with other iron work for one year ended at Michaelmas 1586, £17.15s.1½d.

193. 18 Aug. to Robert Appleby saddler for four dozen leather buckets whereof delivered to my lord mayor half a dozen and to Mr Sheriffs two dozen at 26s.8d. the dozen, £5.6s.8d.

194. 31 Aug. to George Kyrwyn for 30 pieces of oaken timber delivered into the Greenyard at Leadenhall containing 15½ loads and 3½ foot at 18s.4d. the load, all charges borne, £14.5s.5½d.; 19 Sept. and 15 Oct. to Avery Coker and Thomas Thompson carpenters for 16 loads and 37 foot of timber delivered into the Greenyard at 18s. the load £15.1s.6d. and more for 4 loads and 18 foot of timber at 13s.4d. [f.119] the load 57s.8d., and for cranage and carriage of 16 loads 37 foot from the Three Cranes to the Greenyard at 2s. the load 33s.6d., summa £19.12s.8d. Summa totalis £33.18s.1½d.

195. 1 Sept. to John Himsley salter for 12¾C 6 lb of cresset light delivered for store at 7s. the C, £4.9s.7d.

196. To Richard Sampson blacksmith for hasps, hinges, staples, spikings, bars, cramps and dogs of iron and other stuff and workmanship, due for one year ended at Michaelmas 1586, £84.17s.11d.

197. 17 Oct. [1586] to Barnaby Bestowe turner for staves, tampions, stoppers, shovels, spades, scoops and a lighthorn, for one year ended at Michaelmas 1586, £1.15s.1d.

198. [f.119v] To James Harman for the use of William Ethredge of Croydon collier for 8 loads of great coals at 27s. the load, £10.16s.0d.

199. For canvas, tallow, cord, leather, sand, loam, clay, hair, tile pins, billets, faggots, brooms, meat and drink, baskets, Spanish white, packthread, mending the kettle in the scullery, washing of linen, ash poles, boots mending, ragstones and 26 foot of freestone, 1,500 of bricks, gravel, resin, mending the pumps at St Antholin's and Bishopsgate,

candles, links and other necessaries bought and provided weekly as by 37 bills appears, £35.10s.5d.
Margin Weekly emptions.

200 [f.120] 8 Dec. [1586] to William Palmer founder for cocks, washers, stoppers, mending, tinning and setting in divers cocks, and scouring the city's latten squirts with other necessaries done and delivered, for one year ended at Michaelmas 1586, £6.6s.6d.

201. By order of court [15 Nov. 1586, Rep.21, f.358b] to Randolph Bull goldsmith for a double dial by him delivered and set up at Ludgate £13.6s.8d.; to William Kyrwyn by order of court [24 Nov. 1586, Rep.21, f.362b] in respect of such work as he has done in building and beautifying of Ludgate more than he was bound to perform by the covenants of his indentures £100; and more to him by like order [8 Dec. 1586, Rep.21, f.365] for the building of the south part of the gate £30; summa £143.6s.8d.
Margin B. Ludgate. Look backward at A [see **181**].

202. Summa totalis of all the Emptions is £2,043.16s.9d. whereof to be deducted for the account of Sir John Philpott £8.11s.10½d., for the account of Mr John Carpenter 10s., for the account of Sir [*sic*] John Raynewell nil, and for the account of Finsbury nil, summa £9.1s.10½d.
And so to be allowed to the general lands, £2,034.14s.10½d.

[f.120v blank, f.121] 1586

The Foreign Charge [Payments]*

203. To Mr Duffylde[1] for preaching in the Guildhall chapel on Michaelmas day 1585 before the election of Sir Wolstan Dixie knight to the office of mayoralty[2] 10s.; to the wardens of the Parish Clerks for their pains and service the same day there 6s.8d. and for making up the books of the certificates of the weekly reports of all such persons as are weekly born and buried within this city and liberties delivered to the lord mayor and sent to the queen for one year ended at Michaelmas 1585 £3.6s.8d.; to Leonard Largen serjeant of the channel (cannell) for his charges riding to the court to deliver the same certificates £11.15s.6d.; to the vergers of St Paul's for opening and shutting the door of St Dunstan's chapel there at the coming of the lord mayor and aldermen thither on Sundays and other days there tarrying till the sermon time 20d.; to the yeomen of the waterside for keeping [f.121v] clean the said chapel 6s.8d.; to a poor man for keeping clean the circuit of the place where my lord mayor's officers and others sit and stand at the sermon time 8s.; summa £16.15s.2d.

[1] See **97** note 3.
[2] Knighted during his mayoralty on 6 Feb. 1586. See **211**.

*Many of the payments recorded were paid against bills of charges, particularly in the case of junior officers. The frequently recurring phrase 'as by a bill appears' has generally been omitted from the calendar. References to payment by court order, commandment of the lord mayor or in accordance with the journal are always noted.

204. 18 Jan. 1586 to William Edwyn bargeman[1] for serving Mr Alderman Martyn and certain commoners to and from the court 12s.6d.; 24 Jan. to him for serving certain aldermen, Mr Recorder and divers commoners to and from the court 12s.6d.; 22 Feb. to him for serving Mr Recorder and divers commoners to and from the court 12s.6d.; 19 April to him for serving certain aldermen and Mr Recorder to and from the court 12s.6d.; 31 May to him for serving certain aldermen to and from the court 12s.6d.; 15 June for serving Sir Thomas Pullyson and other aldermen to and from the court 13s.6d.; summa £3.16s.0d.

[1] *Margin* 'Barge hire'.

205. [f.122] 9 Oct. to William Edwyn for stuff and workmanship bestowed in dressing the city's little barge 8s.9d.; 26 Oct. to him for dressing the said little barge and the city's great barge 36s.5½d.; 13 Jan. to him for dressing the 2 barges 37s.10d.; 22 March to him for dressing the 2 barges 37s.; 30 June to him for dressing the great barge 30s.8d.; summa £7.10s.8[½]d.

206. More for the boat hire of divers aldermen their servants and other officers of the city travelling about the city's affairs within the time of this account as by the journal and 16 bills appears £11.6s.[3d.]

207. [f.122v] 4 Oct. to Henry Ravenscrofte for his horse hire and other charges riding to and from the court 5s.; 12 Nov. to James Harman for horse hire for Mr Recorder, Mr Sheriff Ratclyffe, Mr Secondary Fytton, three clerks of the compter, with other officers, to and from the court at Richmond to invite guests to the lord mayor's feast £4.1s.4d.; 20 Nov. to William Ravenscrofte for his charges being sent to the court with a letter 2s.10d.; 4 Jan. to him for his like charges to 'Portas' in Essex 12d.; 26 Jan. to Richard Dodd for the charges of himself and certain aldermen's servants at the court 5s.9d.; 29 March to Thomas Sympson for his charges riding to Wouldham (Oldam) in Kent and to Dunmow in Essex with letters for the procuring of preachers in the Easter holy days at St Mary Spital 15s.7d.; 14 June by commandment of my lord mayor and court of aldermen to Thomas Eccles leatherseller, ordinary post for London, for the hire of 123 horse with foot cloths for the ambassador of Denmark[1] and his train at 12d. the piece £6.3s.; 3 Sept. to John Smith [f.123] for his horse hire and other charges sent to the court with a letter 5s.10d.; 17 Sept. to Christopher Darrell servant to Mr Recorder for his diet and horse hire to and from the court at Windsor 3s.; 27 Sept. to Phillip Treherne for his horse hire and other charges in one day riding to the court with a letter 6s.9d.; summa £12.10s.1d.

[1] Henry Ramel, who had arrived at Greenwich on 6 May 1586 (*Cal. SPF 1585–86*, 608). It appears that the city furnished lodgings for him (Rep.21, f.478).

208. 5 Oct. by order of court [28 Sept. 1585, Rep.21, f.211] to Sir Edward Osborne knight and alderman for the redeeming of Hamond Ponde late captive in Barbary £30;[1] more by like order [12 Nov. 1585, Rep.21, f.237b] to Henry Huete clothworker for 8 fine broad cloths of him bought to be sent into Barbary and Turkey for redeeming of captives in the same countries £123.12s.11d.;[2] more by the said order to Sir Edward Osborne for the assurance of £100 of the said sum late employed for the redeeming of captives £8.8s.; summa £162.0s.11d.

[1] By an earlier order of 21 Jan. 1580 Osborne had been promised payment of £30 for the charges in redeeming Hamond, son of Jeffrey Ponde, citizen and bowyer, then a prisoner and captive in Greece as soon as the latter should arrive in England (Rep.20, f.31). Ponde was present in court on 28 Sept. 1585 when the order for payment was made.

[2] The cloths bought of Henry Hewett were despatched in the 'George Bonaventure', master Robert Ryckeman, bound for Algiers where they were to be consigned to John Tipton, consul for the English nation, to be bestowed in presents or otherwise for the redeeming of captives (Rep.21, f.237).

209. For 12 canvas bags to serve for money and accounts 5s.4d.; to Robert Smyth by order of court [29 Sept. 1585, Rep.21, f.211b] for his pains in collecting and engrossing acts of common councils heretofore made into one volume £30;[1] for 24 reams of writing paper bought of sundry persons at divers prices as by the journal appears £5.11s.6d.; summa £35.16s.[10d.]

[1] See **229** note 3.

210. [f.123v] 6 Oct. to William Edwyn bargeman for serving my lord mayor elect to the lord chancellor to be presented to his honour 10s.10d., and to the bargemen in reward 12d., to the keeper of his lordship's chamber door 2s.4d., and to the porter of his watergate 2s.; 29 Oct. to the poor of Westminster when the lord mayor took his oath there 53s.4d., and to the keeper of the exchequer 2s., to the keeper of the chapel door 2s., to the queen's bedemen 2s., to the vergers there 3s.4d., to the sextons 2s., to the marshal's men 5s., to the keeper of Baynard's Castle 10s., and to the porters there 3s.4d.; to William Edwyn bargeman for serving my lord mayor, aldermen and other officers with their retinue the same time to and from Westminster in the city's 2 barges and 2 other barges hired £5.6s., and to the bargemen in reward 2s.; to Henry Ravenscrofte which he paid by commandment of my lord mayor the same time to sundry poor persons of Westminster 16d.; summa £10.8s.6d.

211. 6 Feb. at the court at Greenwich at what time the lord mayor was knighted there viz. to the heralds 20s., the gentlemen ushers of her majesty's chamber 40s., the yeomen ushers 20s., the grooms and pages 20s., the keeper of the great chamber door 6s.8d., the yeomen of the cellars 10s., the yeomen of the buttery 10s. and the porters 20s.; to William Edwyn for serving my lord mayor, aldermen and other officers thither the same time in 2 barges 50s.8d.; summa £9.17s.4d.

212. [f.124] 12 Oct. by order of court [5 Oct. 1585, Rep.21, f.215b] to Mr Wilkes clerk to the council [cf.**73**] for penning and setting down an order before her majesty's council betwixt this city and the lieutenant of the Tower of London £3; 9 Dec. to Robert Smithe for his pains and money by him laid out touching the said matter 12s.; 1 July to him for drawing a breviate of the points of the controversy betwixt the city and the lieutenant 6s.8d.; summa £3.18s.[8d.] [cf.**82**]

213. 13 Oct. to Mr Dalton for his counsel and pains taken touching the city's right in a certain way and passage to and from the back parts of the city's tenements in the parish of St Clement Eastcheap by the churchyard wall there 10s.[cf.**92**]; 6 Dec. to Mr Recorder for his counsel and pains in the same cause 10s.; 18 Jan. to Mr Recorder's man for engrossing an indictment against certain of the parishioners of the said parish for stopping up the way and passage 2s.; 1 April to him for engrossing one other like indictment 2s.; 16 April to Mr Daniell for his pains in the matter 10s.;[1] 28 April to James Lorde for bringing one Arragon before Mr Town Clerk to be examined in the same matter 12d., to Mr Town Clerk for taking depositions of him and copies of the same 5s.4d., and to Robert Smith for his pains therein 17s.6d.; summa £2.17s.10d.

[1] On 12 April 1586 he was appointed to arbitrate in the variance but the matter was still unresolved in Dec. 1586 (Rep.21, ff.282, 369b).

214. [f.124v] 14 Oct. by order of court [7 Oct. 1585, Rep.21, f.216b] to Mr Thomas Ware fishmonger by him to be employed in the service of the city in the ward of Bridge Within wherein he is deputy 40s.; 15 Oct. to Mr Daniell for his pains taken at the chancery bar for the orphanage of the orphans of John Eston grocer deceased 10s. [cf.**93**]; 9 Nov. to Robert Smithe for his pains and for money by him laid out for the recovery of the said orphanage £3.10s.6d.; 16 Oct. to James Lorde for charges in law for condemning, carriage and burning certain corrupt hops 9s.8d.; 23 Nov. for charges in law for condemning the like corrupt hops 22s.6d. and more to James Lorde for charges in burning the said hops and for a dinner for certain persons appointed to search the same and other hops 26s.9d.; 19 Oct. to Robert Smithe for drawing and engrossing a pair of indentures between this city and William Kyrwyn freemason for the new building of Ludgate 10s. [cf.**38**], and for drawing and engrossing divers letters and other things to the several companies to contribute to the building of the same 10s.; the same day by order of court [21 Oct. 1585, Rep.21, f.223] to John Bysshoppe ironmonger by him employed to the city's use 20s.; summa £10.19s.5d.

215. [f.125] 23 Oct. to David Mannynge one of the yeomen of the woodwharves for his charges riding westward for the view of wood 40s.1d., and to Thomas Redknighte one other of the said yeomen for his charges riding into Essex and Kent eastward for the view of wood £3.10s.3d.; 17 Sept. to Davy Mannynge for his charges riding westward for like view of wood 41s.; to Thomas Redknight for his charges riding eastward for the like view of wood £3.6s.2d.; summa £10.17s.[6d.]

216. 28 Oct. to John Shawe for writing a pair of indentures between my lord mayor and this accountant for the city's plate and jewels delivered to the lord mayor 2s.6d., and to two porters for carrying the plate and jewels from the old lord mayor's to the new lord mayor 12d.; 19 March to Richard Mathewe goldsmith for mending and gilding the city's greatest livery pot and gilt bason 10s.; 29 April to Thomas Samon goldsmith for mending the city's sword carried before my lord mayor 12d., and to him for soldering and mending one of the city's livery pots 2s.6d.; this year to divers persons for 8 cormorants' heads 2s.8d., and for 11 otters' heads at 3s.4d. the piece 36s.8d. as by the journal appears [cf.**68**]; summa £2.16s.4d.

217. [f.125v] 8 Nov. by order of court [28 Oct. 1585, Rep.21, f.228] to Lybbeus Barnard in respect of his diligent service heretofore by him done to the city 40s.; 9 Nov. by order of court [26 Oct. 1585, Rep.21, f.225] to Richard Thompkins grocer and William Middleton vintner to either of them 50s. for their pains taken heretofore in looking to the measure of charcoal and apprehending legers (ledgers) and other colliers remaining in and about this city to shoot coals to the great deceit of her majesty's subjects, over and above £5 heretofore paid unto them by like order for their like pains £5 [cf.**107**]; 12 Feb. by order of court [23 Dec. 1585, Rep.21, f.251b] to John Barnard, a Moravian born, to him given of the free gift of this city 40s.; 7 June by order of court to Mr Alderman Barne by him to be delivered to the clerks of Sir Francis Walsingham as of the free gift of the court 40s.; 22 June by order of court [21 June 1586, Rep.21, f.308b] to Margaret Smithe, widow of John Smithe the elder deceased, in consideration of her poverty 40s.; summa £13.0s.0d.

218. 4 Jan. to the Lord Anderson's[1] porter in reward 12d., to the poor there 2d.; 8 Jan. to a pursuivant for bringing the queen's letter to the lord mayor and aldermen declaring her favour and goodwill towards this city 10s.; 22 Jan. to a pursuivant which came on a message from the court for certain aldermen to repair to the court 2s.6d.; 8 Feb. by order of court [3 Feb. 1586, Rep.21, f.261b] to Katherine Lyddus wife of Robert Lyddus (one of the waterbailie's servants) who remains now lunatic in Bethlem towards her relief 20s.; for conveying a letter to Oxford 4d.; [f.126] 17 March to a messenger for carrying a letter to the Lady Gressham to appear before her majesty's council for the repairing of the Royal Exchange 5s.; 22 March to Mr Recorder which he gave to the bishop of Canterbury's porters at Lambeth being there touching Mr Closse the preacher 2s.;[2] 29 July by commandment of my lord mayor to Albert Fyderkin, a Polonian born,[3] toward his relief 10s.; summa £2.12s.0d.

[1] Sir Edmund Anderson, lord chief justice of the common pleas.
[2] On Sunday, 6 March 1586, George Closse, reader at St Magnus, London Bridge, had slandered the lord mayor in a sermon preached at Paul's Cross, charging him with injustice. On 8 March several aldermen and the recorder repaired to the archbishop, and on 10 March Closse, obeying an order of the archbishop, made submission in the court of aldermen (Rep.21, ff.272, 273).
[3] A native of Poland.

219. 13 Nov. for a dinner at the 'Salutacion' at Billingsgate for Mr Chamberlain, Mr Dumer and other officers at what time they viewed, measured and limited out the city's lands at and near Botolph Wharf

15s.4d.; 4 Dec. for a dinner at the 'Flyinge Horse' in Maiden Lane for Mr Chamberlain, Mr Dumer and other officers at the cutting out of winter liveries 26s.5d.; 15 Jan. for a dinner at the 'Harrowe' in Gracechurch (Graciouse) Street for this accountant, Mr Dumer, John Martyn plumber and other workmen and labourers being at Leadenhall weighing out of old lead 13s.2d.; 22 Feb. for a dinner at the 'Harrowe' for this accountant, Mr Dumer, with other officers and workmen being at Leadenhall weighing out new pipes for the conduits in Aldermanbury and Fleet Street 26s.10d.; 14 March for a dinner at the Banqueting House where the conduit heads stand for Mr Chamberlain, Mr Dumer and certain commoners appointed by order of court [8 March 1586, Rep.21, f.272] to view the conduit and the defects thereof 23s.2d.; summa £5.4s.11d.

220. [f.126v] 15 Nov. to Mr Waterbailiff for a search by him made on the river of Thames 9, 10 and 11 Nov. 34s.10d.; 14 Dec. to him for charges in taking up a barge being sunk in the Thames over against Somerset House 7s.6d.; 11 Jan. to him for like search by him made on the river 4, 5 and 6 January 35s.5d.; for like seach made 12, 13 and 14 Feb. 37s.10d.; 22 March for like search made 14, 15 and 16 March 37s.8d.; 21 April for like search made 17, 18 and 19 April 35s.6d.; 15 June for like search made 28, 29 and 30 May 43s.6d.; 19 July for like search made 11, 12 and 13 July 33s.2d.; 27 July to William Lathes under waterbailiff for like search by him made 19 and 20 July 5s.4d.; 19 Aug. to the waterbailiff for like search by him made 18, 19 and 20 Aug. 35s.10d.; summa £15.6s.7d. [cf.**96**]

221. [f.127] 6 Sept. for writs of attendance out of the chancery directed to the sheriffs of Surrey and Middlesex for the summoning of 2 juries out of the said counties to appear before my lord mayor on 19 Sept. at Putney and Fulham to present the annoyances of the river of Thames 20s.; 19 Sept. to William Lathes under waterbailiff for his charges in delivering the writs 5s.6d.; to William Edwyn bargeman for the carrying of the provision of a dinner to Mr Aldersey's house at Putney for my lord mayor and aldermen sitting there 19 September for the same purpose 18s.8d., and for serving my lord mayor and aldermen with other officers thither the same time in the city's great barge 27s., summa 45s.8d.; to Edwyn for dressing the barge 31s.8½d.; for a dinner for my lord mayor and aldermen then and there £10.0s.7d.; to the sheriff of Surrey in reward for his attendance and making warrants for the summoning of a jury there 10s., to three bailiffs for summoning 25 persons which appeared on the same jury 8s.4d., to the said bailiffs for their dinners 3s., to the jurors for their dinners 25s., and to the poor there 17d., to the [f.127v] sheriff of Middlesex in reward for his attendance and making out warrants for summoning a jury at Fulham for the conservancy of the river 10s., to 6 bailiffs for summoning 34 persons which appeared on the said jury 11s.4d., to 7 bailiffs for their dinners 7s., to 26 men sworn on the jury for their dinners 26s., and to the poor there 3s., to Mr. Chalenor's 2 servants[1] in reward 2s., to the ringers of the bells at Fulham church 2s., for boat hire between Putney and Fulham 6d., and in reward to the bargemen 4s.; to Mr Waterbailiff for charges of himself, his men, the under waterbailiff and 12 watermen from Blackwall eastward unto Colney Ditch beyond Staines westward two whole days with the said 2 juries to search out the annoyances of the river with 7s. paid for a towing line and 2 ropes for 2 grapnels £7.6s.8d.; 18 Oct. to the jury of Surrey giving up their verdict in Southwark of the annoyances of the river 20s., to the jury of Middlesex giving up their verdict at Westminster 20s., and to the keeper of the chancery court there for attending and laying the cloth there 2s.6d.; to William Edwyn bargeman for serving my lord mayor and aldermen thither the same time to take the verdicts 11s.6d.; summa £30.16s.8½d. [cf.**96**]

[1] cf.**96** note 2.

222. [f.128] 20 Nov. to Edward ap John for 2 bushels of wheat meal for the trial of the assize of bread to be made by Mr Chamberlain and Mr Aske one of the bridgemasters 7s.8d., and for carriage thereof 2d.; 3 Jan. to Edward Lyle for bread by him and Mr Recorder's man bought at Westminster and within the Duchy[1] court by commandment of my lord mayor 2s.3d.; 18 Jan. by order of court to Robert Rogers servant to Mr Alderman Martyn which he paid to George Grymes brown baker for half a quarter of wheat meal and making trial thereof for the assize of bread 20s.8½d.;[2] summa £1.10s.9½d.

[1] Of Lancaster.

[2] On 18 Jan. 1586 the court ordered payment of 20s.4d. to George Grymes for travelling to Brentford (Braynford) and buying half a quarter of wheat and baking the same for a trial (Rep.21, f.255).

223. 23 Nov. to Mr Recorder for his pains taken two several times in moving the lord chief justice of the common pleas,[1] once privately and once pleading before his lordship and other justices at Westminster at the bar there, for the bringing down of a suit by writ of *procedendo* commenced against William Gardner leatherseller for £300 by him due for that he refused to be sheriff [25 June 1585, Rep.21, f.184][2] 30s.; 3 Dec. to James Lorde for attending and arresting William Gardner for the £300, 2s.6d.; 31 Dec. to Mr Daniell and Mr Owen to either of them 10s. for his pains taken in the council chamber touching the matter 20s.; 1 March to Robert Smithe for his pains and for money by him laid out in the matter 25s.4d.; 17 [f.128v] May to Mr Recorder for his pains at the common pleas bar at Westminster for the bringing down of the matter 20s; 26 May to Robert Smithe for his pains and for money by him laid out in the matter 10s.6d., and to Mr Daniell, Mr Owen and Mr Fuller to every of them 10s. for his pains taken in conferring together 30s.; summa £6.18s.4d.

[1] Sir Edmund Anderson. Orders were given on 17 May and 9 June 1586 for certain aldermen also to wait upon him concerning this suit (Rep.21, ff.296b, 305).

[2] The fine for refusal of the office of sheriff upon election thereto was normally £200 but under the act of common council of 27 May 1585 governing the election of sheriffs rose to £300 if payment was more than three months in arrears.

224. 26 Nov. by act of common council [27 May 1585, Jor.21, ff.437–8] to Mr Anthony Ratclyffe merchant taylor for that he took upon him the office of shrievalty in the stead of Mr Giles Garton ironmonger who lately refused the same £100; more to Mr Henry Prannell vintner by like act for that he took upon him the office of shrievalty in stead of Mr John Lacy clothworker who lately refused the same £200;[1] to George Hannam clerk of the warrants in the common pleas for entering and filing the warrant of attorney for the mayor and commonalty 6s.8d.; and to Humfrey Masterson for entering the warrant of attorney for the mayor and commonalty in the king's bench 3s.4d.; summa £300.10s.0d.

[1] Under the act of 1585 payment for accepting office following another's refusal was £100 but Prannell was allowed a further £100, parcel of a £200 fine which he had paid for an earlier refusal in 1580 (Jor.21, f.453b).

225. [f.129] 1 Dec. by act of common council [30 Nov. 1585, Jor.22, f.5b] to the Earl of Leicester towards his charges into the Low Countries of the free gift and goodwill of this city in new angels £500; to Anthony Marten goldsmith for the exchange of £500 in old angels to be carried and put into the exchequer in place of £500 in new angels delivered to the Earl of Leicester 41s.8d., and to a porter for carrying £500 in white money into the exchequer for the new angels 6d.; summa £502.2s.2d.

226. 9 Dec. to Robert Smithe for money by him laid out and for his pains in the suit commenced against this city by Sir James Acrofte for the office of garbling[1] 23s.8d.; 31 Dec. to Mr Daniell and Mr Dalton to either of them 10s. for his pains taken in drawing a book between Sir James Acrofte and this city for his interest in the office of garbling throughout England (London only excepted) 20s.; 22 Jan. to Mr Owen for his pains and for his counsel at my lord mayor's house with Sir James Acrofte's counsel for agreeing upon a book to be engrossed for the said office 10s.; 19 Feb. to Mr Daniell and Mr Owen to either of them 10s. for his further pains [f.129v] 20s.; 1 March 1586 by order of court [1 March 1586, Rep.21, f.269b] to Joan White widow for one quarter due at Christmas 1585 which Sir James Acroft knight should have paid unto her for the said office £10 and to her for charges in law for passing the foresaid book between this city and Sir James Acroft 40s.; 1 March to Mr Daniell for his pains in the assurance to be made of the office 20s., to Mr Owen for his pains therein 10s.; and to Philip Treherne for calling the committees together for the said matter 3s.4d.; 17 March to Sir James Acrofte for his interest in a letters patent under her highness' great seal for the office of garbling of spices, drugs and other merchandise throughout the realm of England (London only excepted) which letters patent are conveyed over by writing to Mr Anthony Radclyffe and Mr Richard May merchant taylors and other commoners by the consent of common council to the use of this city £666.13s.4d.; to Robert Smithe for drawing and engrossing the said book of assurance made to Mr Radcliffe, Mr Maye and other commoners by Sir James Acrofte of the office of garbling and for drawing and engrossing several obligations for the assurance of one annuity of £40 to Joan White widow for the said office during her natural life and obligations for saving Mr May and the other commoners harmless £3.8s.8d.; summa £687.9s.0d.

[1] See **79**.

227. [f.130] 9 Dec. to Robert Smithe for money by him laid out in the matter depending in the star chamber at the suit of the lord Thomas Howard for the liberties of Christ Church near Aldgate 20s. [cf.**83**]; 1 March to him for his pains and for money by him laid out in a suit brought against the city for the Conduit Meads 8s.2d. [cf.**84**]; 30 April for charges in the arches court for the administration of the goods of Richard Graunt, John Smarte and William Purches to whom with others a lease was made of the Conduit Meads by Sir John Forteskue knight £3.10s.; 26 May to Robert Smithe for his pains and for money by him laid out in the said suit 13s.; 9 Dec. to Robert Smithe for his pains and for money by him laid out touching the quo warranto brought against this city for the office of search of hops, oil, butter, vinegar and soap 10s.8d. [cf.**76**]; 10 Dec. to him by order from Mr Recorder for writing out a long discourse delivered to Sir William Wynter knight by Roger Tyler[1] complaining against the lord mayor and aldermen and containing divers false and scandalous speeches touching the said search 20s.; and for his boat hire in and [f.130v] about the same 16d.; 1 July to Robert Smithe for money by him laid out in the said suit 13s.4d.; 23 April to Mr Eve deputy in the crown office for his travail with Mr Attorney General for the non suiting of several suits prosecuted by quo warranto, viz. for the search of hops, butter, oil, vinegar and soap, and for the liberties of London and Southwark, and the search of Thames £3; 26 May to Robert Smithe for his pains and for money by him laid out in the said suits 56s.10d.; summa £13.13s.4d.

[1] The company of tallow chandlers had granted Tyler, one of their members, a deputation for life of the right to search under their letters patent. See **76** note 1.

228. 9 Dec. to Robert Smithe for money by him laid out in the suit commenced against my lord mayor and aldermen by John Mellowe clothworker 18s.8d. [cf.**95**]; 9 Dec. to him for his pains and money by him laid out in a suit commenced against Sir Thomas Pullyson knight in the exchequer by John Lewys for imprisoning his wife 39s.2d.; 1 March to him for pains and money by him laid out in the said suit 9s.8d.; to him for his pains and money by him laid out in the chancery for the orphanage of the orphans of Thomas Whitlocke merchant taylor deceased [f.131] 10s.8d. [cf.**93**]; 1 March to him for his pains and money by him laid out in the said matter 54s.; 26 May to him for his pains and money by him laid out in the said matter prosecuted by Robert Newdick and George Smedley against Sir Thomas Pullyson and Mr Thomas Aldersey to answer in the name of the mayor and commonalty for the said orphanage 11s.4d.; 1 July to him for money by him laid out in the said suit 4s.6d.; summa £7.8s.0d.

229. To Edward Gyllam waxchandler for 24 pounds of red sealing wax delivered to the city's use for one year ended at Michaelmas 1586 24s; to Hugh Syngleton stationer for 29 pottles and one pint of ink delivered for one year ended at Michaelmas 1586 at 2s.2d. the pottle £3.3s.4½d.; 16 Dec. to him for 300 proclamations by him printed for this city forbidding the inhabitants of Norwich and other infected places to repair to London with their wares [20 Sept. 1585, Jor.21, f.470], and for 500 constables' oaths with additions, and for 12 almanacs 34s.10d.; 2 July to him for 300 books of orders for my lord mayor and aldermen for wearing their apparel,[1] and for 2,800 [f.131v] oaths for freemen, 300 acts of common council against the new erected alleys and inmates £6.0s.10d.; to him for 300 acts of common council showing that all foreigners and strangers should pay fifteenths and other charges and customs with the freemen of this city 25s.; more for 50 proclamations against eating of flesh in Lent 4s.2d.; 17 Jan. to Humfrey Bate stationer by warrant from my lord mayor for 5 paper books delivered to the lord mayor 24s.; 14 March to William Prestwood stationer for 3 small books of paper, one roll of parchment, one book of paper royal for a journal, 2 quires of paper royal and one book of demy paper for orders taken before my lord mayor 45s.10d.; more 31 May for one roll of parchment 10s.; 12 Oct. [1586] to Hugh Singleton stationer for boards, skins, girdling, bosses, plates and new binding for the new written book of oaths and for ink of divers colours for the same 22s.;[2] to him for stuff and workmanship in binding and making up a book in parchment containing the acts of common councils into one volume ⟨since the charter *de condendis legibus*⟩, and for like stuff and workmanship for one book in paper as calendar to the former book, 53s.4d.;[3] summa £21.7s.4½d.

[1] Presumably 'The order of my lord mayor, the aldermen and the sheriffs for their meetings and wearing of their apparel throughout the year' of which a first edition had been printed in 1568. An edition printed by Hugh Singleton in 1586 is listed in T. F. Dibdin's Ames, *Topographical Antiquities*, iv, 1819, 295 but no copy is now known.
[2] The Elizabethan book of oaths, written on parchment and with coloured initials, is extant. It was written by Robert Smith who delivered it into the court of aldermen on 28 Sept. 1586 (Rep.21, f.338. And see note 3).
[3] The volume of acts of common council and the calendar thereto are not known to survive. They also had been engrossed by Robert Smith and delivered on 28 Sept. 1586. They comprised acts of common council from the time of the charter of 15 May 1341 (which gave power to the mayor, aldermen and commonalty to amend defective customs) to 1584–85, 'with a table also to the same book containing the substance thereof and referring to the same after the manner of an alphabet' (Rep.21, f.338). Smith had already received £30 on account of this collection of acts by order of 29 Sept. 1585 (see **209**). It was ordered on 28 Sept. 1586 that he should receive a further £30 for this and the book of oaths, but this payment is not contained in the account for 1585–86. And see **233**.

230. [f.132] 25 Jan. to John Shawe for writing out certain notes out of the wardmote inquests as touch this accomptant to be reformed 30s.; to him for writing and engrossing divers surveys at Botolph Wharf and at the 'Seven Starrs' in Smithfield being entered in the journal 24s.4d.; 15 Jan. to Robert Smith for search and other travail touching the matter of purprestures to maintain the city's title thereunto 10s.; 1 March to him for his pains and for money by him laid out for search and copies of inquisitions of purprestures remaining in Sir Thomas Hennage's office in the Tower[1] and other things touching the same 54s.4d.; 11 Aug. to Mr Daniell for his pains taken touching purprestures and the city's perambulations 10s.; 21 Jan. to William Dalbye and Robert Smithe to either of them 10s. for their pains in searching out of certain old laws and ordinances to see by what warrant the chamberlain may lawfully let leases of the city's lands 20s.; to Mr Recorder for his counsel and pains in a law to be confirmed for the lawful letting and leasing of the said lands 10s.; to Mr Daniell, Mr Owen and Mr Fuller for their pains and counsel in the matter 30s.; summa £9.8s.8d.

[1] Sir Thomas Heneage, keeper of the Tower records.

231. [f.132v] To John Coxe merchant taylor and farmer of the profits of the markets and housing of corn at Queenhithe in consideration of the lack and want of a loft there detained by the company of Grocers and is due for one year ended at Michaelmas 1586 40s.,[1] 28 Jan. to Nicholas Smithe merchant taylor for stuff and workmanship bestowed in making up John Luck's gown and coat[2] against Christmas 10s.4d.; to Robert Durant skinner for furring Luck's gown with fitches 16s.; to Nicholas Smithe for stuff and workmanship bestowed in making up Luck's coat against Whitsuntide 7s.5d.; to Thomas Childe for writing out such orders and decrees out of the repertory as touch this accomptant for one year ended at Michaelmas last past 20s.; to William Ravenscroft for keeping the door passage from the council chamber into the lord mayor's court for one year ended at Michaelmas last past 40s. [cf. **81**]; 20 Dec. to Nicholas Willy gentleman and late waterbailiff in consideration that he did resign the office of waterbailiff to Thomas Somer now deceased due for one quarter ended at Christmas 1585 £5 [cf.**81**]; summa £11.13s.9d.

[1] See **7p** note. On 3 Oct. 1587 the chamberlain was ordered to take possession of that part of the garner at Queenhithe lately occupied by the company of Grocers (Rep.21, f.472b).
[2] See **26g** for other references to John Luck's liveries.

232. [f.133] 23 Dec. to Ann Wytt alias Smithe widow for 6 badges for the 6 waits against Christmas 12s.; 20 May to her for 6 other badges for the waits against Whitsuntide 12s.; 12 Feb. to Arthur Parker servant to my lord mayor which his honour paid and gave to one of the lord of Leicester's servants for bringing 20 warrants unto his lordship for venison 20s.; 3 Nov. 1586 by order of court [27 Sept. 1586, Rep.21, f.352b] to John Deywell common hunt for his own charges and his two men riding to the court to procure warrants for bucks and stags for my lord mayor and aldermen £9.15s.10d.; 20 Feb. by commandment of my lord mayor to Mr Watson clerk of the crown office in the chancery for the commission of oyer and determiner 13s.4d.; to Godfry Fanshawe for a copy out of the exchequer for the rates of every several precinct of every ward within London of the fifteenth due to the queen 7s.; to Robert Smithe for search and other charges by him laid out in the exchequer touching the said several rates in former times 3s.2d.; 1 March to Mr Recorder for penning a law to be confirmed by act of common council for the election of the sheriffs 10s.; summa £13.13s.4d.

233. [f.133v] For the making of 8 obligations, viz. one wherein Mr Robert Withens vintner stands bound for the payment of £100, one wherein Mr Richard Gourney haberdasher stands bound for payment of £100, 3 wherein Mr Richard Barne mercer stands bound for payment of 200 marks and 3 wherein Mr John Taylor haberdasher stands bound for the payment of £300, 4s.;[1] to Robert Smithe for making 4 obligations wherein Mr Robert Howse clothworker, Mr William Elkyn mercer and Mr William Albany merchant taylor late elect sheriffs stood bound 2s.8d.;[2] to William Conradus for drawing great letters in the book of common councils 12d.;[3] by order of court [Rep.21, f.277b] to Hugh Mantell late keeper of the reparation stuff to him allowed by the court 17 March 1586 £20; 26 March for charges in law for the trial of certain lead supposed to be foreign bought and sold 24s.10d.; 28 March to Robert Smithe for a copy of the letters patent made to Sir Thomas Cowarden knight of the late house of the Blackfriars now in the tenure of Sir William Moore knight 5s.; 26 May to him for money laid out touching the city's right in the liberties of the White and Black Friars 25s.; summa £23.2s.6d.

[1] All fines for refusal to serve as sheriff.
[2] Howse and Elkyn served 1586–87, Albany refused 9 June 1586. See **278j**, **280f**.
[3] See **229** note 3.

234. [f.134] To James Harman yeoman of the chamber for mending the lighthorn serving in the Guildhall porch and for bread, ale, beer, wine, strawing, herbs, flowers, perfumes, rushes, small coals, making clean the Guildhall, horse hire, candles, carriage of beer barrels and other measures to and from the Guildhall, and for 16½ yards of mats, carriage of foot cloths, for a bushel to be hanged at Leadenhall, carrying of cushions, watching the city's tent [*sic*], for 18 hassocks and a mat for the house of office, being all due for one year ended at Michaelmas last past as by 4 bills called quarter bills appears £11.18s.; to him for horse hire for the king of Portugal[1] riding on hunting, for Mr Recorder, divers aldermen and other officers to and from the court and other places due for one quarter of a year ended at Michaelmas last past £4.16s.4d.; 8 April for cleansing and carrying away 20 loads of soil out of the lanes passing to St Mary Spital and the Artillery Yard in the Easter holy days 16s.8d.; to James Harman for making clean the house at St Mary Spital and for brooms, rushes, strawing, herbs, carrying of cushions, labourer's wages, a stand of ale, coals and faggots 59s.2d.; summa £20.10s.2d.

[1] Don Antonio, pretender to the Portuguese throne.

235. [f.134v] 1 April by warrant from my lord mayor to Richard Buckley, John Addys, William Harrison and Thomas Davys to every of them 6s.8d. for taking of flesh in Lent 26s.8d.; to John Grove servant to Mr Town Clerk for the charges in putting the certificates into the chancery for the eating of flesh in Lent 2s.; 21 April to Mr Kyrton common serjeant for the charges of a *procedendo* and allowing the same in a suit against Mark Norton for the portion of the orphans of Peter Burcher grocer deceased 12s.; . . . [to Robert Smithe for his pains?][1] and for money by him laid out in the suit prosecuted in the chancery by Thomas Cartwright touching the orphans of Simon Smithe grocer deceased 22s.8d.; to him the same day for money laid out in a suit prosecuted against Thomas Damport and his wife for the orphanage of the orphan of Thomas Hartopp goldsmith deceased 4s.; by order of court to Richard May of Horsemonden, Kent, clothier for so much received 19 October last past for the city's part of one broad cloth being found by a jury to be foreign bought and sold and therefore forfeit 52s.11d.; summa [£6.0s.]3d.[1]

[1] Ms mutilated.

236. [f.135] By the bequest of Mr Taylor late alderman deceased for the discharge of such persons in the ward of Cordwainer Street as are assessed (sessed) at 12d. and under for every fifteenth due to the queen and is now for the second fifteenth granted in the 27th year of her reign, viz. 23 in the parish of St Mary le Bow 20s.2d., 3 in the parish of All Hallows [Bread Street][1] 2s.8d., 17 in the parish of St John [the Baptist] in Walbrook 15s.8d., 7 in the parish of St Benet Sherehog 7s., 14 in [Holy] Trinity parish in Knightrider Street 13s.10d., 28 in the parish of St Mary Aldermary 28s., 26 in the parish of St Antholin 26s., 28 in the parish of St Thomas the Apostle 24s.8d., summa £6.18s.0d. [cf.**97**]

[1] This parish extended from Bread St. into Cordwainer Ward.

237. [f.135v] 14 May for a dinner for Mr Chamberlain, Mr Dumer and other officers and workmen at the measuring out of the ground where the new pipes serving the conduit in Aldermanbury were laid 13s.8d.; for a dinner the 16 May for the auditors of the third account of this accountant[1] 44s.1½d.; 19 May to Ralph (Raphe) Sheperde for his charges in a suit prosecuted against him in the king's bench by John Garfield for eggs seized as forfeit being forestalled by Garfield before they were brought to the market 14s.8d.; 10 June to him which he paid to Garfield by order of the court of king's bench 13s.4d., and for money by him laid out in the suit 17s.4d.; 22 May to Mr Ashebold[2] for preaching at the new churchyard[3] on Whitsunday 13s.4d.; 1 June by order of Mr Webb and Mr Buckell aldermen, Mr Nicholas Spencer and Mr Humfrey Huntley, committees appointed by order of court [22 Feb. 1586, Rep.21, f.267] for reformation of the bushel for measuring of salt upon the water, viz. to the cooper, the smith and the turner for the several stuff and workmanship belonging to the same bushel £5.10s.;[4] summa £11.6s.5½d.

[1] The account for the previous year 1584–85.
[2] See **16d**.
[3] See **97** note 4.
[4] The committee appointed on 22 Feb. 1586 subsequently reported on the inaccuracy of the measures used by the saltmeters at the waterside and recommended that all bushels of salt called watermeasures should contain 5 pecks or 10 gallons. New bushels were ordered (Rep.21, ff.273b–274, 278).

238. [f.136] 24 June by order of court [21 June 1586, Rep.21, f.310] to John Darcye a poor man (being recommended to the city by the queen) as of the free gift of this city £5; 25 June by order of court [23 June 1586, Rep.21, f.310] to Robert Sheperd fisherman (by the hands of Mr Waterbailiff) for a sturgeon fish by him taken in the Thames and presented to the queen 13s.4d.; for the exchange of light, broken and soldered gold and silver received for redeeming of captives, for one fifteenth and mustering of soldiers for the space of 5 years last past, 10s.7d.; to John Grove for charges in putting the certificates of the rate of servants' wages into the chancery 2s.; to Richard Grewe the common hunt's man for killing 1,055 dogs at 1½d. the piece £6.11s.10½d.; 30 July to James Harman for money laid out for the watch on Midsummer Eve at night viz. to 24 cresset bearers and 12 bag bearers at 8d. the piece 24s., for 3 dozen of straw hats at 8d. the piece 24s., for 36 badges with the city's arms 3s., for 3 dozen of staff torches for my lord mayor and Mr Sheriffs 36s., for 100 of cresset lights and exchange of 100 of old cresset lights with other necessaries 21s.3d., summa £5.8s.3d. [cf.**101**]; summa totalis £18.6s.0½d.

239. [f.136v] 26 Aug. to John Grafton and William Aldersey serjeants at mace for their pains taken as sticklers at the wrestling at Bartholomew (Barthewe') day 6s.8d. and to the poor there by commandment of my lord mayor 2s.2d.; 8 September by commandment of my lord mayor to the clerks of St Magnus' parish for making ready the church against his lordship's coming thither on Our Lady day being the fair in Southwark 2s.6d., and by like commandment to the prisoners in the Marshalsea, King's Bench, White Lion[1] and Compter in Southwark[2] the same time 6s.6d., and to the poor there 18d., and to the waits there in reward 2s.6d.; 13 Sept. to a broker for procuring £100 to be taken up at usance of Mr John Barker for the city's use 5s. [cf.**157d**]; summa £1.6s.10d.

[1] The county gaol for Surrey.
[2] The city's prison in Southwark, often known as the Borough compter.

240. To Mr Dumer, Henry Woodwall, John Shawe, Richard Foster, Edward Lyle, James Lorde and Leonard Largen to every of them 6s.8d. for setting out and measuring the ground at Bartholomew Fair 46s.8d., and to Richard Foster, Edmund Lyle and James Lord for weighing of cheese [f.137] at the cheese beam 6s., and for meat and drink for the said officers attending there all the fair time with a dinner at the Fair Eve for Mr Chamberlain and other officers £6.13s.2d., and to a poor man for breaking up the g[round . . . 6d.],[1] for writing 2 copies of the particular [profits][1] 2s.6d., and spent by John Shawe in the leather fair 24s.4d., summa £10.13s.2d.

[1] Ms mutilated (cf.**111**)

241. To Sir Wolstan Dixie knight lord mayor in respect of wax, [herrings and][1] sturgeon wont to be paid by the Easterlings inhabiting the Steelyard £5.6s.8d., and to Mr Anthony Ratclyffe and Mr Henry Prannell sheriffs for like wax, herrings and sturgeon wont also to be paid by the Easterlings £5.6s.8d., and to the sheriffs for a petty toll wont also to be paid by the Easterlings 40s., being all due for one year ended at Michaelmas last past, summa £12.13s.4d. [cf.**109**]

[1] Ms mutilated.

242. 14 Sept. by order of court [8 Sept. 1586, Rep.21, f.331] to John Singwell ironmonger of the free gift of the court £3.6s.8d.; to Mr Chamberlain for his horse hire due for one [f.137v] year ended at

Michaelmas 1586 40s., for his boat hire due for the like time 30s., and to Mr William Dumer comptroller of the chamber for his horse hire for like time 40s.; by order of my lord mayor to William Ravenscrofte and Richard Dodd to either of them 20s. for seeing the bills fixed upon houses infected with the plague and not to be removed and is due for one year ended at Michaelmas 1586 40s.; to John Shawe clerk of the chamber[1] for drawing of this account 13s.4d., and for engrossing the same account 53s.4d. and for engrossing the book of fines 3s.4d.; summa £14.6s.8d.

[1] 'John Shawe clerk of the chamber' written over 'this accountant's clerk', struck through.

243. To Sir Wolstan Dixie knight lord mayor for the measuring of linen cloth due for one year ended at Michaelmas 1586, £50.0s.0d. [cf.**7n**]

244. Summa totalis of the Foreign Charge is £2,119.8s.11d.

245. [f.138 blank, f.138v] *Margin* New Year's Gifts
a.To Sir Thomas Bromley knight, lord high chancellor, £20 and to the keeper of his chamber door and to his porter 4s., summa £20.4s.0d. To Sir William Cycyll lord high treasurer £20.0s.0d. To Mr John Popham attorney general £10.0s.0d. For the exchange of white money into gold for the said gifts 4s.2d. and for 3 purses for the same 18d., summa 5s.8d.
b. 17 Nov. 1585 to Sir Wolstan Dixie lord mayor in recompense of 4 tuns of wine [as **115b**], £40.0s.0d.
c. Summa totalis £90.9s.8d.

246. [f.139] *Margin* Winter Liveries[1]
a. To John Alington draper for 31 yards of London russet at 8s.8d. the yard £13.8s.8d., 32 yards at 10s.6d. the yard £16.16s., 31 yards at 11s.6d. the yard £17.16s.6d., 28 yards at 12s. the yard £16.16s., 27½ yards at 13s. the yard £17.17s.6d., 33 yards of fine London russet at 13s.8d. the yard £22.11s., 32¼ yards at 15s. the yard £24.3s.9d., 32½ yards at 15s.8d. the yard £25.9s.2d., 20 yards at 15s.4d. the yard £15.6s.8d., and for 12 yards of black cotton at 8d. the yard 8s.; summa £170.13s.3d.

[1] The first entry under this heading 'To John Alington draper for 20 yards of fine London russet at 15s.4d. the yard £15.6s.8d.' is deleted with a marginal annotation 'quia po. .' [mutilated].

b. To Stephen Mabb' draper for 6¼ yards of pheasant colour for John Luck's gown and coat[1] at 10s. the yard £3.2s.6d. and for 7½ yards of broad green baize to line the same at 2s.2d. the yard 16s.3d.; summa £3.18s.9d.

[1] See **26g** for other references to John Luck's liveries.

c. Summa for all the cloth for winter liveries £174.12s.0d.

247. *Margin* Money paid instead of cloth for winter liveries
To Mr Chamberlain 53s.4d., Mr Common Serjeant 53s.4d., Mr Dumer 53s.4d., Mr Kytchyn 40s., Mr Dalton 40s., Mr Owen 40s., Mr Fuller 40s.,

Mr Common Cryer 53s.4d., [f.139v] Mr Waterbailiff 53s.4d., Mr Common Hunt 53s.4d., the renter of Mr Raynewell 31s., the steward of Finsbury 24s., the renter of Finsbury 24s., the bailiff of Finsbury 24s., this accountant's clerk 30s., the keeper of the star chamber door 32s., Robert Maskall carpenter 28s., William Browne foreign taker 28s., Stephen Cowley mealweigher 28s.

Summa of the money paid for cloth for winter liveries £36.9s.0d.

248. *Margin* [Paid] for Summer Liveries

a.To John Alington draper for 17 yards of broad sad new colour at 7s.4d. the yard £6.4s.8d., 32 yards at 7s.6d. the yard £12, $17\frac{3}{4}$ yards at 8s. £7.2s., $18\frac{1}{4}$ yards at 8s.6d. the yard £7.15s.$1\frac{1}{2}$d., $31\frac{3}{4}$ yards at 8s.6d. £13.9s.$10\frac{1}{2}$d., $31\frac{1}{2}$ yards of fine broad sad new colour at 10s.8d. the yard £16.16s., $11\frac{1}{4}$ yards of the same at 9s. the yard £5.1s.3d., and for 12 yards of black cotton at 8d. the yard 8s., summa £68.16s.11d.

b. To Stephen Mabb' draper for 2 yards of broad cloth of French colour tawny for John Luck's coat at 11s. the yard 22s. and for $2\frac{1}{4}$ of broad baize to line the same at 2s.2d. the yard 4s.10d.; summa 26s.10d.

c. Summa totalis of the money paid for cloth for summer liveries £70.3s.9d.

249. [f.140] *Margin* Money paid instead of cloth for summer liveries

To Mr Chamberlain 53s.4d., Mr Common Serjeant 53s.4d., Mr Dumer 53s.4d., Mr Common Cryer 53s.4d., Mr Waterbailiff 53s.4d., Mr Common Hunt 53s.4d., the renter general 32s., the renter of Mr Raynewell 31s., Edward Lyle 32s., John Shawe 32s., James Harman 32s., Henry Woodwall 32s., the accountant's clerk 30s., Mr Common Serjeant's clerk 26s.8d., Robert Maskall carpenter 28s., David Mannynge 28s.

Summa totalis £31.3s.8d.

250. Summa for all the cloth and money paid for winter and summer liveries £312.8s.5d.

whereof to be deducted for the account of Mr Carpenter £5.16s.$8\frac{1}{2}$d., for the account of Mr Raynewell £3.2s., for the account of Finsbury £3.12s., summa £12.10s.$8\frac{1}{2}$d.

And so to be allowed to the general account £299.17s.$8\frac{1}{2}$d.

251. [f.140v] *Margin* Allowances

First this accountant asks allowance of £10 to him given by act of court and of £10 more given at the audit, of 20s. paid to the comptroller and clerk of the chamber for casting and examining of this account, of £6.13s.4d. paid to the comptroller of the chamber for his reward at the audit, and of 17s. for purses and counters for the examination and casting of this account; of £200 delivered by commandment of my lord mayor and court of aldermen to Mr John Lacye clothworker 4 March 1586 which he paid into the chamber on 1 March [cf.**158f**] in the name of a fine for that he refused to be sheriff and for which sum he stands bound in 3 several obligations to repay the same into the chamber at the 3 next several feasts of Michaelmas following by even portions; of £4 paid to John Benson for keeping and engrossing the account of orphanage for 2 years ended at Michaelmas 1586; and of £19.17s.4d. being parcel of a more sum upon him charged in this account for one fifteenth granted by act [f.141] of common council [cf.**157b**] for that the same was not received (unreceived) due by the several wards following, viz. of Castle Baynard 17s., Bread Street 3s.4d., Broad Street 40s., Candlewick Street 13s.8d., Coleman Street 3s.11d., Cordwainer Street £4.7s.10d., Cheap 28s.4d., Cripplegate 8s.4d., Dowgate 5s., Farringdon Within 49s.3d., Farringdon Without 22s.8d., Langbourn 13s.4d., Portsoken 30s., Queenhithe 52s.6d., Tower 16s., and Walbrook 6s.2d.; summa £252.7s.[8d.]

252. *Margin* Orphanage [Payments]
Paid to the use of divers orphans from Michaelmas 1585 unto Michaelmas 1586, as particularly appears by an account thereof kept by John Benson by sundry books the one called the ledger, folio 47, and the other called the journal, folio 42, as by the repertory kept in the inner chamber of the Guildhall and acquittances made by the receivers thereof, £2,048.4s.7d.

253. [f.141v] *Margin* Orphans their Finding
More paid within the time of this account to sundry persons for finding divers orphans whose portions remain in the chamber, as appears as well by the said journal kept by John Benson as also by sundry acquittances made by the persons receiving the same, £301.5s.4d.

254. Summa totalis of the discharge £8,273.5s.4d.
And so it is found that the commonalty owes unto this accountant upon the general account £1,035.1s.3¾d.
And this accountant owes unto the commonalty upon this account 16 peppercorns.

255. [f.142] The account of the chamberlain for the lands and tenements late of Sir John Philpott knight for the year aforesaid
[Receipts]
a. Arrearages by this accountant due upon the foot of the last account, £252.5s.2d.
b. As **125b**, £72.3s.4d.
c. Of Robert Medley goldsmith in part of £90 being the rest of £120 for a fine of his house and shop in West Cheap in the parish of St Vedast late in the tenure of John Lonyson goldsmith deceased and also a back room behind the same tenement late in the tenure of Marston[1] deceased, £30.0s.0d. [cf.**125d**]

[1] 'John' struck through, 'Marston' inserted in a different hand. The previous account has 'John Marsham'.

d. Of John Wilson goldsmith in part of £60 being parcel and rest of £80 for a fine of his shop in West Cheap in the parish of St Vedast late demised with other things to John Lonison goldsmith deceased, £20 [cf.**125e**]
e. Summa totalis of the charge £374.8s.6d.

256. [f.142v] The Discharge [Payments]
a. As **126a** except that the sum is paid for the year ended Michaelmas 1586, 6s.6d.
b. As **126b**, £4.3s.4d.
c. As **126c**, £19.15s.5d.
d. To masons, carpenters, plumbers, bricklayers, plasterers and labourers for their several days wages working and labouring in and upon the tenements as by one bill appears, 2s.2d. [cf. **176m**]
e. For stone, timber, boards, quarters, lathes, lead, solder, gravel, loam, sand, cleansing of privies and other necessaries spent and bestowed upon the tenements as by the weeks' bills appears, £8.11s.10½d. [cf.**202**]
f. Summa totalis £32.19s.3½d.

257. And so due to the city upon this account £341.9s.2½d.

258. [f.143] The account of the chamberlain for the lands and tenements of Mr John Carpenter sometime common clerk of this city for the year aforesaid.

[Receipts]
a. Arrearages by this accountant due upon the foot of the last account, £14.13s.10½d.
b. As **128b**, £34.0s.0d.
c. Summa totalis of all [the charge] £48.13s.10½d.

259. The Discharge [Payments]
a. As **129a** except that the sums are paid for the year ended Michaelmas 1586, 8s.0d.
b. [f.143v] As **129b**, 13s.4d.
c. As **129c**, £1.3s.4d.
d. As **129d**, £4.0s.0d.
e. As **129e**, £9.2s.0d.
f. For 5¾ yards of London russet for the coats of the 4 children against Christmas 1585 at 10s.6d. the yard £3.0s.4½d., 5½ yards of new colour for the coats of the children against Whitsuntide 1586 at 7s.4d. the yard 40s.4d., for 24 yards of black cotton for the lining of the 8 coats at 8d. the yard 16s., and to James Harman yeoman of the chamber which he laid out for buttons and for making of the 8 coats 10s.4d.; summa £6.7s.0½d.
g. [f.144] For wages of workmen and labourers for reparations done upon the tenements of Mr Carpenter as by 3 bills appears, £1.14s.10d. [cf.**176m**]
h. For timber, solder, lead, paving stone, brick, lime, sand, gravel, loam, cleansing of privies and other necessaries spent in repairing the tenements this year as by 2 bills appears, 10s.0d. [cf.**202**]
i. Summa totalis of the discharge £23.18s.6½d.

260. And so due to the city upon this account £24.15s.4d.

261. The account of the chamberlain for the lands and tenements sometime of Sir John Raynewell knight [*sic*] sometime lord mayor for the year aforesaid.

[Receipts]

a. Arrearages by this accountant due upon the foot of the last account, £205.17s.8d.
b. As **131b**, £125.3s.4d.
c. Summa totalis of the charge £331.1s.0d.

262. [f.144v] The Discharge [Payments]
a. To Nicholas Kennam, sub-dean of St Paul's, to the use of the petty canons of St Pauls for the chantry of Gilbert Folyate, £1.0s.0d. [cf.**132a**]
b. As **132b** except that the sum is paid for the year ended at Michaelmas 1586, £1.0s.0d.
c. As **132d**, £9.15s.4d.
d. As **132e**, £2.0s.0d.
e. As **132f** except that the sum is paid for one year ended at Michaelmas 1586, 10s.0d.
f. To Mr Anthony Radclyffe and Mr Henry Pranell sheriffs for a discharge of a toll of London Bridge due for one year ended at Michaelmas 1586, £8.0s.0d. [cf.**132g**]
g. [f.145] As **132h** except that the sum is paid for the year ended at Michaelmas 1586, £10.0s.0d.
h. To Benedict Barnam draper, Percival Hassall skinner and Simon Bourman haberdasher, high collectors for the second fifteenth granted to the queen in the 27th year of her reign to be paid within the city of London, by the bequest of Sir [*sic*] John Raynewell, viz. for the ward of Aldgate £5, Billingsgate £31.10s., and Dowgate £28, being all for the discharge of all the inhabitants within the said wards, £64.10s.0d. [cf.**132 i**]
i. Summa of the discharge £96.15s.4d.
263. And so rest due to the city £234.5s.8d.

264. [f.145v] The account of the chamberlain for the diet of masterless men taken up and sent into the Low Countries for her majesty's service.

[Receipts]

7 Oct. received of Mr Richard Huddilstone treasurer of the queen's wars in the Low Countries for the diet of such masterless men as late were and now are taken up within the city of London, county of Middlesex and other places for her majesty's service in the Low Countries, £150.

265. The Discharge [Payments]
7 Oct. to Mr Roger Warfield treasurer of Bridewell for the diet of such masterless and vagrant persons as late were and now are taken up for her majesty's service as is aforesaid as pioneers soldiers £48; 20 Oct. by warrant from my lord mayor to Henry Barker gentleman for a new supply of the new victualling of 120 masterless men shipped to be sent to Flushing for pioneers £12; 26 Oct. by warrant from my lord mayor to Mr Warfield for the diet and charge of the said masterless men £34.15s.1d.; [f.146] by like warrant to Simon Padyam underbailiff of Southwark towards his loss

and hindrance sustained by lodging certain of the said masterless men 40s., and by like warrant to William Lathes under waterbailiff which he laid out about the said masterless men 3s.4d.; 24 Dec. by commandment of my lord mayor to Thomas Sympson for the diet of 96 masterless men taken up and sent to Leadenhall in November last for her majesty's service in the Low Countries £5.1s.9d.; by like commandment to Robert Lyddus for the diet of the said masterless men 59s.6d. and for candle and other necessaries 12s.6d., summa £3.12s.; 1 March by order of court [1 March 1586, Rep.21, f.269b] to Andrew Kyrwyn freemason for his charges in conveying 7 Spaniards to Dunkirk by the council's order out of such money as remains to be employed for press (prest) and diet of masterless men £9.2s.4d.; summa £114.14s.6d.

266. And so due to the city upon this account £35.5s.6d.

267. [f.146v] The account of the chamberlain for horse hire for the Estates of the Low Countries

[Receipts]

2 Oct. received of Henry Ravenscrofte, one of the yeomen of the waterside, which he received of Sir Thomas Hennage knight, treasurer of her majesty's chamber, for the hire of 643 horses taken up by William Goffe, ordinary post for London, to serve the Estates of the Low Countries at their being in London, as by 2 warrants from her majesty's council appears £60, whereof deducted for the charges of the same paid to Sir Thomas Hennage, the clerk of the council and others £4.2s.6d., so rest due to be charged £55.17s.6d.

268. The Discharge [Payments]

To divers innholders, hackneymen and others for the hire of 462 horse to serve the Estates of the Low Countries to and from the court at 16d. for every horse by the day, viz. to Maurice (Morrys) Johnes for 41 horse 54s.8d., widow Roffe for 4 horse 5s.4d., William Hill of Hackney for 4 horse 5s.4d., Edward Porter for 50 horse £3.6s.8d., Lawrence Gorye for 2 horse 2s.8d., Henry Warleye for 22 horse 29s.4d., James Leather for 12 horse 16s., Richard Wyttrans for 66 horse £4.8s., Richard Horne for 12 horse 16s., Davy Wylson 10 horse 13s.4d., Griffith Bennett for 4 horse 5s.4d., Peter Burcheley for [f.147] 26 horse 34s.8d., Edward Mackarys for 15 horse 20s., John Methingham for 46 horse £3.1s.4d., John Nycolls for 3 horse 4s., Robert Wyllett for 7 horse 9s.4d., John Nicholson alias Whiteheade for 4 horse 5s.4d., Thomas Steward for 4 horse 5s.4d., John Wickins for 6 horse 8s., Richard Marlton for 28 horse 37s.4d., Arthur Norton for 6 horse 8s., John Johnson for 3 horse 4s., James Fells for 6 horse 8s., Matthew Chamberlen for 3 horse 4s., Gregory Pattricke for 7 horse 9s.4d., Susan Suckley for 6 horse 8s., Richard Gyll for 3 horse 4s., Andrew Smithe for 7 horse 9s.4d., Roger Banckes for 2 horse 2s.8d., William Whaffourthe for 8 horse 10s.8d., John Chaplyn for 3 horse 4s., Henry Clark for 2 horse 2s.8d., Henry Elkes minister for 4 horse 5s.4d., Richard Flettcher for 2 horse 2s.8d., Henry Lodge for one horse 16d., John Hall for 2 horse 2s.8d., Robert Griffyn for 6 horse 8s., William

Ravenscrofte for 9 horse 12s., Robert Cowper for 2 horse 2s.8d., Roger Dekyn for 2 horse 2s.8d., Robert Wheateley for 6 horse 8s., Robert Androwes 3 horse 4s. and Joan (Johan) Jackson widow for 3 horse 4s.; to William Goffe ordinary post for London in part of a more sum by him demanded for horse meat, horse hire and guides for the said Estates as by his bill appears which bill [f.147v] has since been found untrue £4; to Philip Bennett servant to Sir Francis Walsingham for his pains in procuring the council's hands to a warrant for money to be paid for the said horse hire 40s.; summa £36.16s.0d.

269. And so due to the city upon this account £19.1s.6d.

270. And so it is found by the right honourable Sir George Barne knight lord mayor,[1] Sir Wolstan Dixie knight late lord mayor, Sir Rowland [Hayward],[2] Sir Lionel Ducket,[3] Sir Thomas Ramsey knights, Thomas Starky and George Bonde aldermen, John Harbye skinner, Thomas Ware fishmonger, Thomas Wilford merchant taylor and William Store[4] haberdasher, auditors and surveyors of this account, that the commonalty owes unto this accountant upon the general account, £1,035.1s.3¾d. [cf.**254**]
And that this accountant owes upon the account of Sir John Philpott, £341.9s.2½d. [cf.**257**]
Also he owes upon the account of Mr John Carpenter, £24.15s.4d. [cf.**260**]
Also he owes upon the account of Sir [*sic*] John Raynewell, £234.5s.8d. [cf.**263**]
Also he owes upon the account of Finsbury £129.17s.2d. and 4 red roses.[5]
Also he owes upon the account for the diet for masterless men, £35.5s.6d. [cf.**266**]
Also he owes upon the account of horse hire for the Estates of the Low Countries £19.1s.6d. [cf.**269**]
Also he owes unto the commonalty upon the general account 16 peppercorns. [cf.**254**]
And so it is found by the auditors that the commonalty owes unto this accountant as before is declared, £250.6s.11¼d.
And it is also found that this accountant owes unto the commonalty upon the general account, 16 peppercorns and 4 red roses.

[1] 1586–87.
[2] Surname omitted in Ms.
[3] Not listed among the auditors in **281**.
[4] *Recte* 'Stone' as in **281**. Foster, p. 172, lists William Stone haberdasher as a common councilman 1586–88.
[5] For the Finsbury account, see p. xxvii.

271. *At the foot of the page* See after the debts at this letter A the foot general of all these accounts which is in the engrossed book of this year, and is to be observed the next year and so forward.

[f.148] More owing to the City

272.a. As **136a**, £3.6s.8d.

b. As **136b**, £10.0s.0d.
c. As **136c**,[1] [£100.0s.0d.]

[1] The entry here ends: 'whereof he did assure to the city's use one lease of a messuage near Fleet Bridge which lease is redelivered unto him'.

d. As **136d**, £50.0s.0d.
e. As **136e**, £74.8s.5d.

273.a. [f.148v] As **137a**, £24.0s.0d.
b. As **137b**, £2.0s.0d.
c. As **137c**, £25.0s.0d.
d. As **137d**, £400.0s.0d.
e. As **137e**, £33.6s.8d.
f. As **137f**,[1] £32.0s.0d.

[1] Save that William Dent is here described as 'butcher'.

g. As **137g**, £27.0s.0d.[1]

[1] Amount of the debt reduced since the previous year, see **158s.** This item is entered on f.149 but the letter A in the margin against it and B against the next item indicate that it should be taken here.

274.a. As **138a**, £1,463.0s.10¾d. and 28 peppercorns.
b. As **138b**, £10.0s.0d.
c. [f.149] As **138c**, £20.0s.0d.[1]

[1] The next entry is calendared above, see **273g**.

d. As **138d**, £1.10s.0d.
e. As **138e**, £25.0s.0d.
f. As **138f**, £100.0s.0d.
g. [f.149v] As **138g**,[1] £7.10s.0d.

[1] Save that Nicholas Willy is described as 'now deceased'.

275.a. As **139a**, £200.0s.0d.
b. As **139b**, £66.13s.4d.
c. As **139c**, £120.0s.0d.[1]

[1] Amount of the debt reduced since the previous year, see **158a**.

d. As **139d**, £50.0s.0d.
e. As **139e**, [f.150] £291.6s.8d.[1]

[1] The amount of the debt had been left blank in 1584–85.

f. As **139f**, £114.0s.0d.[1]

[1] The period of the debt is now 9 years. The total had been left blank in 1584–85.

276.a. As **140b**, £40.0s.0d.[1]

[1] Amount of the debt reduced since the previous year, see **158n**.

b. As **140c**,[1] £10.0s.0d.

[1] Save that the debt is here given as in respect of the year ending Michaelmas 1582, not 1583.

c. As **140e**,[1] £5.0s.0d.

[1] With the addition that the garden is 'against the Minories without Aldgate'.

d. As **140g**, £4.0s.0d.
e. As **140j**, £5.0s.0d.[1]

[1] In 1584–85 the amount of the debt, the figures of which have been altered, is given as £2.8s.0d.

f. As **140 l**, £5.0s.0d.
g. As **140m**, £20.0s.0d.
h. [f.150v] As **140n**, £10.0s.0d.
i. As **140p**, £40.0s.0d.[1]

[1] Amount of the debt reduced since the previous year, see **158h**.

j. As **140q**, £37.0s.0d.[1]

[1] Amount of the debt reduced since the previous year, see **158p**.

277.a. As **141b**, £300.0s.0d.
b. As **141g**, £200.0s.0d.
c. As **141h**, £200.0s.0d.
d. As **141i**, £200.0s.0d.[1]

[1] This sum had been paid by the debtor, John Lacy, into the chamber on 1 March 1586 and repaid to him on 4 March, see **158f** and **251**.

e. As **141k**, £300.0s.0d.[1]

[1] Amount of the debt reduced since the previous year, see **158 l**.

f. As **141 l**, £200.0s.0d.
g. As **141m**, £88.17s.10d.[1]

[1] Amount of the debt reduced since the previous year, see **158e**.

278.a. As **142a**, £33.6s.8d.[1]

[1] Amount of the debt reduced since the previous year, see **158b**.

b. [f.151] As **142b**,[1] £50.0s.0d.[2]

[1] With the addition that Hytchcocke's house is 'at Billingsgate'.
[2] Amount of the debt reduced since the previous year, see **158r**.

c. As **142c**, £60.0s.0d.[1]

[1] Amount of the debt reduced since the previous year, see **255c**.

d. As **142d**, £40.0s.0d.[1]

[1] Amount of the debt reduced since the previous year, see **255d**.

e. John Beste cutler for the rest of £20 for the lease of a house in the Old Bailey, £10.0s.0d. [see **156b**]
f. The parson and churchwardens of St George in Southwark for the arrearages of rent due for the tenements 'Red Crosse' in Southwark for 4 years ended at Michaelmas 1586, £4.0s.0d.
g. Anthony Percey haberdasher and William Dent butcher for the farm of certain sheds at Broken Wharf and customs of rushes there and other places due for half a year ended at Midsummer 1586, £7.0s.0d.[1]

[1] A lease of the custom of rushes of £14 p.a. had been granted to Percey and Dent 3 Nov. 1584 (Rep.21, f.108. And see **153c**).

h. As **142e**.
i. Owing by divers wards for the fifteenth granted towards the purchasing of the queen's letters patent for the office of garbling throughout England (London only excepted) viz. [sums for individual wards as listed in **251**], £19.17s.4d.
j. [f.151v] Mr William Albany merchant taylor for his fine for that he refused to be sheriff [9 June 1586, Rep.21, f.305] £200.0s.0d.

279. Plate and jewels remaining in the hands of the now chamberlain
As **143** with this addition in a different hand:
[f.152v] Two dozen of silver trenchers parcel gilt with the arms of the city engraven, given by the bequest of the Lady Nycholas deceased, late wife of Sir Ambrose Nycholas late knight and alderman deceased,[1] weighing 194½ oz.

[1] Lord mayor 1575–76.

280. Debts owing by the City
a. There remains for the redeeming of captives by several collections as by the last account and this account appears, £103.11s.1¼d.[1]

[1] The money held at the close of the previous account was £193.18s.3¼d. (**144a**) and expenditure shown in this account totals £162.0s.11d. (**208**). This leaves a balance of only £31.17s.4¼d. but although neither sum is charged in the general account this year the chamberlain received £6.8s.10d., the surplus of a collection the greater part of which was paid direct to certain former captives (Rep.21, f.237), and £65.4s.10d. from the collections at the Easter sermons in 1586 (Rep.21, f.294).

b. As **144b**, £600.0s.0d.
c. To divers orphans as appears in the book called the journal kept by John Benson, £6,092.13s.8½d.
d. [f.153] As **144d**, 100 marks.
e. To Mr John Barker of Ipswich, Suffolk, esquire, of him received in prest, £102.10s. [see **157d**, **239**]
f. To Mr Robert Howse one of the sheriffs in consideration that he took upon him the office of shrievalty [14 June 1586, Rep.21, f.306] in the place of Mr William Albany merchant taylor who lately refused the same, [see **278j**], £100.0s.0d. [f.153v blank]

281. [f.154] Summa totalis of the charge of the account general and of the several charges of the accounts particular before mentioned in this account and also of the charge of the account of Finsbury, £8,405.0s.5¼d. and 16 peppercorns and 4 red roses.

Summa totalis of the several discharges of all the same several accounts, £8,655.7s.4½d.

And so it is found by the right honourable George Barne lord mayor, Sir Wolstan Dixie knight late lord mayor, Sir Rowland Hayward, Sir Thomas Ramsy knights, Thomas Starkey and George Bonde aldermen, John Harby skinner, Thomas Ware fishmonger, Thomas Wilford merchant taylor and William Stone haberdasher, auditors and surveyors of this account, that the commonalty owes unto this accountant upon the several accounts, £250.6s.11¼d. and 16 peppercorns and 4 red roses.[1]

[1] Cf. **270** in which the list of auditors includes also Sir Lionel Ducket and the peppercorns and roses are shown, correctly, as being due from the chamberlain to the commonalty.

APPENDICES

(Extracts from Chamber Accounts 1)

282. As explained in the Introduction Chamber Accounts 1 consists chiefly of draft and fragmentary accounts, bound in considerable confusion. An attempt has been made to date the material and a tentative guide to the volume, by date, is available in CLRO. Nevertheless, it must be emphasised that, without further research into the internal evidence, a degree of uncertainty attaches to some of the attributions of date between 1562 and 1578, and consequently to a few of the selected extracts and references in these appendices, although it is unlikely that any errors in dating will exceed a year or two.

All folio references are to the sequence of numbers at the foot of the leaves of the manuscript.

A.

ACCOUNT OF THE CHAMBERLAIN'S CLERK 1535–36

283. This account for the financial year Michaelmas 27 Henry VIII–Michaelmas 28 Henry VIII (1535–36) is the earliest in Chamber Accounts 1 and contains a number of entries in respect of chantries and obits and the payment of quitrents to monastic houses which do not, of course, appear in the post-Reformation accounts. It is not the city's cash account but a subsidiary account, kept quarterly by Richard Maunsell, 'Mr Chamberlain's clerk and servant',[1] which would have been one of several preliminary accounts used in compiling the chamberlain's account for that year. It contains a record of certain payments, made in respect not only of the general account but also of the Philipot, Carpenter and Reynwell estates,[2] and of the monies received by Richard Maunsell to balance his disbursements. Each quarter of the account contained 3 sections. First, a brief, untotalled, list of sums received on the vigil of the quarter day, most of which were rent farms. Second, the very much longer list of payments, which were almost exclusively of a kind which would recur from year to year, such as fees paid to officers and artificers as well as quitrents, annuities, charitable alms and obits;[3] many were paid quarterly, some half yearly and a few annually. The third section showed the amounts received by Maunsell by way of the receipts of the rent farms listed in the first section, plus money received directly from the chamberlain, plus also, if necessary, an allowance upon his indenture as rent gatherer of the city lands, to make up the total which he is recorded in the second section as having disbursed. The account was examined and annotated by the chamberlain, George Medley, who marked a small number of items 'pd per me' and one, the rent for the prebendal manor of Finsbury, as paid by William Vere, the rent gatherer of the manor, and also supplied some of the sectional totals. It appears to be Medley's hand which supplied the figures to be found in the bottom corner of most of the pages, occasionally preceded by an abbreviation which would seem to stand for *probatur* [agreed or examined]; these figures give a total for the page, sometimes distinguishing between the amount paid by the chamberlain and Vere and that paid by Maunsell. The total expenditure for the year, whether disbursed by

Maunsell, the chamberlain or Vere, viz. £557.16s.1d., is given at the end of the account.

[1] So described 17 June 1535 (Rep.9, f.112). The description of him a few weeks later (*ibid.* f.115) as 'clerk of the chamber' can mean no more than a clerk in the chamber. William Brown held the senior office of 'the clerk of the chamber' at this time and received an annual fee out of the chamber. Maunsell's remuneration and tenure of office as clerk and also as rent gatherer of the city lands, which duties he had exercised for the past 7 years, were at the pleasure of the chamberlain (*ibid.*, f.115).

[2] The source is not usually given in the text but, where a payment has been identified as issuing out of one of the charitable estates, this is indicated in a note.

[3] In the 1560s and 1580s, and very possibly at this date also, most of such payments would be entered in the chamberlain's account in the sections of the general account headed 'Salaries of Priests', 'Rents and Quitrents', 'Inward Fees' and 'Outward Fees', and in the accounts of the charitable estates. None of the payments in Maunsell's account is of a kind to be found in 'Foreign Charge'.

284. The account is calendared in its reconstructed order and not in the sequence of the folios as at present bound. The entries, which in the manuscript are generally single line entries, are grouped in paragraphs. Where there is no natural division the entries on one page have been placed in one paragraph since most pages have the sum of the entries at the foot. Annotations by George Medley, the chamberlain, are given within angle brackets ⟨ ⟩. Nearly all the entries in the original are marked in the left margin with a cross, not reproduced in the calendar, which apparently indicated actual payment or receipt; /// represents a symbol used occasionally in the original when the amount of the fee was not entered; *di' ai'* is rendered as 'half a year'. Any explanatory footnote is given only on the first occurrence of the relevant item in the account.

285. The beginning of this account, probably including a heading as well as the list of receipts on the vigil of the Nativity of Our Lord, is missing.

286. [f.90] Payments upon the said [Christmas] eve

a. To Mr Roger Chomley recorder for his fee this quarter £20; Mr Medley chamberlain ///;[1] Robert Southworth[2] common serjeant £5, margin ⟨by me to Ryc'⟩; Thomas Russheton common clerk £5; Thomas Haies under chamberlain[3] £5; Walter Smyth swordbearer £3; John Burton common hunt 50s. and for fuel 6s.8d., 56s.8d.; Sebastian Hillary waterbailie 50s.; John Hallyday common cryer 15s.; William Wever carver 15s. and for weighing bread 6s.8d., 21s.8d.; Richard Hoore[4] 15s.; John Throughgood[4] 15s.; John Waase[5] 10s.; Thomas Abbot[5] 10s.; Christopher Fowke[5] 10s.; Ric[hard Benet][6] serjeant of the market [10s.];[6] the renter general ///;[7] William Broun[8] 16s.8d. and for writing the indentures of the wardmote 30s., 46s.8d.; William Veer[9] 25s.; Richard Lambe keeper of Leadenhall ///; William Middelton[10] for divers businesses 24s.2d.; William Plumpton[11] 6s.8d.; Thomas Mundy under waterbailie 13s.4d.; Thomas Cosby yeoman of the market 8s.4d.; Thomas Lidiat yeoman of the waterside 6s.8d.; John Murton yeoman there 6s.8d.; Dave Griffyn yeoman there 6s.8d.; Geffrey Aleyn yeoman there 6s.8d.; *bottom corner of the page* ⟨pd *per* Ryc' £56.4s.[2d.]⟩

[1] On 26 Oct. 1535 the chamberlain was granted during pleasure of the court £10 above the accustomed fee of £20 p.a. (Rep.9, f.133).

[2] *Recte* Southwell.

[3] The underchamberlain was the comptroller of the chamber.

[4] Serjeant carver.

[5] Serjeant of the chamber.
[6] Ms mutilated.
[7] This office was held by the chamberlain.
[8] Clerk of the chamber.
[9] Clerk of the works.
[10] Yeoman of the chamber and keeper of guildhall.
[11] Yeoman of the chamber.

b. [f.90v] To Robert [blank] the swordbearer's servant 6s.8d.; Adrian Burton the common hunt's servant 6s.8d.; Henry Gowle[1] the common cryer's servant 6s.8d.; Thomas Bullice foreign taker 6s.8d.; John a Wood foreign taker 6s.8d.; William Dumkyn beadle of the beggars 13s.4d.; John Mowse his page 6s.8d.; Thomas Furde his page 6s.8d.; the 6 waits: John[2] Strachon 20s., John Frith 20s., Thomas Bell 20s., Edmund Dier 20s., Robert Norman 20s., Richard Bacon 20s., £6; sir Joh[n Chu]rch[3] priest of the library 35s.;[4] [sir Rich]ard[3] Harris priest of the same 35s.;[4] the custos for wine and wax 10s.;[4] Mr Church tutor to the children 3s.4d.;[4] for the costs of the children this quarter 22s.1d.;[4] Nicholas Man clerk of the chapel 16s.8d.;[4] Thomas Grove clerk there 6s.8d.;[4] sir Nicholas Knowlles priest of the charnel 40s.;[5] sir Edmund Brograve priest there 13s.4d.;[5] sir John Joye priest at St Swithin's 26s.8d.;[6] the vicar of Gillingham in Kent 16s.8d.;[7] the 2 priests at Edmonton (Edelmeton) £3.10s. [cf.**15a**.]; the parson of St Peter's in Cornhill 20s. [cf.**16d**.]; the same parson and wardens of the Trinity altar there 25s.; the king for rent farm 25s.; *bottom corner of the page* ⟨pd *per* Ryc' £27.5s.5d.⟩

[1] 'Gold' in later entries.
[2] 'Richard' in later entries.
[3] Ms mutilated.
[4] Payable out of the Carpenter estate (*Cal. P & M Rolls 1458–1482*, x).
[5] Payable out of the Reynwell estate (*Cal. Wills* ii, 577). There was a chapel above the charnel house in St Paul's churchyard (*ibid.*; Stow i, 329).
[6] Payable under the will of Roger de Depham enrolled Feb. 1359 (H.R. 87(20)).
[7] Payable out of the Philipot estate (*Cal. Wills* ii, 275–6).

c. [f.91] To the churchwardens at St Dunstan's in the East 20s. [cf.**16g**]; the wardens of the Mercers for the Conduit Meadows [cf.**16e**], *margin* ⟨pd by me⟩; sir William Carre chantry priest at St Paul's for a quit rent 3s.4d.; Dr Wolman prebendary (prebender) at Finsbury £8.6s.8d., *margin* ⟨*per* William Vere⟩;[1] Henry Lomnour for his annuity half a year £10;[2] William Palmer for keeping the Moorgate and the posterns (postrons) 6s.8d.; Nicholas Glossop 6s.8d.;[3] Mr Henry 'Desart' 6s.8d.;[4] Henry Warwick for the grate at Holborn Bridge 20d.; Ball's widow for Lothbury grate 15d.; William Strile[5] for the grates at London Wall and Lothbury 3s.4d.; George Giles for keeping Aldersgate[6] 2s.6d.; William Sewen founder for trimming the conduit cocks 6s.8d.; the same for keeping the great conduit 20d.; Richard Johnson carpenter 5s.; the keeper of the conduit without Cripplegate 20d.; the parson of St Swithin's for Depham's obit[7] 6s.8d.; my lord mayor for being at the said obit 10s., *margin* ⟨pd by me⟩; Mr Recorder for like cause 6s.8d., *margin* ⟨pd by me⟩; the sheriffs for half toll of London Bridge £4;[8] the churchwardens of St Michael at Quern for Mr John Horwod's obit 6s.8d.; Robert Dynne gentleman for an annuity to him granted by the mayor and aldermen for life for a quarter 10s.; for embroidering (embrotheryng) the waits' sleeves 12s.; to the keeper of the grates at Aldgate and Crossed Friars 20d.; *bottom corner of the page* ⟨*per* Ryc' £19.3s.11d.; *probatur* £29.7s.5d.⟩

[1] William Vere, clerk of the city's works, was also rent gatherer of Finsbury (Rep.8, f.246b–7).
[2] Payable out of the rent received from Sir William Sidney for the great beam, lately restored to the city by Henry VIII and leased to Sidney and Lumnour (R. R. Sharpe, *London and the Kingdom*, i, 387; Birch, 99–105).
[3] On 17 Dec. 1521 Nicholas Glossop, servant of the archbishop of Canterbury, was granted 26s.8d. p.a. (Rep.4, f.107).
[4] Henry Patenson 'desart' in later entries, see **289c** note 5.
[5] 'Stile' in later entries.
[6] i.e. the grate(s) at Aldersgate, cf.**289d**.
[7] Will of Roger de Depham enrolled Feb. 1359 (H.R. 87(20)).
[8] Payable out of the Reynwell estate.

d. [f.91v] Philpott's alms: William Veer, Thomas Grove, Richard Milles, John Freer, Richard Abram, Richard Wright, Richard Claybrok, William Pery, Joan Osbourne, Maud Skif, Anne Lowen, Margaret Walwyn, Margaret Lamyman, to every of them 7s.3d., ⟨£4.14s.3d.⟩; ⟨pd *per* Ryc' £4.7s.0d.⟩.

e. ⟨Summa totalis pd *per* Ryc' £107.0s.6d.⟩
⟨Summa totalis pd £117.11s.9d.⟩

287.a. [f.92] Received of my master towards the said payments, first in ready money £25, and that he paid to Thomas Haies £5; of Clemence Rutland £7.10s.; of Peter Starky £8.6s.8d.; of the Steelyard £17.10s.10d.;[1] summa £63.7s.6d., *per me Ricardum Maunsell*

[1] Rent payable by the Hanse merchants to the Reynwell estate, see p. xxvi.

b. More towards the said payments, of ready money paid to Mr Common Serjeant £5; of Mistress Bootes £20; of William Middelton 36s.4d.; of the 3 serjeants of the chamber for ale silver with Pope beer brewer and for their pains allowed £13.14s.3d.; of Walter Thomas 50s.; of William Stodard and Robert Lang 20s.; summa £44.0s.7d.

c. Summa totalis received by me Richard Maunsell £107.8s.1d. ⟨Received again 20 March by me George Medley 7s.7d.⟩[1]

[1] Maunsell had disbursed only £107.0s.6d., see **286e**.

d. ⟨Total paid £117.11s.9d.⟩

288. [f.92v] Receipts in the vigil of the Annunciation of Our Lady 27 Henry VIII [1536]

Of Peter Starky for a quarter farm of Blackwell Hall £8.6s.8d.; of Clemence Rutland for the passage of barges £7.10s. [cf.**7e**]; of William Middelton for weights and measures 28s.8d.; of Walter Thomas for custom of rushes 50s.; of William Stodard and Robert Lang for gauging of fish 20s.; of Alis Johnson for sealing (sealdage) of leather half a year £5; of William Awdwyn for Billingsgate and Queenhithe £3, ⟨*margin* R' by me⟩.

289 [f.83] Payments upon the said eve of the Annunciation of our Lady

a. To Mr Roger Chomley recorder for this quarter £20, *margin* ⟨pd by me⟩; Mr George Medley chamberlain ///; Mr Robert Southwell common serjeant £5; Mr Thomas Russheton common clerk £5; Mr Haies £5, *margin* ⟨pd by me⟩; Walter Smyth swordbearer £3; John Burton common hunt 50s. and for fuel 6s.8d., 56s.8d.; Sebastian Hillary waterbailiff (waterbayly) 50s.; John Halliday common cryer 15s.; William Wever carver 15s. and for weighing bread 6s.8d., 21s.8d.; John Throughgood [15s.]; Richard Hoore 15s.; John Waase serjeant of the chamber 10s.; Thomas Abbot 10s.; Christopher Fouke 10s.; Richard Benet serjeant of the market 10s.; the renter general ///; William Broun 16s.8d.; William Middleton for divers causes 24s.2d.; William Plumpton 6s.8d.; Thomas Munday under waterbailie 13s.4d.; Mathew Penrith yeoman of the market 8s.4d.; William Veer 25s.; Richard Lambe ///, *bottom corner of the page* ⟨pd £53.7s.6d.; *per* Ryc' £28.7s.6d.⟩

b. [f.83v] To Thomas Lidiatt yeoman at the waterside 6s.8d.; John Murton yeoman there 6s.8d.; Dave Griffyn yeoman there 6s.8d.; Geffrey Aleyn yeoman there 6s.8d.; Thomas Bullice foreign taker 6s.8d.; John a Wood foreign taker 6s.8d.; William Yates the swordbearer's servant 6s.8d.; Adrian Burton the common hunt's servant 6s.8d.; Henry Gold the common cryer's servant 6s.8d.; the 6 waits: Richard Strachon, John Frith, Thomas Bell, Edmund Dier, Robert Norman and Richard Bacon, £6; sir John Church priest of the charnel [*recte* library][1] 35s.; sir Richard Harris priest of the same 35s.; the custos for wine and wax 10s.; Mr Church tutor of the children 3s.4d.; the same for costs of the children 21s.2d.; Nicholas Man clerk of the chapel 16s.8d.; Thomas Grove clerk there 6s. 8d.; sir Nicholas Knowlles priest of the charnel 40s.; sir Edmund Brograve priest of the same 13s.4d.; sir John Joye priest at St Swithin's 26s.8d.; the churchwardens of St Dunstan's in the East 20s., *bottom corner of the page* ⟨*probatur* £20.7s.10d.⟩

[1] cf.**286b**.

c. [f.84] To the 2 priests at Edmonton (Edelmeton) £3.10s. and for an obit 20s., £4.10s.; the vicar of Gillingham in Kent 16s.8d.; the parson of St Peter's in Cornhill 20s.; the same parson and churchwardens 25s.; the king for rent farm 25s.; the wardens of the Mercers for the Conduit Meadows 20s., *margin* ⟨to pay by me⟩; the petty canons of St Paul's for Foliatt's chantry half a year 10s.;[1] sir William Carry chantry priest at St Paul's 3s.4d.; the prior of Elsing Spital for the highway behind the Guildhall (Yeldhall) 20s., *margin* ⟨pd by me⟩; the prior of Lewes for quitrent out of Philpott's lands half a year £3.6s.8d.;[2] the Lady Coke for her annuity half a year £13.6s.8d.;[3] Mr Williams for half a year £5; [Doctor][4] Wolman for Finsbury a quarter £8.6s.8d., *interlineated* ⟨William Vere must be allowed of this £8.6s.8d. by me in his indenture⟩; William Dumkyn 13s.4d., John Mowse 6s.8d., Thomas Fourd 6s.8d., William Palmer 6s.8d., Nicholas Glossop 6s.8d., Richard Johnson carpenter 5s., Sewen founder for the trimming of the conduit cocks 6s.8d., the same for the great conduit 20d., Mr Henry Patenson 'desart'

6s.8d.;[5] Henry Warwick for the grates at Holborn Bridge 20d.; Bawle's widow for Lothbury grates 15d.; *bottom corner of the page* ⟨*probatur* £44.12s.11d.; *per* Ryc' £34.6s.3d.⟩

[1] Payable out of the Reynwell estate, cf.**132a**.
[2] *Cal. Wills* ii, 275–6.
[3] A descendant of John Reynwell? He charged his property with an annual payment of 40 marks to his son William and the lawful heirs of his body.
[4] Ms mutilated.
[5] Henry Patenson was Sir Thomas More's fool. More gave the jester to his father, Sir John More, and after Sir John's death, to the lord mayor and his successors (*Correspondence of Sir Thomas More*, ed. E. F. Rogers, 1947, 529n).

d. [f.84v] William Stile for the grates at Lothbury 3s.4d.; George Giles for the grates at Aldersgate 2s.6d.; the keeper of the conduit in Aldermanbury half a year 3s.4d.; the keeper of the conduit in Fleet Street half a year 3s.4d.; the keeper of the conduit in Gracechurch (Gracious) Street half a year 3s.4d.; the embroiderer (imbrotherer) for the waits' sleeves 12s.; the keeper of the conduit at Cripplegate a quarter 20d.; Mr Dynne by act of court 10s.; the keeper of the grates at Aldgate and Crossed Friars 16d.; the keeper of the conduit in Cornhill half a year 3s.4d.; How organ maker for the organs at the chapel 12d.;[1] summa £2.5s.2d.

[1] For other references to How, see **301i**.

e. Philpott's alms: William [Veer],[1] Thomas Grove, Richard Milles, Richard Abram, John Freer,[2] Richard Wright, Richard Claybrok, William Pery, Joan Osbourne, Maud Skyf, Anne Lewen, Margaret Walwyn, Margaret Lamyman, to every of them 7s.6d., £4.17s.6d.; *bottom corner of the page* ⟨£7.2s.8d.⟩

[1] Ms mutilated.
[2] This name entered by a different hand.

f. [f.85] Reynwell's obits:[1] my lord mayor 20s.; Mr Recorder 6s.8d.; Mr [blank] alderman of the ward of Dowgate 6s.8d.; Mr [blank] alderman of the ward of Billingsgate 6s.8d.; Mr Bowier alderman of the ward of Aldgate 6s.8d.; Mr Monmothe and Mr Cootes sheriffs 6s.8d.; Mr Crull and Mr Draper bridgemasters 6s.8d.; Mr Chamberlain 13s.4d.; the churchwardens of St Botolph next Billingsgate 13s.4d.; the churchwardens of St Andrew Undershaft 13s.4d.; the churchwardens of All Hallows the Great 13s.4d.; summa £5.13s.4d. ⟨per me⟩.

[1] Annual payments to city officers and for obits in 3 city churches as specified in the will of John Reynwell (H.R. 207(31)).

g. *bottom corner of the page* ⟨Total £131.4s.3d., whereof pd by me £41 and by Ryc' £90.4s.3d.⟩.

290.a. [f.85v] Received of the Steelyard £17.10s.10d.; of Mr Starky £8.6s.8d.; of Clemence Rutland £7.10s.0d.; summa £33.7s.6d., *per me Ricardum Maunsell*

b. Received more the last day of March to pay Mr Southworth[1] and Mr. Russheton £10, *per me Ricardum Maunsell*

[1] *Recte* Southwell.

c. Received more by William Middelton 28s.8d.; of Walter Thomas 50s.; of Stodard and Lang 20s.; summa £4.18s.8d., *per me Ricardum Maunsell*
d. Received of Johnson's widow for the sealage of leather which she owes to me Richard Maunsell £5, *per me Ricardum Maunsell*; *margin* 19 day
e. Total £53.6s.2d.
⟨And pd by me and to be pd with the £8.6s.8d. by Ver, total £41⟩
Received upon the indenture of Christmas quarter and received 19 May 28 [Henry VIII, 1536] for the said payments and allowed to me for that I paid more than I received as appears, summa £36.18s.1d., *per me Ricardum Maunsell*,
⟨Summa totalis paid and allowed with the money that is to be paid for the obit, the Mercers, and Elsing Spital £131.4s.3d.⟩.
Margin against these items ⟨per me G M⟩

291. [f.86] Receipts on the vigil of St John Baptist 28 Henry VIII [1536]
Of William Brothers for half a year's farm of the packership £33.6s.8d., *margin* ⟨R' by me⟩; of Sir William Sidney for the great beam half a year £25;[1] of Margaret Bootes for the gaugership[2] half a year £20, *margin* ⟨R' by me⟩; of Peter Starky for Blackwell Hall a quarter £8.6s.8d.; of Clemence Rutland for passage of barges a quarter £7.10s.; of William Awdwyn for wharfage at Billingsgate and Queenhithe £3, *margin* ⟨R' by me⟩; of Walter Thomas for the custom of rushes at Queenhithe 50s.; of William Stodard and Robert Lang for gauging of fish 20s.; of William Middleton for weights and measures 30s.10d.

[1] See **286c**, note.
[2] Of wine and oil, cf. **7j**.

292. [f.86v blank, f.93] Payments upon the said eve of St John Baptist
a. To Sir Roger Chomley knight,[1] recorder, for this quarter £20; Mr George Medley chamberlain ///; Mr Robert Southewell common serjeant £5; Mr Russheton town clerk £5; Mr Haies £5, *margin* ⟨by me pd⟩; Walter Smyth swordbearer [£3 and] for his jornet (jorynet) 20s., £4; John Burton common hunt 50s. and for fuel 6s.8d., 56s.8d.; Sebastian Hillary waterbailie 50s.; John Halliday common crier 15s.; William Wever carver 15s. and for weighing bread 6s.8d., 21s.8d.; John Throughgood 15s.; Thomas Cosby[2] 15s.; John Waase serjeant of the chamber 10s.; Thomas Abbot 10s.; Christopher Fooke 10s.; Richard Bennet serjeant of the market 10s.; the renter general ///; William Broun 16s.8d.; William Middelton for divers causes 24s.2d.; William Plumpton 6s.8d.; William Veer 25s.; Thomas Mundy under waterbailie 13s.4d.; Mathew Penrith yeoman of the market 8s.4d.; Richard Lambe keeper of Leadenhall ///; *bottom corner of the page* ⟨£54.7s.6d.⟩

[1] Not knighted until October of this year (Beaven i, 289); Maunsell's account must have been written up later.
[2] Now a serjeant carver, formerly yeoman of the market, see **286a**.

b. [f.93v] To Thomas Lidiat, John Murton, Dave Griffyn, Geffrey Aleyn, yeomen of the waterside, 26s.8d.; Thomas Bullice foreign taker 6s.8d.; John a Wood foreign taker 6s.8d.; William Gaates the swordbearer's servant 6s.8d.; Adrian Burton the common hunt's servant 6s.8d.; Henry Gold the common crier's servant 6s.8d.; the 6 waits: Richard Strachon, John Firth, Thomas Bell, Edmund Dier, Robert Norman, Richard Bacon, £6; William Dumkyn beadle of the beggars 13s.4d.; John Mowse his page 6s.8d.; Thomas Fourd his page 6s.8d.; Nicholas Glossop 6s.8d.; Mr Henry Patenson 'desart' 6s.8d.; sir John Church priest of the library 35s.; sir Richard Harris priest there 35s.; the custos for wine and wax 10s.; Mr Church tutor of the children 3s.4d.; the costs of the same children 22s.1d.; Nicholas Man clerk of the chapel 16s.8d.; Thomas Grove clerk there 6s.8d.; *bottom corner of the page* ⟨£17.8s.9d.⟩

c. [f.94] To sir Nicholas Knowlles priest of the charnel 40s.; sir William [*sic*][1] Brograve priest of the same 13s.4d.; sir John Joye priest at St Swithins 26s.8d.; the vicar of Gillingham in Kent 16s.8d.; the 2 priests at Edmonton (Edelmeton) £3.10s.; the churchwardens of St Dunstan's in the East 20s.; the parson of St Peter's in Cornhill 20s.; the same parson and wardens of the Trinity altar there 25s.; the wardens of the Mercers for the Conduit Meadows ⟨20s.⟩, the same for a quit rent out of the Compter Alley 13s.4d.; the king for rent farm 25s.; sir William Carre chantry priest at St Paul's 3s.4d.; the almoner of Westminster for 2 lb pepper 3s.8d. [cf.**16s**]; Henry Lomnour for his annuity out of the great beam £10; Doctor Wolman prebendary (prebender) of Finsbury £8.6s.8d., *margin* ⟨paid by me £5 and by Ryc' £3.6s.8d.⟩; William Palmer for keeping the Moor ditches 6s.8d.; Henry Warwick for the grates at Holborn Bridge 20d.; Ball's widow for keeping Lothbury grates 15d.; William Stile for cleansing the same grates 3s.4d.; Sewen founder for trimming the conduit cocks 6s.8d.; the same for keeping the great conduit 20d.; George Gil[es][2] for the grates at Aldersgate 2s.6d.; Richard Joh[nson][2] carpenter 5s.; the keeper of the [conduit][2] without Cripplegate 20d.; Robert Dynne [servant to][2] my lord chancellor 10s.; my lord mayor towards 4 jackets (jakettes) 13s.4d.; the cresset bearers, bagbearers and fillers and for cresset light *per* bill £7.5s.6d. ⟨by me 46s.8d.⟩, *bottom corner of the page* ⟨£43.2s.11d.⟩

[1] *Recte* Edmund? cf. **286b**, **289b**, **295c**.
[2] Ms stained.

d. [f.94v] Philpott's alms: William Veer, Thomas Grove, Richard Abram, Richard Milles, [blank], Richard Wright, Richard Claybrok, William Pery, Joan Osbourne, Maud Skef, Anne Lowen, Margaret Walwyn, Margaret Lamyman, to every of them 7s.7d., summa ⟨£4.18s.7d.⟩

e. ⟨Summa totalis for this quarter paid £119.17s.9d.
whereof is paid by me with the 33s.4d. to pay to the Mercers £14.
So rest paid by Richard Mansell £105.17s.9d.
and thereof he has received as appears upon the other side £85.15s. and allowed upon the other side £20.2s.9d., summa £105.17s.9d.⟩

293.a. [f.95] Received of my master the chamberlain towards the said quarter's payments 23 June 28 Henry VIII [1536] in gold, £16.0s.0d.
b. Received by the hands of Mr Starky for Blackwell Hall £8.6s.8d. and of Clemence Rutland £7.10s., summa £15.16s.8d.
c. Received more in white money the said day, £6.6s.8d.
d. More of the Steelyard for a quarter's rent ended at midsummer £17.10s.10d.; and of Sir William Sidney for the great beam half a year £25; summa £42.10s.10d.
e. More of William Middelton 30s.10d.; and of William Stodard and Robert Lang 20s.; summa £2.10s.10d., *per me Ricardum Maunsell*
f. Summa totalis £83.5s.0d.
More of Walter Thomas, £2.10s.0d.
Summa totalis £85.15s.0d. *per me Ricardum Maunsell*
⟨Paid more to Ryc' Manssell 19 August 28 Henry VIII [1536] by indenture allowed to him £20.2s.9d. And quit for this quarter⟩
⟨Total paid £119.17s.9d.⟩

294. [f.95v] Receipts in the vigil of St Michael the Archangel 28 Henry VIII [1536]
Of Peter Starky for a quarter farm of Blackwell Hall £8.6s.8d.; of Clemence Rutland for a quarter farm of the barges £7.10s.; of Walter Thomas for a quarter of the custom of rushes 50s.; of Alis Johnson widow for half a year's farm £5; of William Middelton for weights and measures 18s.; of William Stodard and Robert Lang for gauging of fish 20s.; of William Awdwyn for wharfage at Billingsgate £3, *margin* ⟨R' by me⟩; of the brewers, tipplers and innholders called ale silver £14.8s.8d.; of the beer brewers 40s.; of the strangers basket makers 26s.8d., *margin* ⟨R' by me⟩; of oystermen for their signs 2s. *margin* ⟨R' by me⟩; of Richard Lambe for standing of wools at Leadenhall £20.4s.11d.; of the clerks of the mayor's court for deeds and testaments nil; of the wardens of the Taylors for strangers botchers 13s.4d.; of Mr Crayne for the little beam[1] 30s. Paid to the 3 serjeants of the chamber 40s.[2]

[1] The small beam 'commonly called the silk beam' (Rep.15, f.101 (1562)). William Crane was weigher of raw silk (Rep.9, f.102b).
[2] Out of the receipts of ale silver above, see **296e**.

295. [f.96] Payments upon the said eve of St Michael *anno* 28
a. To Sir Roger Chombley recorder for his fee this quarter £20; Mr George Medley chamberlain ///; Mr [blank][1] Broke common serjeant £5; Mr Thomas Russheton common clerk £5, *margin* ⟨and 50s., summa £7.10s.⟩; Mr Thomas Haies £5, *margin* ⟨pd by me⟩; Walter Smyth swordbearer £3; John Burton common hunt 50s. and for fuel 6s.8d., 56s.8d.; Sebastian Hillary waterbailie 50s.; John Halliday common crier 15s.; William Wever carver 15s. and for weighing of bread 6s.8d., 21s.8d.; John Throughgood carver 15s.; Thomas Cosby carver 15s.; John Waase serjeant of the chamber 10s.; [Thomas Abbot 10s.];[2] Christopher Fouke 10s.; Richard Bennet serjeant of the market 10s.; to the renter general ///; William Broun 16s.8d.; William Middleton yeoman of the chamber for divers causes 24s. 2d.;William Plumpton yeoman there

6s.8d.; William Veer 25s.; Richard Lambe ///; Thomas Munday under waterbailie 13s.4d.; Mathew Penrith yeoman of the market 8s.4d.; *bottom corner of the page* ⟨*probatur* £55.7s.6d.⟩

[1] Robert Broke, elected 11 July 1536.
[2] Ms mutilated and a line missing.

b. [f.96v] To Thomas Lidiat yeoman of the waterside 6s.8d.; John Moreton yeoman there 6s.8d.; Dave Griffyn yeoman there 6s.8d.; Geffrey Aleyn yeoman there 6s.8d.; William Gayttes the swordbearer's servant 6s.8d.; Adrian Burton the common hunt's servant 6s.8d.; Henry Gold the common cryer's servant 6s.8d.; Thomas Bullice foreign taker 6s.8d.; John a Wood foreign taker 6s.8d.; John Busshe mealmeter 26s.; R [blank] Bucer mealmeter (mealmeate) 26s.; William Dumkyn beadle of the beggars 13s.4d., John Mowse his page 6s.8d.; Thomas Fourd his page 6s.8d.; William Wattes for keeping the Moor gate and ditches 6s.8d., [. . . 6s.8d.],[1] Henry Patenson 'desart' 6s.8d.; the 6 waits: Richard Strachon 20s., Thomas Bell 20s., John Frith 20s., Edmund Dier 20s., Robert Norman 20s., Richard Becon 20s., £6, *bottom corner of the page* ⟨*probatur* £13.8s.8d.⟩

[1] Ms mutilated and a line missing.

c. [f.87] To sir John Church priest of the library 35s.; sir Richard Harris priest of the same 35s.; the custos for wine and wax 10s.; Mr Church tutor of the children 3s.4d.; the same for the costs of the children 10s.6d., Nicholas Man clerk of the chapel 16s.8d.; Thomas Grove clerk there 6s.8d.; sir Nicholas Knowlles priest of the charnel 40s.; sir Edmund Brograve priest of the same 13s.4d.; sir John Joye priest at St Swithin's 26s.8d.; the vicar of Gillingham in Kent 16s.8d.; the 2 priests at Edmonton (Edelmeton) £3.10s.; the churchwardens of St Dunstan's in the East 20s.; the parson of St Peter's in Cornhill 20s.; the same parson and wardens of the Trinity altar there 25s.; the wardens of the Mercers for the Conduit Meadows ///,[1] the wardens of St Peter's in Cornhill by Mr Carpen's bequest 33s.; the churchwardens of St Clement's in Eastcheap 12s.; the petty canons of St Paul's for Foliatt's chantry half a year 10s.; the chamberlain of St Paul's for Mr Barton's obit 40s.; the dean and chapter of St Paul's for a quit rent 3s.; the same for certain quit rent 6s.6d.; sir William Carre chantry priest at St Paul's 3s.4d.; the chamberlain of Westminster for 2 several quit rent [cf.**129a**] 8s.; *bottom corner of the page* ⟨*probatur* £23.4s.8d.⟩

[1] The Conduit Meads were acquired from the Mercers by the Crown in 1536, see **16e**.

d. [f.87v] To sir John Aleyn knight now mayor towards 4 tuns wine £26.13s.4d.[1] *margin* ⟨pd by me⟩; the sheriffs in discharge of the toll of London Bridge half a year £4, *left margin* ⟨pd by me £4 and by Ryc' £4⟩, *right margin* ⟨pd by Ryc'⟩; my lady Coke of Gloucester for her annuity half a year £13.6s.8d.; Mr Williams of the king's house half a year £5; Dr Wolman for the prebend of Finsbury £8.6s.8d., *margin* ⟨pd by William Vere 25 October⟩; the prior of Lewes for quitrent out of Philpott's lands

£3.6s.8d.; the prior of Tortington for quit rent 40s. [cf.**16a**], *margin* ⟨pd by me⟩; the prior of Hurley for Philpott's obit 13s.4d.,[2] *margin* ⟨pd by me⟩; the prior of Christchurch in Canterbury 10s.; the king for quit rent out of the compter in the Poultry late to Elsing Spital 22s.8d.;[3] the king for quitrent out of tenements at St Michael le Quern late to the nunnery at Kilburn 8s.; the abbot of Waltham for 2 several quit rents 46s.8d.; to William Broun mercer for quit rent 33s.4d.; the bridgemasters for quitrent 34s.4d. [cf.**16r**]; Giles Pollibere for quit rent out of the Rood Alley 10s.;[4] the vicar of St Lawrence Jewry 5s.; Henry Warwick for the sluice of Holborn Bridge 20d.; Giles Polibere for Aldersgate grates 2s.6d.; William Stile for the grates at London Wall and Lothbury 3s.4d.; Ball's widow for keeping the grates there 15d.; Fowle pewterer for keeping the chains (chynes) in Lombard Street 13s.4d.; the keeper of the grates at Aldgate ⟨2s.8d.⟩; Robert Dynne servant to my lord chancellor 10s., *margin* ⟨pd by me⟩; the prior of St Mary Spital 10s.; Thomas Barnwell steward of Finsbury 20s.; John Burton for the ground that the bricks is made upon 6s.8d.; *bottom corner of the page* ⟨*probatur* £75.8s.1d.⟩[5]

[1] See **115b**, note.
[2] *Cal. Wills* ii, 275–6.
[3] Elsing Spital, otherwise the Hospital of St Mary within Cripplegate, had been suppressed earlier this year under the act of March 1536 for the dissolution of the smaller monasteries (*V.C.H. London* i, 536).
[4] Payable out of the Reynwell estate (cf. **132f**, **324c**).
[5] £73.18s.9d. written above.

e. [f.88] To Mr Broun serjeant at the law[1] for his fee this year 20s., *margin* ⟨pd by me⟩; Mr Willoughby serjeant at the law[2] for his fee 20s., *margin* ⟨pd by me⟩; Mr Roper attorney in the king's bench 20s., *margin* ⟨pd by me⟩; Mr Joynour attorney in the common pleas (place) 20s.; John Darnald attorney in the exchequer 20s.; William Martyn of counsel in the Guildhall (yeldhall)[3] 20s., *margin* ⟨pd by me⟩; Doctor Trignnell of the arches 20s., *margin* ⟨to pay by me⟩; the escheator of London for his fee 40s.; Thomas Dockerey proctor (propter) of the arches 13s.4d.; the keeper of the star chamber door 6s.8d.; Thomas Acon plumber 40s.; John Hilmer mason 20s.; ⟨Richard Johnson⟩ carpenter 5s.; William Hawles for Marylebone (Marybourne) 21s.4d.; [. . . 12s.][4] William Sewen founder for trimming the conduit cocks 6s.8d.; the same for keeping the great conduit 20d.; the keeper of the conduit in Cornhill half a year 3s.4d.; the keeper of the conduit at Gracechurch half a year 3s.4d.; the keeper of the standard in Cheap ///, the keeper of the little conduit in Cheap 6s.8d.; the keeper of the conduit in Aldermanbury half a year 3s.4d.; the keeper of the conduit in Cripplegate 20d.; the keeper of the conduit in Fleet Street half a year 3s.4d.; *bottom corner of the page* ⟨*probatur* £15.8.4d.⟩[5]

[1] Humphrey Browne, serjeant at law, was admitted of counsel, 16 June 1523 (Rep.4, f.153b). He became a judge of the common pleas 1542 (E. Foss, *Biographia Juridica*, 1870).
[2] Thomas Willoughby became a judge of the common pleas 1537 (Foss, *op.cit.*)
[3] Martyn, one of the common pleaders (Rep.3, f.213), was to be of counsel towards the chamberlain (28 Oct.1519, Rep.4, f.28).

[4] Ms mutilated and a line missing; 12s. is the sum required to make the total correct.
[5] £15.5s.0d. written over.

f. [f.88v] Philpott's alms: William Veer, Thomas Grove, Richard Milles, Richard Abram, [blank], Richard Wright, Richard Claybrooks, William Pery, Joan Osbourne, Maud Skef, Anne Lowyn, Margaret Walwyn, Margaret Lamyman, to every of them 8s.1d., £5.5s.1d. *probatur*
g. Summa totalis of all this quarter's payments £189.2s.4d. whereof paid by my master and Veer £44.10s. and to pay in 5 parcels £4.11s.8d. And received more by me Ric[hard] M[aunsel] at divers times of my master and others as appears on the other side, summa £92.17s.6d. Summa *per* M[aster] Car' £141.19s.2d. And received 20 Dec. 28 Henry VIII [1536] and allowed to me in the indenture of the rents due at Michaelmas last past, summa £47.3s.2d.
Summa totalis £189.2s.4d.
bottom left of page ⟨pd by me £43.10s. and more £68.7s.6d., summa £111.17s.6d.⟩
bottom right of page ⟨*Probatur* total £189.2s.4d.⟩

296a. [f.89] Received of my master the chamberlain 28 Sept. 28 Henry VIII [1536] in gold and money £20, *per me Ricardum Maunsell*
b. Received money that I received of the Steelyard the said day £17.10s.10d.; of Peter Starky £8.6s.8d.; of Clemence Rutland for the passage of barges £7.10s.; summa £33.7s.6d., *per me Ricardum Maunsell*
c. Received more in crowns of 5s. 30 Sept. 28 Henry VIII [1536] £10, *per me Ricardum Maunsell*
d. Received more in ready money 8 Sept. 28 Henry VIII [1536] towards the said payments which was delivered to pay Nelson glazier with, £5, *per me Ricardum Maunsell*
e. More received of Walter Thomas 50s.; of William Middelton 18s.; of Johnson's widow £5; of the ale silver £12.8s.8d. and the serjeants paid; of Pope beer [brewer][1] 40s.; of the merchant taylors 13s.4d.; and William Stodard and Robert Lang 20s.; summa £24.10s.0d., *per me Ricardum Maunsell*

[1] Ms mutilated.

f. More received 20 Dec. 28 Henry VIII [1536] by allowance upon my indenture as appears by the same and on the other side, summa £47.3s.2d. I say £140.0s.8d. sterling. Summa totalis received and allowed £140.0s.8d.
g. ⟨Summa totalis paid £189.2s.4d.⟩

297. ⟨*probatur* Summa totalis paid by these 4 quarters £557.16s.1d. sterling⟩

B.

RECEIPTS EXTRAORDINARY 1564–65

298. [f.136] Receipts Extraordinary

a. Of Mr Edward Gilbert goldsmith, late alderman, for a fine by him appointed to be paid by the lord mayor and aldermen at a court held 16 Nov. 1564 [Rep.15, f.394] for his discharge of as well the room of an alderman as of the room of shrievalty hereafter, to be executed by him in full payment of £266.13s.4d., £66.13s.4d.

b. Of Dame Elizabeth Lion widow for so much bequeathed by Sir John Lion late alderman towards the erecting of a house at Queenhithe,[1] £100.0s.0d.[2]

[1] Sir John Lyon, lord mayor 1554–55 and alderman of Queenhithe ward 1547–64, died 8 Sept. 1564. On 28 Nov. 1564 a committee viewed the city's void ground at Queenhithe to appoint a site for a market house. On 8 Jan. 1566 the new house was viewed and by orders of 12 Feb. and 12 Nov. 1566 Queenhithe was appointed the place of sale for shellfish, grain, salt and fruit brought to the city for sale from the west (Rep.15, ff.399, 513b; Rep.16, ff.10, 133. And see **316**).

[2] The words, 'as appears in the account following', have been inserted following 'Queenhithe' and this sum in the margin is struck through. It would seem to have been transferred to a special account, which has not survived, for 'building of a market place and new garner at Queenhithe', kept separately from the general account 1564–65. The sum of £97.7s.0d. was deducted from expenditure upon 'Emptions of Reparation Stuff' to be charged to this special account (Chamber Accounts 1, f.220v).

c. Of Jane Poynter widow and executrix of the testament and last will of Richard Poynter citizen and draper of London[1] of his bequest to be employed within 2 years next after his decease by the advice of his overseers towards the repairing of the water pipes for the better conveyance of the water of the conduits in the city of London which were then in decay, £20.0s.0d.

[1] Warden of the Drapers' company 1562–63 and member of the Russia company (A. H. Johnson, *History of the Worshipful Company of Drapers of London*, ii, 1915, 185, 470).

d. Of the wardens of the Greytawyers by order of court 16 March [*recte* 12 April] 1565 [Rep.15, f.437b] for that 30 of them, being the whole company of the Greytawyers, that they with their apprentices should be set over to the company of the Skinners and for their translation do pay, £6.13s.4d.[1]

[1] The court had had the union of the two companies under consideration for some months (Rep.15, ff.396b, 400, 403, 408, 435).

e. For certain great stones for bases and ashlar stone and elm timber occupied about the foundation of the new house or market place erected at Queenhithe being of the city's store, £16.13s.2d.

f. [f.136v] of William Besewick draper by order of court 10 July last [Rep.15, f.443] to be discharged as well of the room of alderman as of all other offices for ever, £500.0s.0d.

g. Of Nynion Coxton, John Flete and Thomas Worlege, alnagers and searchers of woollen cloths, for the profits of the office this year to the use of the queen £84.16s.5d., and for the fee farm of the office due also to the queen for one whole year £60, and for the profits due to the city by the same office £85.2s.0¼d., and with £13.6s.8d. due and wont to be paid to John Aylewoth esquire for a pension out of the said office during his life and now redeemed to the use of this city as by the account ended at Michaelmas 5 Elizabeth [1563], £243.5s.1¼d.[1]

[1] cf. **8h** and note thereto. The city had bought out Aylewoth (Aylward)'s interest in the office of alnager in return for an annuity of 20 marks (Rep.14, ff.386b, 396b).

h. Of Mr Ambrose Nicholas salter, treasurer of St Bartholomew's Hospital, for timber brick lime sand and other reparation stuff, wages of workmen and labourers bestowed for repairing divers the storehouses in Blackwell Hall and to this accountant allowed among other things in his last account, £25.14s.6d.

i. Of Anthony Sylver deputy of Farringdon Without and Christopher . . . ansted[1] for so much by them gathered of the inhabitants . . . in Smithfield, £7.0s.0d.

[1] Ms trimmed with some loss of text. It is not certain that the section is complete.

C.

OUTWARD FEES 1562–63

[f.117] Outward Fees [Payments]

299.a. To Sir Thomas Saunders knight one of the queen's remembrancers in the exchequer for a yearly reward, £2.0s.0d.

b. To Mr Gerrard the queen's attorney for like reward for a year and a half at 53s.4d. by year, £4.0s.0d.

c. To Mr Rosewell the queen's solicitor for like reward a year and a half at 40s. the year, £3.0s.0d.

d. To Mr Chidley for his fee, £1.6s.[8d.]

e. To William Roper attorney in the king's bench for 2 years 40s., to Mr Leonarde attorney in the common pleas (place) for 2 years 40s.,[1] to Mr Greke attorney in the exchequer for this year's fee 20s.,[2] summa £5.0s.0d.

[1] John Leonarde (Lennard(e)) (*Cal. PR 1560–63*, 306, 322).

[2] Thomas Greke (Greeke) held this appointment from 1558 until being made a baron of the exchequer in 1576 (Rep.14, f.89b; Rep.19, f.35b).

f. To Mr Houne of the learned counsel of this city 20s.,[1] to Henry Fanshawe under escheator 40s., and to the keeper of the star chamber door for his fee 6s.8d., summa £3.6s.[8d.]

[1] William Hone (Houne), common pleader since 9 Aug. 1542 (Rep.10, f.269).

g. To Mr Serjeant Carrows, Master Gilbert Gerrard, Mr Edward [*recte* Edmund] Plowden, Mr Manwood, Mr Bromeley and Mr Wray[1] to every of them for a year and a half £3 and to Mr Buxton[2] for one half year being of the learned counsel of this city 20s., summa [£19.0s.0d.]

[1] For biographical references to the six foregoing men, see p. xxii, note 43.
[2] Robert Buxton, admitted one of the learned counsel 18 Feb. 1563 (Rep.15, f.197).

h. [f.117v] To Philip Paskyn master mason for his year's fee 20s., to John Howtinge master carpenter for his fee 26s.8d. and to William Axe plumber for his fee 40s., summa £4.6s.8d.

i. To the 6 waits to every of them for his fee £6, summa £36.0s.0d.

j. To Richard Strachey late one of the waits for a yearly pension, £2.13s.4d.[1]

[1] Granted 29 Jan. 1555 in respect of age and infirmity (Rep.13(1), f.255b).

k. To the accountant's clerk for his fee, £3.6s.8d.

l. To Nicholas Bingham keeper of Leadenhall for his fee, £5.0s.0d.

300.a. To the raker of Coleman Street and Broad Street wards for carrying away the filth gathered at the grates at London Wall and Lothbury 13s.4d., to the keeper of the grate at Lothbury for keeping clean the grate 5s., to the keepers of the grates at Aldersgate 10s., to the keeper of the postern called Moorgate and the ditches there 26s.8d., to the keeper of the grates of Aldgate and the late Crutched Friars 6s.8d., to the keeper of the new grate at Bishopsgate 6s.8d., to the keeper of the sluice in Holborn Bridge 6s.8d., to Nicholas Williams for keeping clean the channel between Bishopsgate and St Mary Axe and to him granted by act of court 26 March in the mayoralty of Sir William Hewet [1560, Rep.14, f.318] 13s.4d.,[1] to Thomas Gitton for keeping clean the grate at Petty Wales also by decree of court 9 Dec. in the mayoralty of Sir William Harper [1561, Rep.15, f.22] 20s.,[2] summa £5.8s.4d.

[1] Williams, a serjeant carver, was to appoint a poor honest man to do the work who would receive 13s.4d.
[2] By the order the keeper of the grate was to be appointed by the alderman of Tower ward or his deputy.

b. [f.118] To the keepers of the conduits at Gracechurch, Cornhill, the great conduit in Cheap, the standard there, the little conduit in Cheap, the conduit in Aldermanbury, the conduit in Lothbury, the conduit at Bishopsgate, the conduit at Cripplegate, the conduit in Fleet Street and the conduit in Holborn, to every of them 6s.8d., and to John Sewen founder for overseeing of the cocks of the conduits this year 26s.8d., summa £5.0s.0d.

301.a. To Nicholas Umfrey foreign taker for his fee this year, £1.6s.8d.

b. To Simon Thompson and Henry Smert meters of meal at the markets of Leadenhall and Newgate after the rate of 2s. weekly to every of them, £10.8s.0d.

c. To the 2 keepers of the chains in Lombard Street this year, 13s.4d.

d. To the scavenger of Lime Street ward for keeping clean the market place within Leadenhall, £1.0s.0d.

e. To the widow of Sebastian Hilary, late waterbailie for her annuity granted by act of court [16 Feb. 1545, Rep.11, f.145b] during her life, £2.0s.0d.
f. To John Chese broiderer for embroidering of 6 badges with the arms of the city and the lord mayor worn by the waits this year, £1.4s.0d.
g. [f.118v] To Roger Nicolles poulter for his attendance to be used to wait upon the lord mayor to survey poultry wares granted *per curiam* 28 March *tempore* William Hevet knight mayor [1560, Rep.14, f.320] to see the prices thereof set by the lord mayor and his brethren and [*sic*] aldermen to be well observed, £6.13s.4d.
h. To the late wife of Thomas Ferrour for a yearly annuity to her granted, 13s.4d. [cf. **25c**]
i. To John How organ maker for keeping and tending the organs in the Guildhall chapel, 2s.0d.[1]

[1] On account of his age and infirmity the payment to How was increased to 20s. a year on 9 July 1566 (Rep.16, f.79) and is shown at this rate in later accounts (Chamber Accounts 1, ff.196, 232, 128). He also received payments for mending the organs in the chapel which were entered under the Foreign Charge and which are probably to be dated 1563–64, 1564–65 and 1566–67 (Chamber Accounts 1, ff.112v, 163, 231). He is probably the same How, organ maker, mentioned in 1536 (**289d**). A John Howe the younger was translated by order of 29 Aug. 1532 from the dissolved company of organ makers to that of the Skinners (Rep.8, f.242b).

j. To Philip Brusselles for his attendance at the gaol delivery at Newgate to interpret divers languages spoken by strangers there, 13s.4d.[1]

[1] Brusselles (Brisselles, Bryssell) received a similar fee in other years, probably for 1564–65, 1565–66, 1566–67 and 1567–68 (Chamber Accounts 1, ff.218v, 196, 232, 128).

k. To Nicholas Nashe farmer of Finsbury for his pains yearly to see the rakers and others resorting to the laystall (laystow) there with dung and filth to bestow the same upon the laystall and not to annoy (noy) the fields nor ways with the same, 13s.4d. [cf.**25d**]
l. To John Hogdeson beadle of the beggars in full recompense for such charges as he shall sustain about the punishment of vagabonds and others idle persons, £1.0s.0d.
m. [f.119] To John Evans and Hugh (Hught') Grymes, searchers appointed at the waterside for the ordering of billets, faggots, tall wood and other fuel brought to be sold to this city by water, to every of them for his fee, 33s.4d., summa £3.6s.8d.

302.a. To Edward Bawme for one yearly pension granted by act of court [27 Oct. 1552, Rep.12(2), f.541b], £1.6s.8d.

b. To Anthony the clocksmith for tending the clock this year, 6s.8d.[1]

[1] He received a similar fee in other years, almost certainly 1564–65, 1565–66 and 1566–67 (Chamber Accounts 1, ff. 229, 196v, 232).

c. To John Haywood gentleman late measurer of linen cloth for an annuity to him granted for life in recompense of his office which he has lately surrendered to the di[sposition][1] of the lord mayor and aldermen, £13.6s.[8d.]

[1] Ms mutilated, cf. other accounts. A committee was appointed to treat with Haywood concerning the terms of his resignation, 7 Feb. 1555 (Rep.13, f.261).

d. To Mr Blackwell common clerk and clerk of the peace for the city of London for a yearly reward to him granted by act of court in consideration of such fees as to him belong as clerk of the peace by the poor prisoners at Newgate at the time of their delivery for that such as be not able to pay their fees should not remain [f.119v] prisoners for the same, £3.6s.8d.; to Henry Clerck clerk of the peace in the county of Middlesex for like consideration, £3.6s.8d.; to Edmund Mundes keeper of Newgate in like case, £3.6s.8d.; and to the swordbearer, marshal there, for like case, 13s.4d.; summa £10.13s.4d. [cf.**23c**]
e. To Robert Cause late one of the sheriffs' officers by order of court 16 July 1562 [Rep.15, f.103] granted for term of his life yearly, £2.13s.4d.
f. To Lucy (Luce) Lyvers for her right and title of dower which she claims out of the house wherein William Bowmar late dwelt at Billingsgate for term of her life by act of court [24 July 1561, Rep.14, f.514],[1] £2.0s.0d.

[1] This order describes her as Luce Lyvers, widow of William Hall, mercer, and gives the tenant's name as William Dowmer.

Summa £159.9s.0d.

D.

ARTIFICERS, SUPPLIERS, CARRIERS AND MAKERS OF GOODS 1563–77

303. [The following names have been abstracted from such portions of the 'Emptions' section of the chamberlain's accounts as survive for the period 1563–77. The folio reference is given in brackets after the date. For observations on the tentative dating of the accounts, see **282**. A few of the payments were made in respect of goods supplied earlier than the year of the account.]
a. *Armourer* [. . .],[1] 1576–77 (77)

[1] Ms mutilated.

b. *Barge* Thomas Norwell and Nicholas Myllwarde, shipwrights, 1576–77 (64).
c. *Blacksmith (ironwork)* Richard Sampson (Samson), 1563–64 (120v), 1564–65 (219v), 1565–66 (192), 1566–67 (224), 1568–69 (24v).
d. *Bricks* Mr Bramston, mercer, 1568–69 (25); Thomas Cobbe, 1568–69 (25); Richard Austen of Hoxton (Hogeston), Middlesex, moneyer, 1575–76 (2v).
e. *Buckets* Launcelot Mannering, 1576–77 (63v).
f. *Founder* John Seven (Sevyn, Sewen Shewyn), 1563–64 (120v), 1564–65 (220), 1565–66 (192), 1566–67 (224v), 1568–69 (25v); William Palmer, 1568–69 (26), 1576–77 (77v).

g. *Glazier* Garret (Garrett, Garrard) Hone (Hoen, Honne), 1563–64 (120v), 1564–65 (220), 1565–66 (192), 1566–67 (224v), 1568–69 (25); Oliver Wallett, 1576–77 (62).

h. *Ironmonger (nails)* Peter Whaley (Whalley), 1563–64 (120), 1564–65 (219v), 1566–67 (223v), 1568–69 (24); John Etheridge, 1568–69 (24).

i. *Joiner* John Christian, 1566–67 (224), 1568–69 (24), 1576–77 (62).

j. *Lead* Mr Thomas Dalton alderman of Hull, 1568–69 (24v); Sir Christopher Draper, 1568–69 (24v); William Wyggens, 1576–77 (77v).

k. *Lime* Thomas Dryver (Dryvar, Dyvar) of Limehouse, 1563–64 (120), 1564–65 (219), 1566–67 (223); from Bridewell, 1566–67 (223), 1568–69 (23v); William Vaughan, 1576–77 (74).

l. *Nightwork* Jeffery Lovejoye (Loveioye), 1563–64 (121), 1564–65 (220v), 1565–66 (192v), 1566–67 (224v, 12v), 1568–69 (26v); Ethelbert Thorne, 1576–77 (62v–63).

m. *Paviour* Jeffery North, 1563–64 (121), 1564–65 (220v), 1566–67 (223v), 1568–69 (26–26v); Thomas Stacye (Stace), 1576–77 (74v–76v).

n. *Plumber* William Axe, 1563–64 (120v), 1564–65 (220), 1565–66 (192), 1566–67 (224), 1568–69 (24v), 1576–77 (77v).

o. *Pumps* Robert Albanye merchant taylor, making 1576–77 (63v); Thomas Lymby, painting 1576–77 (63v); Robert Mascall carpenter, 1576–77 (63v).

p. *Ropes* Clement Draper 1568–69 (26); John Coxe, 1568–69 (26); Robert Maskall, 1576–77 (63v); Richard Hewson 1576–77 (63v).

q. *Stone (including carriage)* John Tulle of London tiler, 1563–64 (120); Philip Pasken (Paskine, Paskyn) mason, 1564–65 (226v), 1566–67 (223v), 1568–69 (23v), 1576–77 (74); Robert Wight draper 1564–65 (219); William Hichecokes salter, 1568–69 (23v); Bartholomew Parrott (Parrat), 1568–69 (23v); Thomas Shotton, 1568–69 (23v,24); Thomas Spencer bricklayer, 1568–69 (23v); Thomas Wilkinson, 1568–69 (23v, 24); Sir Christopher Draper, 1568–69 (23v); Richard Benson tiler, 1568–69 (23v); Jeffery North paviour, 1568–69 (24); [. . . Ford?][1] freemason, 1568–69 (23v); John [?], 1568–69 (24).

[1] Ms mutilated.

r. *Tiles* Robert Northe of Hampstead, Middlesex, yeoman, 1564–65 (219), 1566–67 (223), 1568–69 (24),[1] 1575–76 (2v).

[1] Described this year as of Shootup Hill (Shote Up hill), Hampstead.

s. *Timber (including wharfage and carriage)* Robert Strowdewick of 'Awstade', Surrey,[1] 1563–64 (106), 1564–65 (226); Christopher Rydeldon carpenter, 1563–64 (106); John Northe of Hampstead, Middlesex, 1563–64 (106v); John Hilliarde carpenter, 1563–64 (106v), 1564–65 (226v); Rowland Felde of Strood (Strode), Kent, yeoman, 1564–65 (226, 220v), 1566–67 (222v); Peter Pett shipwright, 1564–65 (226); Thomas Samon of 'Yeling', Kent,[2] yeoman, 1564–65 (220v), 1566–67 (222v); John Dance?, 1564–65 (220v); William Strowdwick (Strowdewyk) of Kirdford (Kurford, Kyrdeford),[3] Sussex, 1566–67 (222v), 1568–69 (16v); Robert Palmer of 'Myle Hale', Kent,[4] yeoman, 1566–67 (222v); Richard Snowe, 1566–67 (222v); Thomas Hewett of 'Lawrence Okarne', Berks.,[5] 1566–67

(222v); Thomas Browne of Uxbridge, Middlesex, 1566–67 (222v); Roger Larkin of 'Yeling', Kent,[2] yeoman, 1566–67 (222v); alderman Sir William Hewett deceased, 1568–69 (16v); John Hawarde, 1568–69 (16v); Christopher Darell merchant taylor, 1568–69 (23); Henry Store woodmonger, 1568–69 (23), 1575–76 (1, 1v); Anthony Webbe salter, 1575–76 (1); Richard White of Reading, Berks., bargeman, 1575–76 (1); William Mawbourne of Reading, Berks., bargeman, 1575–76 (1); Thomas Wilkes of Waltham St Lawrence (Laurence Walton), Berks., yeoman, 1575–76 (1v); Henry Strowdewick of Kirdford (Kurford), Sussex, boardman, 1575–76 (2).

[1] Ashtead or Oxted?
[2] Yalding?
[3] On f.222v 'Kurford' is deleted and 'Chyddingford' written above.
[4] Hayle Mill in the parish of Loose?
[5] Not identified. Perhaps Waltham St Lawrence where the baptismal registers of the 1590s have entries for the children of a Thomas Hewett. I am indebted to the County Archivist of Berkshire for this information.

t. *Turner (tampions and staves for the conduits)* Agnes Perkins widow, 1563–64 (121), 1564–65 (220), 1565–66 (192), 1566–67 (224v), 1568–69 (26); Barnaby Bestney, 1576–77 (77).

E.

EXTRACTS FROM THE FOREIGN CHARGE 1563–71
[PAYMENTS]

Some of the extracts given below relate to entries in the draft accounts which have been amended in the original manuscript. Usually these amendments served only to provide greater detail and in most cases only the final version is given in the following calendar. The date of the account to which the entry has been attributed is given in italics following the serial number. For observations on the tentative dating of the accounts in Chamber Accounts 1, see **282**. Some attributions of date may derive from another entry, not calendared, on the same folio.

304. *1563–64* [f.121v] To the wardens of the parish clerks for their pains taken at the ministration of the communion when Sir John White mayor was elect on the day of St Michael the Archangel[1] 6s.8d.; to Mr Crowley[2] for a sermon made that day by my lord mayor's commandment 13s.4d.; more to the wardens for making of certificates this year as well to the queen as to every alderman of the city of the persons weekly born and buried within the liberties of the city 20s.; to Leonard Largyn for his expenses in carriage of the certificates this year to the court £13.10s.8d.; to the vergers of St Paul's in reward for opening and shutting the door of St Dunstan's chapel at the repair thither of the lord mayor and aldermen on Sundays and other days 20d; to the yeomen of the waterside for keeping clean of the same chapel 6s.8d.; to William Boxall a poor man for keeping clean of the circuit of the place where the officers and others sit and stand before the lord mayor and aldermen in St Paul's churchyard at the sermon time 3s.4d.; summa £16.2s.4d. [cf.**63**]

[1] Knighted during his mayoralty (Beaven ii, 34; Chamber Accounts 1, f.110).
[2] Robert Crowley, author, printer, and divine and prebendary of Mora in St Paul's, and at this date rector of St Peter le Poor (*DNB*; G. Hennessy, *Novum Repertorium Ecclesiasticum Parochiale Londinense*, 1898, 38, 376).

305. *1563–64* [f.111] *Margin* [Pre]sent[1] given to [the] Ambassador of France[2] To divers persons for a present provided by this accountant to be given in the name of the lord mayor, aldermen and citizens to the lord ambassador of France and to him delivered at Winchester Place in Southwark, that is to say: to Richard [A]dams and John Wolstone [butcher]s for one ox weighing 5½ C and 5 lb at 14d. the stone £4.10s.3¼d., 6 muttons at 10s.6d. the piece and 4 muttons at 10s. the piece £5.3s., 2 veals at 12s. the piece 24s., 6 lambs at 3s.4d. the piece 20s., and for carriage of the same thither 16d., whereof paid by the order of my lord mayor only £11.16s.4d. as by one bill appears; to John Berden and John Preston wardens of the Poulters for 8 pheasants at 3s. the piece 24s., 30 capons at 2s.4d. the piece £3.10s., 5 dozen chickens at 5s. the dozen 25s., 5 dozen of quails at 8s. the dozen 35s. [*sic*], 3 dozen of runners (ronners) at 3s.4d. the [do]zen 10s., 12 herons at 2s.6d. the piece, 12 shovellers at 2s.6d. the piece and 12 brewes at 2s. the piece £4.4s., and for two flasks and one tray to carry the poultry wares 2s.4d., summa as by the bill of the said [pou]lters corrected by the lord mayor appears £12.10s.4d.; also for 11 gallons and one [po]ttle of hippocras (ipocras) at 5s. the gallon 57s.6d., and for the runlet 6d., and for a firkin of sturgeon 28s., summa as appears by a bill £4.6s.; to William Bodnam grocer for [. . .] loaves of sugar weighing 53½ lb at 12½d. the lb 55s.8d. and for one box marmalade weighing 3¼ lb 6s.6d. and for one other box marmalade 3 lb 3 oz 6s.4½d., summa as by his bill appears £3.8s.6½d.; to John Howllande waxchandler for one quarter and 20 lb weight of wax at £4 the C 33s.4d., to Norton the comfitmaker for biscuits and caraways, long comfits and subtleties (subtlettes) with the boxes, barrels and carriage thereof as by a bill appears 27s.2d., for 6 marchpanes of 3 lb the piece garnished with fine gold and conceits (conseytes) and cinnamon comfits at 4s. the piece 24s., for the hire (higher) of 25 geldings which the ambassador and his train of gentleman had 2 days as by the journal appears 20s., for flaskets and carts and porters to bear the present from the butchers (bawchers) and poulters to the ambassador's and for drinking money to them and others that took pains as by the journal appears 16s.4d., summa £6.0s.10d. Summa totalis £38.2s.0½d.[3]

[1] Ms trimmed.
[2] Paul de Foix. On 13 June 1564 it was ordered that the chamberlain should have allowance upon his next account of all money which had been laid out upon the present for the French ambassador (Rep.15, f.348). Had the gift perhaps been made to atone for the 'wrong' done to the ambassador at the lord mayor's feast? (*Cal. SPF 1563*, 578).
[3] Gifts of sugar, poultry, wax and claret were given to the Swedish ambassador in 1566–67 (Chamber Accounts 1, f.189v).

306. *1563–64* [f.112v] To William Prestwood stationer for binding of two great books containing the accounts of George Medley, Thomas Hayes and John Sturgeon, late chamberlains,[1] £3.3s.0d.

[1] The three predecessors of George Heton, the chamberlain in office, who had been elected on 1 August 1563.

307. *1563–64* [f.101v] To Thomas Norwall shipwright for making of a new boat and mending the old boat for Moor Ditch, £2.13s.4d.

308. *1563–64?* [f.103] To Mr Waterbailie's men and others taking pains at Moor Ditch fishing there, 10s.0d.

309. *1563–64* [f.97] Paid unto Mr [*blank*] Mallorye alderman immediately after he was elected lord mayor the sum of £200 being the money which was received of Mr Hardinge and Mr Walkynden for refusing the office of shrievalty being thereunto lawfully elect,[1] which sum by order of my lord mayor and divers of my masters of the grey cloaks[2] was lent unto him to be repaid at [Michaelmas?][3] following, £200. [*This entry deleted*]
This to be allowed in the foot of the account as a debt due to be paid by obligation.

[1] Robert Harding, elected as sheriff by the commonalty on 1 Aug. 1564, paid his fine for refusal on 29 Aug. Geoffrey Walkynden was elected in his stead on 30 Aug. and paid his fine on 31 Aug. (Rep.15, ff.369b, 371). Richard Mallory became lord mayor elect on 29 Sept. 1564.

[2] The aldermen who had served the mayoralty.

[3] Ms mutilated.

310. *1564–65?* [f.163] To George Thuneton ironmonger[1] for his pains and charges for riding to Rye and Hastings to see and enquire the cause why fresh fish was brought no more plentifully (plentifuller) to London, £2.13s.4d.

[1] See **324j**.

311. *1564–65*? [f.163] To John Smith armourer and William Staples cordwainer for their charges riding into Norfolk to enquire there the store of wheat there being and make report thereof and other the city's affairs, £6.13s.4d.

312. *1564–65*? [f.175] To Robert Talboyes goldsmith for the exchange of a basin and ewer heretofore given by Sir William [Denham][1] knight late alderman poz' 126 oz and delivered to him at 5s.4d. the oz and receiving another all gilt poz 129½ oz at 6s.10d. the oz which extends the 5s. to him allowed for the amels (ammels) of the new basin and ewer over and beside the value of the old basin and ewer as by his bill appears,[2] £10.17s.11d.

[1] Surname omitted in the Ms.

[2] A basin and ewer of the new weight of 129½ oz is listed in the earliest surviving inventory of the city's plate, 1567 (Masters, 307). Many early pieces of city plate underwent such exchanges (*ibid.*, 301).

313. *1565–66* [f.211v] Paid by order of court [23 April 1566, Rep.16, f.41b] to Doctor Dale,[1] William Saye and John Lewes, proctors of the arches, and William Boyer keeper of the records in the [Tower][2] taking pains for the defence of the city in their causes now in question at Bruges

(Brygges) at that present diet at Bruges (Brydges) by the subjects of king Philip as more particularly by a bill appears, £36.17s.4d., *margin* Note to see the bill before this be entered; to Doctor Awbery[3] by order of court [16 July 1566, Rep.16, f.82b] for his pains about the diet in Flanders being there for the space of 94 days after the rate of 10s. the day, £47.0s.0d.[4]

[1] Valentine Dale, D.C.L., an eminent civil lawyer and diplomatist (*DNB*).
[2] Ms mutilated.
[3] William Aubery, LL.D., an eminent civil lawyer (*DNB*).
[4] Between Feb. 1565 and June 1566 the city was concerned with the defence of its franchises before commissioners at a diet in Bruges held for the determination of matters at variance between Flemish and English merchants (Rep.15, ff.423b, 424b, 425b; Rep.16, ff.41b, 57, 60, 82b).

314. *1566–67*? [f.180] Paid for a dinner at the conduit heads for my lord mayor and his brethren the aldermen with the lady mayoress and other ladies and gentlewomen, the wardens of the 12 chief companies of the city being there, 15 Sept. as by a bill appears, £26.8s.1d.; also to Robert [W]ayte[1] and his companion playing there on the drum and flute 6s.8d., and in reward there to labourers taking pains there 2s.; summa £26.16s.9d.[2]

[1] Ms mutilated. Anthony Castell (see **25i**) was appointed drum player in succession to Robert Wayte, 13 May 1568 (Rep. 16, f.359b).
[2] And see **316**, **321**.

315. *1566–67* [f.231] Paid by order of my lord mayor to him that brought a letter from Mr Lambert touching his answer of a letter to him sent by the lord mayor and aldermen for the obtaining of him the use of some part of his ground at Dowgate for the making of a well and pump there for the receipt of water out of the river of Thames to be conveyed to a cistern for a conduit there to be made, £1.0s.0d.[1]

[1] For the conduit and pump at Dowgate, see Stow i, 230, 232. Stow gives the date of the making of the conduit as 1568. In the account for 1568–69 John Hawarde was paid 23s.4d. for a piece of timber, ready bored pumpwise and 28½ feet in length, bought of him and laid in the Thames near Dowgate for conveying water from the river to the well newly erected to serve the conduit (Chamber Accounts 1, f.16v).

316. *1566–67*? [f.230] To John Aspline painter stainer for painting work at the new house of the conduit heads,[1] £5.8s.4d.; [f.230v] more to him for painting and gilding of the city's arms, Sir John Lyon's and my lady's arms and for painting and writing 2 tables upon the new market house at Queenhithe[2] as by a bill appears, £3.6s.6d.

[1] Soon to become known as the Banqueting House. Order had been given on 18 Sept. 1565 for the building of a good, handsome, room at the conduit heads (Rep.15, f.468; P. E. Jones, 'The Estates of the Corporation of London: property records as a source for historical, topographical and economic research', *Guildhall Miscellany*, i, no.7, Aug. 1956, 10–14).
[2] See **298 b**.

317. *1568–69*? [f.152v][1] 13 Oct. to a yeoman of my lord keeper's house who went and warned my lord of Ely's counsel to be at the star chamber to join with the counsel of this city to show what they had to say for the maintenance of their pretended liberties claimed in Holborn[2] 5s.; 14 Oct. to William Cooke of Westminster for dinner at his house for Mr Recorder, Mr Alderman Haward, Mr Bacon alderman, this accountant with divers others who gave attendance upon the counsel for the hearing of the said cause as by a bill appears 23s.; in reward to Mr Stanton's servants 12d.; at another time to 2 of my lord keeper's servants for their pains in warning the bishop of Ely's counsel and Mr Wiskins to be at the star chamber 6s.8d.; 5 Nov. to Mr Serjeant Manwood, Mr Plowden and Mr Recorder to every of them for their pains giving attendance upon the said counsel 20s., summa £3, and to Mr Hone also being there 10s.; the same day to William Cooke for a dinner at Westminster at his house there for divers aldermen, Mr Recorder, this accountant, with the learned counsel of the city and also their servants giving their attendance 'eftsones' for the hearing of the matter in the star chamber before the lord keeper and others appointed there for the hearing of the matter as by a bill appears £5.1s.6d.; in reward to one of the servants in the house 4d.; also in reward to the officers of the star chamber for their attendance and for beer and ale bestowed upon the aldermen, counsellors and other officers of the city 4s.; 2 Feb. to Mr Skipwich, one of my lord keeper's gentlemen, for warning the bishop's counsel to be at my lord keeper's the 5th February following 5s.; to Edmund Hardye, one of Mr Recorder's clerks, for looking out the book of the matter 2s.; 5 Feb. for a dinner [f.152][1] at Westminster for divers the aldermen, Mr Recorder, Mr Serjeant Manwoode, Mr Plowden, with divers other the learned counsel of this city and others attending upon them £4.16s.5d.; the same day to Mr Serjeant Manwoode for his counsel therein 20s.; in reward to the servants of the house where they dined 20d.; to one of my lord keeper's gentlemen for his pains in warning my lord of Ely's counsel and Wiskins to be at my lord keeper's 3s.6d.; in reward to the yeomen of my lord keeper's cellars 6s.; to Master Martyn, keeper of the lord keeper's chamber, for his friendly furtherance in the city's suits at divers the repair thither of this accountant 5s.; 17 June to Mr Recorder, Mr Solicitor, Mr Serjeant Manwood and Mr Mounson of the city's counsel retained for their pains and travail taken at my lord keeper's house for the matter to every of them 20s., summa £4; the same day to William Cooke for a dinner at Westminster for Mr Recorder, divers the aldermen, the learned counsel of the city, this accountant and others tarrying there attending there 'eftsones' for the hearing of the matter as by a bill appears £4.6s.5d.; and to Cooke at [an]other [time] for a dinner there for like cause £3.11s.3d.;[3] to Mr Solicitor, Mr Serjeant Manwood and Mr Recorder to every of them for their attendance the said [time] 20s., summa £3; to Robert Hodgeson[4] for that he paid to Mr Joneys[?] the examiner for the examining 4 witnesses [f.153] for the [. . .][5] of the city and making copies of the same and paid to Mr Marten, register to my lord keeper, for a copy of the order betwixt the city and the bishop concerning the liberties pretended by the bishop as by a bill appears 55s.;[6] for boat hire as well for divers aldermen, Mr Recorder, the learned counsel of this city, this accountant, Mr Dommer[7] with divers others as also their servants at sundry times in travelling about the matter as by the journal appears 26s.; and in reward to my lord keeper's porter 12d.; summa £36.10s.9d.

[1] This leaf has been guarded and filed by its original fore-edge. The present recto is a continuation from the present verso.
[2] The bishop of Ely, his tenants and officers, claimed that Ely Rents in the parish of Holborn was without the jurisdiction of the city and offered resistance to Sir Roger Martin, lord mayor 1567–68, when he tried to exercise his office there. The matter was referred to the arbitration of the lord keeper and others before whom counsel for both sides appeared many times, and it was subsequently agreed that the cause should be referred to the two lord chief justices, who on 9 June 1570 in the star chamber found for the city (Letter Book V, f.297b).
[3] A deleted but fuller version of this clause, which is here inserted, occurs on f.153: 24 June for a dinner at Westminster for Sir William Chester, Sir John White and divers other aldermen, Mr Serjeant Manwood, Mr Recorder, Mr Plowden, with divers their servants attending at Westminster £3.11s.3d.
[4] A clerk of the mayor's court.
[5] Ms faded and illegible.
[6] This clause has been amended. Deletions indicate that the examiner was paid 50s. and the register 5s.
[7] William Dummer, comptroller of the chamber.

318. *1570–71?* [f.47v] Paid to Mr Gonter[1] for hangings occupied at the Spital in the chamber there where the lady mayoress and other ladies and gentlewomen remain to hear the sermons there preached 3s.4d., for bread, ale, beer, *aqua cum poseta*, and other necessaries provided for the said ladies and gentlewomen 4s., to 7 porters for their pains taken three days in keeping the doors at the Spital 6s.8d., and more to the gunner's servants for keeping the gates in the artillery yard 3s.4d., and to an old man that keeps the yard 20s. [cf.**100**]

[1] A list of expenses at the Spital from another account, to which a date has not been attributed, includes a payment to Philip Gunter for hiring of hangings of arras work (Chamber Accounts 1, f.161).

319. *1570–71* [f.36] Paid to Mr Dyster, deputy to the clerk of the crown in the chancery, for a commission of sewers made to Rowland Haward then lord mayor [1570–71] and others concerning Turnmill Brook and other the common sewers in London and three writs of attendance for the same 41s.; and more to him at another time for amending (mending) the said commission and making it to serve the lord mayor for the time being 5s.4d.; summa £2.6s.4d.[1]

[1] The commission was presented to the court of aldermen by the chamberlain on 1 August 1571 (Rep.17, f.182b). It was not until 1667, after the Great Fire, that the city had a permanent court of commissioners of sewers.

320. *1570–71* [f.36] *Margin* The charges for making of one new collar of SS of silver for [*blank*] Seger a Dutchman lately admitted into the number of 7 waits of the city[1] and for new repairing and mending of 6 old collars and the small scutcheons of the same and for 7 new scutcheons fair new made and parcel gilt with the arms of the city.
First paid to John Wright goldsmith for silver to the new collar 13 oz and to the 7 new scutcheons with the city arms 7½ oz 2 dwt and to the amendment of the old SS and little scutcheons 2 oz 5 dwt, whereof abated

[. . .]$\frac{3}{4}$[2] oz unto him delivered in the old scutcheons [. . .] rest of new silver 18$\frac{3}{4}$ oz which at 3s.10d. the [oz] amounts unto £4.12s.2d.; for making the new collar which had great workmanship 20s., for mending the 6 old collars and ameling of them anew 20s., for making of the 7 new great scutcheons and gilding of them being very fair and well wrought 25s., whereof abated 6$\frac{1}{2}$d.; summa as by a bill appears, £7.16s.8d.

[1] On 10 Oct. 1570 it was agreed that Segar Van Pilkam, stranger, should have the same yearly wages and livery as the other waits (Rep.17, f.63).
[2] Ms mutilated.

321. *1570–71* [f.36v] *Margin* Charges of the lord mayor and ladies and gentlewomen and other citizens in going to view the conduits and conduit heads at Marylebone (Marybone) and Paddington being west from the city.
To Robert Browne yeoman of the [chamber][1] for hire of horses, wagons, wages of wagoners, their meat, rushes and perfumes as well to serve at the Banqueting House as in wagons where the ladies and gentlewomen went, as by his bill appears 55s.6d.; to Thomas Wheler[2] steward and provider of a dinner there had for the lord mayor and others there assembled as by his bill appears £37.14s.9$\frac{1}{2}$d.; to Simon (Symond) Polier master bearward at Paris Garden for his pastime showed there with his bears, bulls and dogs 13s.4d.; and for horse hire and other charges for sending to Cranebery Park[3] being for 5 days for a buck to serve there 30s.; in reward to Sir Roger Marten's man bringing thither half a buck 16d.; in reward to the keeper of Marylebone Park for a buck which he brought to the conduit heads and given to the lord mayor by Mr Johnson clothworker 10s.; and given to the poor there 10s.; to the drum [and] flute there 6s.8d.; to [blank] Stone [. . .] hurt taken there [. . .] 20s.; to Francis Partridge barber surgeon, being there then present, for dressing the said wound 6s.8d.; and more to Stone in consideration of a further relief of his hurt 40s.; summa as by the bills aforesaid and journal appears £47.8s.3$\frac{1}{2}$d.

[1] Ms mutilated.
[2] Clerk of the city's works. From the late 16th century to 1724 this officer held the close at the conduit heads and the Banqueting house thereon as one of the perquisites of office and was responsible for maintenance of the house and the conduit heads and pipes (B. R. Masters, 'City Officers iv: The City Surveyor, the City Engineer and the City Architect and Planning Officer', *Guildhall Miscellany*, iv, no.4, April 1973, 240, 242).
[3] Cranbury Park in the parish of Hursley, Hampshire, near Winchester.

322. *1570–71* [f.78v] Paid for a dinner at Westminster for Mr Chamberlain, Mr Dummer, Mr Spillman, clerk of the parliament house, and others attending there following the cause of the water of Lee 11s.2d., and to Mr Spylman in reward to further the bill exhibited for the said water 20s.; the same day in reward to certain officers in the parliament house and for boat hire 11s.; at another time for a dinner for Mr Chamberlain, Mr Dummer and their servants in giving their attendance upon the parliament house concerning the river of Ley 8s.8d.; the same day to the keepers of the parliament chamber door and for boat hire 3s.8d.; for a dinner for Mr Chamberlain, Mr Dummer, Mr Spillman, clerk of the parliament house, and others 11s.6d., and in reward to officers of the parliament [f.79] house 2s.6d.; for another dinner for Mr Recorder, Mr Chamberlain, Mr Dummer, and Mr Spillman 24s.6d., and to the keepers of the parliament house door 12d.; to James Aldaye for giving his attendance in the parliament house divers times and making declaration to the lords in the higher house of the table which he drew describing the river of Ley 20s.;[1] more for a dinner for Sir Ralph (Raff') Sadler knight and others of the parliament house being committees to confer as well with divers aldermen as Mr Recorder and others of the learned counsel of the city there also being to consider of the bill exhibited by the city for the [water of][2] of Lye [. . .] Westminster and given in reward at the [parliame]nt £3.12s.10d., and in reward to the yeoman [that ke]pt the door at the lords' house attending upon the table [or plo]t of the said water and there hanged up for [the bett]er instructing of the lords of the parliament £6.5s. [. . .d. and] for other rewards and boat hire there spent and bestowed [. . .s.] 4d.; to the clerk of the lower house for engrossing of certain provisos 2s.; for a supper for Mr [f.79v] Chamberlain, Mr Dummer, Mr Hodgeson and others at Stratford in travelling to view the river of Ley 11s.4d., and to Mr Osbourne, one of my lord keeper's gentlemen, that went from Westminster to see the plot from my lord keeper's to Westminster 6s.8d.; to Mr Serjeant Wraye, speaker of the parliament house, for the bill which passed for the river of Ley[3] £5; to Mr John Onslowe, clerk of the lower house, for his fee demanded for a proviso in the bill against usury[4] [10s?] and for the bill of the water of Lee that passed 40s., and for an ordinary reward by him demanded 40s., summa as by his bill appears £4.10s.; to Mr Spillman, clerk of the higher house, in consideration of the act passed for the water of Lye 40s., for the enrolling and exemplification of the same act 50s., and to the gentlemen ushers of the parliament 10s.6d., and for [f.68] putting the same act into print being left out at the first printing of the statutes 10s.; to my lord keeper in consideration of the act passed concerning the river of Ley, being due to him *ex officio* £10; to James Basendyne 'Scottishman' for his travail three days to consider how the river of Ley might best be conveyed from Hoddesdon (Hogesden) to the Mantells and so into Fleet Ditch and other expenses bestowed upon him and others about the same 14s.8d.;[5] more to him and Thomas [blank] the late servant of Albert Stuges joining and conferring together to make the instrument perfect to take the level of the ground from Hoddesdon (Hoggesden) near to Holborn Bridge, and for measuring and setting out [f.68v] the distance from station to station which occupied them sundry days, for their reward in money 23s. 4d. and for suppers, drinkings and other repasts for them 10s.6d., and in reward to a poor man 6d.; to Jaques Furrier Frenchman for making of a new plot for the river of Ley out of the plot which my lord keeper had out of the parliament house 30s.;[6] to Mr Dyster, deputy to the clerk of the crown in the chancery, for the receiving in and filing the writ and return for the parliament as by Mr Moseley's[7] bill appears 8s.; to Sir John Whyht knight and alderman, one of the knights of the parliament for the city, for his fee and livery for his chaplain and 4 servants attending upon him the time of the parliament £14.10s.10d., and to him for boat hire for 58 days at 12d. the day 58s.; to Mr. Thomas Wilbraham esquire,[8] another knight of the parliament, for his fee and livery for himself and 4 servants attending upon the said parliament [. . .], and more to him for boat hire by like time and rate 58s.; to John [Me]rsshe mercer and Thomas Norton[9] [. . .], burgesses for the city, for their fee and for liveries of their 2 servants £12.13s.4d., and to them for their boat hire for 58 days £5.16s.; and to James Peele by commandment of the lord mayor for charges in drawing of a bill put into the parliament house touching the gifts to all corporations[10] drawn by Mr Bowyer of the Temple and preferred by Norton as by a bill subscribed by the then lord mayor appears 12s.

[1] The same James Alday (1516–76) who had been chief assistant to Sebastian Cabot? (E. G. R. Taylor, *The Mathematical Practitioners of Tudor and Stuart England*, 1954, 168).
[2] Ms mutilated or faded. Here and below, *lacunae* are where possible supplied in square brackets.
[3] An act for bringing of the river of Lee to the north side of the city of London, 13 Eliz. c.18. For the city's proposals for the Lea, see K. Fairclough, 'A Tudor canal scheme for the river Lea', *London Journal*, v, no,2, 218–27, and the revision thereof in the light of information in Chamber Accounts 1 in 'A Tudor canal scheme for the river Lea: a note', *London Journal*, viii, no.1, 90–1. I am indebted to Mr. Fairclough for the references in notes 5 and 6 below.
[4] An act against usury, 13 Eliz. c.8.
[5] James Bassantyne, Scottish subject, obtained letters of denization 3 June 1562 (*Cal. PR 1560–63*, 457); Jas Bassendine and two others were commissioned by Thomas Randolph, ambassador in Russia, to undertake a voyage of discovery from the river Peckora eastward, 1568 (*Cal. SPD Addenda 1566–79*, 53).
[6] Furrier (Fure, Furrey, Fraier) of Tournai had come to London in *c.*1568 and was then resident with his wife and child in Broad Street ward. From 19 Nov. 1572 to 2 Feb. 1576 he was a deacon of the French Church (*Returns of aliens*, ed. R. E. G. and E. F. Kirk, Huguenot Soc. of London, quarto series, x, 1902–7, pt.2, 40, pt.3, 352; *Actes du consistoire de l'église française*, ii, ed. A. M. Oakley, *ibid.*, xlviii, 1969, 94, 176).
[7] Humfry Moseley, secondary of Wood Street compter.
[8] The recorder.
[9] The city's first remembrancer.
[10] An act against fraudulent deeds, gifts, alienations, etc. 13 Eliz. c.5?.

F.

ACCOUNT OF THE REYNWELL ESTATE 1565–66

[f.204v] The account of the chamberlain for the lands of Mr John Raynewell sometime mayor of this city

323. The Charge [Receipts]

a. Arrearages due by this accountant upon his last account, £233.3s.4½d.
b. Receipts of the rents of Mr Raynewell, vacations and desperates allowed, as by the renter appears, £123.16s.8d.
c. Of Thomas Sares haberdasher for the fine of a lease of the Black Hoop being a brewhouse wherein he dwells in Lime Street in the parish of St Andrew Undershaft for 21 years beginning at Michaelmas 1565, £20.0s.0d.
d. Summa totalis £377.0s.0½d.

324. The Discharge [Payments]*

a. To William Fermer to the use of the petty canons of St Paul's for Foliat's chantry, £1.0s.0d.
b. To the chamber of London for quitrent out of the vestry of St Botolph Billingsgate charged in the rental of the general lands in the title of Tower Street and Bridge Street, £1.0s.0d.
c. [f.205] To Agnes Kelley widow for quitrent out of Holy Rood Alley near Billingsgate sometime paid to Giles Polyver,[1] 10s.0d.

[1] *Sic.* Pollibere in 1535–36, see **295 d**.

d. To the comptroller of the chamber for overseeing this account, £2.0s.0d.
e. To the renter for gathering the rents and potation money, £6.13s.4d.
f. To him for his liveries this year, £2.13s.4d.
g. To Mr John Ryvers and Mr James Hawes aldermen late sheriffs [1565–66] in discharge of the toll of London Bridge for this year, £8.0s.0d.
h. To James Lorde attorney, accountant in the exchequer at Westminster, to the use of the queen for the fee farm of Southwark ended at Michaelmas last past, £10.0s.0d.
i. [1]To Thomas Canata, Venetian, by order of court 11 July [1566, Rep.16, f.81b] for attending upon the same court and offering his service for the devising of means and ways for the cleansing the shelves of the river of Thames, £2.0s.0d.[2]

[1] The remaining items are written in a different hand. This and the next three items are lettered in the margin A, C, B, D, respectively, presumably indicating the order of entry in the final account.
[2] Under Reynwell's will the residue of the profits from his estate, after payment of specific trusts, could in part be used for the removal of sandbanks and other obstructions in the Thames (HR 207(31)). The Reynwell account for 1564–65 contains a payment of 40s. to Thomas Camata [*sic*], Venetian, for making an instrument for cleansing the Thames, the aldermen having agreed on 30 Aug. 1565 to make use of his lesser instrument for cleansing rivers from 'shelves and other risings of sand and earth' and to talk with him further about his greater instrument (Chamber Accounts 1, f.142v; Rep.15, f.462b). In 1572 Thomas Canata, Venetian, sought licence of the queen to export 200 tons of beer on condition of his making known to her certain inventions useful for the defence of the realm (*Cal. SPD 1547–80*, 453).

j. To Richard Sampson blacksmith for an iron cart or instrument devised by George Thorneton for the removing of the shelves in the river of Thames, £14.1s.8d.[1] and more to him for ironwork bestowed in the repairing the lands of Mr Raynewell 22s.10d., summa £15.2s.6d. [*sic*]

[1] George Thorneton ironmonger, governor of Bridewell, was ordered in Jan. 1566 to devise an instrument for cleansing the Thames and presented an estimate (no details given) in March 1566. Vagabonds from Bridewell were employed on the work (Rep.15, f.516; Rep.16, ff.29b, 137b, 148, 153).

k. To George Thorneton for so much by him paid for the hire of 2 lighters to be occupied at divers times for the trial of the said instrument before the lord mayor and aldermen and for the reward and wages of divers

*For the first eight of these payments, cf. **132a–b, d–h**.

persons labouring in the lighters with the instrument to show a trial thereof to the lord mayor and aldermen, £2.8s.11½d.

l. For timber, boards, quarters, lathes, hard stone, paving stone, bricks, tiles, lime, sand, paving work, night work, nails of sundry sorts and other necessaries spent about the reparations of the lands, £18.19s.7d.

m. [f.205v] For the wages of masons, carpenters, tilers, bricklayers, plasterers and labourers working about as well the necessary reparations of the lands and tenements as also in cleansing and removing the shelves in the river of Thames this year as by 8 bills called weeks' bills appears, £22.6s.10d.

n. Summa totalis of all the discharge £92.14.6½d.

325. And so due upon this account £284 5s. 6d.

INDEX

Various entries have been gathered under the headings 'companies', 'trades and occupations' and 'wards'. In some cases trades may indicate membership of a company rather than an actual occupation. Offices are listed individually in the index but cross references to many city offices will be found grouped under 'city officers'. Cross references from an office to the names of the office holders are given only if the latter provide additional references.

References in Roman numerals are to pages of the Introduction; Arabic numerals denote entries in the calendar. An asterisk (*) indicates a footnote in the Introduction or a note in the calendar.

Index

LONDON RECORD SOCIETY

The London Record Society was founded in December 1964 to publish transcripts, abstracts and lists of the primary sources for the history of London, and generally to stimulate interest in archives relating to London. Membership is open to any individual or institution; the annual subscription is £7 ($15) for individuals and £10 ($23) for institutions, which entitles a member to receive one copy of each volume published during the year and to attend and vote at meetings of the Society. Prospective members should apply to the Hon. Secretary, Miss Heather Creaton, c/o Institute of Historical Research, Senate House, London, WC1E 7HU.

The following volumes have already been published.

1. *London Possessory Assizes: a calendar*, edited by Helena M. Chew (1965)
2. *London Inhabitants within the Walls, 1695*, with an introduction by D. V. Glass (1966)
3. *London Consistory Court Wills, 1492–1547*, edited by Ida Darlington (1967)
4. *Scriveners' Company Common Paper, 1357–1628, with a continuation to 1678*, edited by Francis W. Steer (1968)
5. *London Radicalism, 1830–1843: a selection from the papers of Francis Place*, edited by D. J. Rowe (1970)
6. *The London Eyre of 1244*, edited by Helena M. Chew and Martin Weinbaum (1970)
7. *The Cartulary of Holy Trinity Aldgate*, edited by Gerald A. J. Hodgett (1971)
8. *The Port and Trade of Early Elizabethan London: documents*, edited by Brian Dietz (1972)
9. *The Spanish Company*, by Pauline Croft (1973)
10. *London Assize of Nuisance, 1301–1431: a calendar*, edited by Helena M. Chew and William Kellaway (1973)
11. *Two Calvinistic Methodist Chapels, 1743–1811: the London Tabernacle and Spa Fields Chapel*, edited by Edwin Welch (1975)
12. *The London Eyre of 1276*, edited by Martin Weinbaum (1976)
13. *The Church in London, 1375–1392*, edited by A. K. McHardy (1977)
14. *Committees for Repeal of the Test and Corporation Acts: Minutes, 1786–90 and 1827–8*, edited by Thomas W. Davis (1978)
15. *Joshua Johnson's Letterbook, 1771–4: letters from a merchant in London to his partners in Maryland*, edited by Jacob M. Price (1979)
16. *London and Middlesex Chantry Certificate, 1548*, edited by C. J. Kitching (1980)

17. *London Politics, 1713–1717: Minutes of a Whig Club, 1714–17*, edited by H. Horwitz; *London Pollbooks, 1713*, edited by W. A. Speck and W. A. Gray (1981)
18. *Parish Fraternity Register: fraternity of the Holy Trinity and SS. Fabian and Sebastian in the parish of St. Botolph without Aldersgate*, edited by Patricia Basing (1982)
19. *Trinity House of Deptford: Transactions, 1609–35*, edited by G. G. Harris (1983)
20. *Chamber Accounts of the sixteenth century*, edited by Betty R. Masters (1984)

All volumes are still in print; apply to Hon. Secretary. Price to individual members £7 ($15) each; to institutional members £10 ($23) each; and to non-members £12 ($28) each.